T0334019

The Private Collector's Museum

The Private Collector's Museum connects the rising popularity of private museums with evolving models of collecting and philanthropy, and new inter-relationships between private and public space. It examines how contemporary collectors construct museums to frame themselves as cultural arbiters of global distinction.

By exploring a range of in-depth contemporary case studies, the book aims for a more complex understanding of the private collector's museum, assessing how it is realised, funded and understood in a broader cultural context. It examines the ways in which this particular museum model has evolved within a historical Western tradition of collecting and museum-building, and considers how private museums will endure alongside their public counterparts. It also sheds light on the shifting patterns of collecting, such as the transition of personal art collections into the public sphere. The developments are situated within the wider context of private–public engagement in general.

Providing a new analysis of philanthropy, public access and the museum, *The Private Collector's Museum* is essential reading for scholars and students interested in the private museum, and key reading for those interested in related issues.

Georgina S. Walker is an Honorary Fellow at the University of Melbourne, Australia. She teaches in Art History, Curatorial and Museum Studies and her research interests include the recent and fast-growing number of private, national and international museums that have emerged in China and the Gulf Region.

Routledge Research in Museum Studies

https://www.routledge.com/Routledge-Research-in-Museum-Studies/book-series/RRIMS

The Private Collector's Museum
Public Good Versus Private Gain

Georgina S. Walker

Routledge
Taylor & Francis Group

LONDON AND NEW YORK

First published 2019 by Routledge

2 Park Square, Milton Park, Abingdon, Oxon, OX14 4RN
605 Third Avenue, New York, NY 10017

Routledge is an imprint of the Taylor & Francis Group, an informa business

First issued in paperback 2020

British Library Cataloguing-in-Publication Data
A catalogue record for this book is available from the British Library

Library of Congress Cataloging-in-Publication Data
A catalog record has been requested for this book

ISBN: 978-1-138-55535-8 (hbk)
ISBN: 978-0-367-72886-1 (pbk)

Typeset in Sabon
by Newgen Publishing UK

For my dad
Harry Strintzos
(1930–2016)

Contents

viii   *Contents*

Figures

Chronological listing of key private museums

House museums

Museum	Location	Established
Sir John Soane	London, UK	1837
The Wallace Collection	London, UK	1900
Isabella Stewart Gardner	Boston, USA	1903
The Phillips Collection	Washington DC, USA	1921
Vizcaya and Gardens	Miami, USA	1925
The Barnes Foundation	Merion, USA	1925
Huntington Art Gallery	San Marino, USA	1928
The Frick Collection	New York, USA	1935
Dumbarton Oaks	Washington DC, USA	1940
Hill-Stead	Connecticut, USA	1946
Peggy Guggenheim Collection	Venice, Italy	1951
Hyde Collection	Glens Falls, USA	1952
Foundation E.G. Bührle Collection	Zürich, Switzerland	1960–2015
Kettle's Yard	Cambridge, UK	1966
Oskar Reinhart Collection 'Am Römerholz'	Winterthur, Switzerland	1970
Getty Villa	Los Angeles, USA	1974
Frederick R. Weisman Art Foundation	Los Angeles, USA	1982
Coninx	Zürich, Switzerland	1986–2013

Museum	Location	Established
The Johnston Collection	Melbourne, Australia	1986
Villa Flora	Winterthur, Switzerland	1995–2014
Villa Panza	Varese, Italy	1996
The Rachofsky Collection	Dallas, USA	1996
Hoffmann Collection	Berlin, Germany	1997
Glenstone	Potomac, USA	2006
Julia Stoschek Collection	Düsseldorf, Germany	2007
The Philip Johnson Glass House	New Canaan, USA	2007
Boros Collection	Berlin, Germany	2008
Lyon Housemuseum	Melbourne, Australia	2009
Justin Art House Museum (JAHM)	Melbourne, Australia	2016
The David Roche Foundation	Adelaide, Australia	2016

Stand-alone museums

Folkwang	Hagen, Germany	1902–1921
Folkwang	Essen, Germany	1922
Morgan Library and Art Gallery	New York, USA	1924
The Walters Art Museum	Baltimore, USA	1934
Kröller-Müller	Otterlo, Netherlands	1938
Guggenheim	New York, USA	1939
Oskar Reinhart 'Am Stadtgarten'	Winterthur, Switzerland	1951
Louisiana Museum of Modern Art	Humlebæk, Denmark	1958
Amon Carter	Fort Worth, USA	1961
Marguerite & Aimé Maeght Foundation	Nice, France	1964
Kimbell Art Museum	Fort Worth, USA	1972
Foundation Pierre Gianadda (Léonard Gianadda Collection)	Martigny, Switzerland	1978
Emanuel Hoffman Collection – Schaulager	Basel, Switzerland	1980

Insel Hombroich	Neuss, Germany	inception 1982 and founded 1996
Allen for Neue Kunst	Schaffhausen, Switzerland	1982–2014
The Burrell Collection	Glasgow, Scotland	Gifted 1944, opened 1983
The Saatchi Gallery	London, UK	1985
Menil Collection	Houston, USA	1987
Hess Art Collection	Napa Valley, USA	1989
Gibbs Farm	Makarau, New Zealand	1991
The Rubell Family Collection	Miami, USA	1993
Goetz Collection	Munich, Germany	1993
Migros Collection	Zurich, Switzerland	1996
Fondation Beyeler	Riehen, Switzerland	1997
Getty Centre	Los Angeles, USA	1997
Essl Collection	Vienna, Austria	1999–2016
MKM Küppersmühle for Modern Art – Ströller Collection	Duisburg, Germany	1999
Marguilies Collection	Miami, USA	1999
Würth	Künzelsau, Germany	2001
Neue Galerie	New York, USA	2001
Jumex Foundation	Mexico City, Mexico	2001
Leopold	Vienna, Austria	2001
Haubrok Collection	Berlin, Germany	2002
Rosengart	Lucerne, Switzerland	2002
CIFO Art Spaces	Miami, USA	2002
Daros Latinamerica Collection (Stephan Schmidheiny family Collection)	Zurich, Switzerland	2002–2011
Fondazione Sandretto Re Rebaugengo	Turin, Italy	2002
DIA: Beacon	New York, USA	2003

Nasser Sculpture Centre	Dallas, USA	2003
TarraWarra Museum of Art	Yarra Valley, Australia	2003
La Maison Rouge	Paris, France	2004–2018
Aldrich Contemporary Art	Connecticut, USA (non-collecting)	2004
Langen Foundation	Neuss, Germany	2004
Frieder Burda	Baden-Baden, Germany	2004
Dacra – Art & Design Collection (Craig Robins Collection)	Miami, USA	2005
Elgin	Istanbul, Turkey	2005
Schaufler Collection – Shauwerk Sindelfingen	Sindelfingen, Germany	2005
Crystal Bridges	Arkansas, USA	2005
Inhotim Centre for Contemporary Art	Brumadinho, Brazil	2005
Ritter (Marli Hoppe-Ritter Collection)	Waldenbuch, Germany	2005
Arthur de Ganay Photographic Collection	Berlin, Germany	2006
Palazzo Grassi	Venice, Italy	2006
Frank Cohen – Initial Access	Wolverhampton, UK	2007–2012
Anita Zabludowicz Collection – Chalk Farm	London, UK	2007
Kunsthalle Weishaupt	Ulm, Germany	2007
Vanhaerents Art Collection	Brussels, Belgium	2007
Kunstwerk Klein (Peter and Alison Klein Collection)	Eberdingen,Germany	2007
Celine & Heiner Bastien	Berlin, Germany	2007–2017
Philara-Sammlung zeitgenössischer Kunst	Düsseldorf, Germany	2008
Falckenberg Collection	Hamburg, Germany	Original building 2001; current building 2008

Liaunig	Neuhaus, Austria	2008
KAI 10	Düsseldorf, Germany	2008
Anita Zabludowicz Collection – 1500 Broadway (art space)	New York, USA	2008
De La Cruz Collection Contemporary Art Space (Rosa & Carlos de la Cruz)	Miami, USA	2009
The Brant Foundation Art Study Centre	Greenwich, USA	2009
Punta della Dogana	Venice, Italy	2009
White Rabbit Gallery	Sydney, Australia	2009
Brandhorst	Munich, Germany	2009
Thomas Olbricht – *me*, Collectors Room	Berlin, Germany	2010
Pier 24	San Francisco, USA	2010
The Museum of Old and New Art (MONA)	Hobart, Australia	2011
Anita Zabludowicz Collection (art space)	Sarvisalo, Finland	2012
David Roberts Art Foundation	London, UK	Current space 2012
Modern Art Hünfeld (Jürgen Blum Collection)	Hünfeld, Germany	2014
Foundation LV	Paris, France	2014
FLAG Art Foundation (art space)	New York, USA	2015
Fondazione Prada	Milan, Italy	2015
Newport Street Gallery (Damian Hirst)	London, UK	2015
MORE	Gorssel, Netherlands	2015
The Broad	Los Angeles, USA	2015
Stavros Niarchos Foundation Cultural Center	Athens, Greece	2016
Voorlinden	Hague, Netherlands	2016
Julia Stoschek Collection Berlin	Berlin, Germany	2016
DSL Collection (online)	Paris, France	2016

Modern Contemporary (Moco)	Amsterdam, Netherlands	2016
The Feuerle Collection	Berlin, Germany	2016
The Skulpturenhalle (Thomas Schotte)	Neuss, Germany	2016
Stiftung Nantesbuch	Bad Heilbrunn, Germany	2017
Centro Botín	Santander, Spain	2017
Barberini	Potsdam, Germany	2017
Frieda Burda – Salon Berlin	Berlin, Germany	2017
No Hero	Delden, Netherlands	2018
LUMA Arles (Maja Hoffman Foundation)	Arles, France	2018 (opening in stages until 2020)
Housemuseum Galleries	Melbourne, Australia	2019
Musée Pinault	Paris, France	2019
The Lucas of Narrative Art (George Lucas Collection)	Los Angeles, USA	2021

Acknowledgements

This project has benefitted from the invaluable contribution of many individuals and organisations. I wish to take this opportunity to personally thank them and to express my gratitude.

As the extensive research that has led to this book started out its life as a PhD, I would like to start with thanking my supervisors for their critical perspectives, expertise and constant support. I am greatly indebted to associate professors Christopher R. Marshall and Alison Inglis. As my colleagues at the University of Melbourne, their continuing encouragement and mentorship has also proven crucial to my professional development as an academic and early career researcher. I also thank them for reading and commenting on drafts and engaging in numerous discussions. A personal thank you to Alison Inglis for her assistance with proofreading.

This book could not have been written without the extraordinary contribution of many individuals who offered their time and openly shared their knowledge. It is with great pleasure that I here recognise the contributions and extend my appreciation and thanks to Dr Tobia Bezzola, Director Museo d'arte della Svizzera Italiana, Lugano and formerly Director, Museum Folkwang, Essen; Dr Christoph Becker, Director, Kunsthaus Zürich; Harald Falckenberg, Founder, Falckenberg Collection, Hamburg; Dr Ulf Küster, Curator, Fondation Beyeler, Riehen; Dr Marc Fehlmann, Director Historisches Museum Basel and formerly Director, Oskar Reinhart Museum 'Am Staatgarten', Winterthur; Randy Schulman, Vice President of Development, The Huntington Library, Art Gallery and Botanical Gardens, San Marino; Dr Michael Brand, Director, Art Gallery of New South Wales; Tony Elwood, Director, National Gallery of Victoria; Dr Gerard Vaughan, Former Director, Australian National Gallery; John Kaldor AM; Mark Fraser, Founding Director, MONA; Victoria Lynn, Director, Tarra Warra Museum of Art; Maudie Palmer AO, Inaugural Director, Tarra Warra Museum of Art; Anthony Fitzpatrick, Curator, Tarra Warra Museum of Art; Doug Hall AM, Former Director, Queensland Art Gallery, and Kelly Gellatly, Director, The Ian Potter Museum of Art, University of Melbourne.

I would also like to acknowledge the contribution of Carmen McElwain, Partner, MinterEllison Tax Controversy law practice in Melbourne and

Daniel Slater, Senior Associate, Maddocks Tax Controversy law practice in Melbourne. Their explanations and outline of the Australian and international tax laws was vital. Randy Schulman also provided an overview of the various tax laws in the United States, as did Dr Michael Brand. Dr Tobia Bezzola, Dr Christoph Becker and Dr Ulf Küster provided a greater insight into German and Swiss philanthropic developments and tax laws.

I have benefitted greatly from a number of Australian and international collectors and their staff who kindly shared information and freely provided access to material and photographs. I would like to thank the Menil Collection; Corbett Lyon, Lyon Housemuseum; Charles and Leah Justin, Justin Art House Museum; Judith Neilson, White Rabbit Gallery; David Walsh and the Museum of Old and New Art (MONA); Julia Stoschek Collection; Boros Collection; Museum Frieder Burda; The Frick Collection; Staatliche Kunsthalle Baden-Baden; Kunsthaus Zürich; Museum Folkwang, Essen; Kröller-Müller Museum and Louisiana Museum of Modern Art.

I would also like to acknowledge the assistance of Monika Kerkmann, Director, Julia Stoschek Collection; Juliet Kothe, Director, Boros Collection; Luise Guest, Research Manager, White Rabbit Collection and Kara Thoreson, Menil Collection.

Access to archival material was made possible through the generosity of numerous people. At the Menil Collection, Houston, I was assisted by the curatorial, registrar and archival staff who shared their knowledge and answered my many questions. I would particularly like to thank Archivist Lisa Barkley. She openly shared her knowledge and information about the institution and insights into its founder. A special thanks to Susan Sutton, Former Curator, Menil Collection, and Lisa Barkley for allowing me to visit the de Menil house in River Oaks, Houston. Visiting the house stimulated my thinking and nourished my research in multiple ways that they might not have realised at the time. The Menil Collection's Treasure Rooms was one of the highlights of my field trips to the United States. The other was Schaulager in Basel – many thanks to Andy Blättler. I would also like to extend my gratitude to Jennifer Allan Goldman, Curator, Manuscripts, and Institutional Archivist, The Huntington Library, Art Gallery and Botanical Gardens, San Marino; Susan Chore and Shannon Yale Morelli, Associate Archivists, The Frick Collection/Frick Art Reference Library Archives; Helen Jones, Library Cataloguer, Wallace Collection Library and Archives; and Frieda Midgley, Archivist, Kettle's Yard.

One of the greatest influences on my thinking and undertaking this study have been my encounters with museums (private and public), art collections, exhibitions and the personal experiences. There are, therefore, a great number of people (all over the world) to whom I owe a debt for their passion and ongoing ability to make things so truly memorable (for me and other museum visitors).

At Routledge, special thanks are owed to the editorial staff: Heidi Lowther, whose judgement, interest in and commitment to this project I have greatly appreciated, and Marc Stratton, for whose sense of timing and attentive follow up of this project I am grateful. Sincere thanks are also due to the anonymous reviewers of the manuscript for their generous yet probing reading of my work together with John Bowdler for assistance with copy editing and proofreading of the book. I would also like to thank Kiruthiga Sowndararajan for her professional and timely communication during the production process. I am greatly indebted to the specialist assistance provided by Jane Brown from the Visual Cultures Resource Centre of the University of Melbourne.

My parents – Harry and Anastasia Strintzos – have continued to support and encourage me in this undertaking as in all others. My final debt of gratitude is to Fraser Walker, who has accompanied me on this wonderful journey – thank you for your love and support and constant voice of encouragement.

An introduction to the private collector's museum

The private collector's museum has become a highly visible and aspirational model for a growing number of influential wealthy collectors over the last two decades. Its *raison d'être* is often justified on 'philanthropic' grounds with collectors citing 'public access' as being vitally important in opening up personal collections to local and global audiences. This sense of public-spiritedness is frequently expressed through the notion of 'the museum' rather than other forms of cultural benefaction – that is, gifting signifi-cant works of art or donations of money to existing public institutions. By constructing one's own art museum, wealthy collectors are afforded the autonomy to actively manage their holdings and public personae within the public realm and in their own lifetime. Within this context the terms *philan-thropy, public access* and *museum* can be used to evoke a perception of civic duty, a democratic zeal and sense of cultural authority.

However, for all the focus on individual collector's claims of giving back to society and making private collections publicly available, the terms *phil-anthropy, public access* and *museum* can often be used loosely. At other times they are used opportunistically, as justification for the influence that their immense wealth and works of art can exert within the public sphere and elite museum circles. The use of the word 'museum' can be equally confusing and misleading as not all private collections warrant their own museum or offer what Swiss museum director Dr Tobia Bezzola refers to as a 'full service museum'. Dr Bezzola argues 'many of these private museums provide a restricted service and have a limited understanding of what it means to be a museum, that is, the true concept of a museum'.[1] The museo-logical expertise required in the management of museums and works of art cannot be underestimated. It is for this reason that most European private collectors prefer to employ the terms 'Collection' or 'Foundation'. In the literature, there is a surprising lack of critical assessment of the evolution of the private museum in the twenty-first century: little awareness exists of their philanthropic nature, their cultural contributions presently and in the future or the reasons why they have (re)emerged as a major influence on the global museum stage.

This book seeks to offer such an assessment by asking some fundamental questions. What are the similarities and differences between current and past collectors and their philanthropic gestures and how does the development of private museums play out within a contemporary context? Why has the private museum become a dominant entity in the last two decades and what are the implications for the public museum sector? To what extent are individual collectors challenging and redefining the notion of philanthropy, public access and museum? Lastly, how fiscally sustainable is the private collector's museum beyond the original founder's lifetime? Answering these questions is a crucial step to understanding and defining the framework of the private collector's museum.

Rethinking the development and future trajectory of the private museum is crucial within the already challenging public museum sector and rapidly evolving global stage where museums not only compete vigorously with other museums for their audiences and the patronage and benefaction of wealthy collectors, but also for ongoing government funding to ensure they remain financially viable and relevant to their audiences. More recently, fiscally challenged cities and museums have looked to offset declining budgets and endowments by deaccessioning notable works of art from their holdings. In February 2018, the Berkshire Museum of Art in Pittsfield, Massachusetts was given the approval by the Supreme Court to proceed with the sale of up to 40 works of art in an attempt to raise $55 million dollars to secure the museum's future. This controversial decision sparked international condemnation, but it is not an isolated incident and in Chapter 6 I will examine how a number of public museums in Germany have undertaken a similar path. The (re)emergence of the private museum – established as a counterpoint to the public museum – further complicates the current fragile museum terrain throughout parts of Europe, the United States, England and Australia. This book examines the implications of a more complex understanding of the private museum; how it is realised, funded and understood in the broader cultural context. An examination of the ways in which this particular museum model has evolved within a historical Western tradition of collecting and museum building will also shed light on shifting patterns of collecting, like the transition of personal art collections into the public sphere. Furthermore, this analysis of the impact on the public museum sector of various international taxation laws will enhance the capacity of museum managers and private benefactors to better understand and plan future funding strategies in more productive ways.

One of the first issues raised by the relationship between today's collectors and their predecessors is how the understanding of cultural benefaction has altered over time. While the late-nineteenth and early-twentieth-century collectors were actively involved in building their self-image through their collections of fine art, their choices in determining the method of benefaction were clearly limited: to build their own house museum to gift to the public;[2] bequeath their vast art collections to an existing public institution such as the Metropolitan Museum of Art;[3] or donate their collection to help found a public museum.[4] Henry Clay Frick's (1849–1919) will formally entrusted a board of trustees to see through the 'formation' and 'organisation' of The Frick Collection which was intended as a permanent public institution.[5] A $15 million endowment fund accompanied Frick's bequest. Under Section 17 of the Decedent Estate Law of the State of New York, it states that a person with immediate next of kin – wife, husband, child or parent – is able to bequeath more than 'one-half and no more' of their estate, after payment of any debts or taxes to any charitable organisation. Frick's direct heirs were required to waive and renounce further access to the Estate of Henry C. Frick.[6] Although Frick's mansion was built for the single purpose of being a 'gallery of art', it was not intended to be open to the public within the collector's lifetime. The Frick residence was opened to the public as a museum, in 1935 – 16 years after Frick's death.

This delay is because such acts of benefaction were usually undertaken towards the later part of the collector's life or in consultation with the institutions they supported. As a result, the trajectory of their collection into the public sphere was clearly defined and the source or motivation plainly articulated: to establish a permanent memorial to themselves as a notable connoisseur and collector of fine art and to establish significant art collections and institutions that would be accessible to the public.

Posthumous acts of benefaction have become less appealing for many contemporary collectors who elect to manage the transition of their collection into the public sphere, by way of their private museum. Hence, private collections are being made publicly accessible without necessarily gifting them to the state or the nation or even at the death of the collector. This paradigm shift indicates a significant point of departure from earlier philanthropic conventions as now private museums are increasingly created with the public in mind. Entrepreneurs such as American art collector and philanthropist Eli Broad, are no longer satisfied with the traditional and passive form of philanthropy and seek to redefine the notion of giving to one that they regard as being more relevant to today's changing view of arts philanthropy. Eli Broad's 'philanthropic' relationship with the Los Angeles County Museum of Art (LACMA) and Museum of Contemporary Art (MOCA) in Los Angeles is discussed in Chapter 9. His longstanding association with LACMA and MOCA informed the construction of The Broad and raise questions around complex practices between private and public and what is understood by the term 'philanthropy'.

Central to this shift in cultural benefaction, and to the relationship between private and public sectors was art historian Carol Duncan's past criticism of American public museums as they have eagerly embraced restrictive donations offered to them by wealthy benefactors seeking to immortalise their private collection and themselves in dedicated museum wings.[7] More specifically, she points to the proliferation of what she terms 'donor memorials' within museums such as the Metropolitan Museum of

Art, dedicated to various private collections of varying quality and art historical significance. Duncan puts this down to museum trustees' unwillingness to guard the museum's principles as a public institution.[8] In seeking to establish a public home for their personal collections, wealthy collectors can often put their interests of self-commemoration and personal pursuits ahead of genuine altruism and the interests of the public institutions they are seeking to support. More recently, the debate between private and public priorities has intensified as public institutions are reluctant to subscribe to inflexible private demands that often include the permanent display of a private collection. Furthermore, it is becoming more difficult for public institutions to readily accommodate large collections of art that have expanded dramatically in size and breadth over relatively short periods of time.[9] This has prompted very wealthy contemporary collectors to look at the private museum model to exhibit their holdings.

The rhetoric coming from some private collectors attempts to position the private museum as not only embodying a different relationship with art, artistic practice and the public but also, a new relationship with its own history. One of the key outcomes of this current debate on the role of private collections has been the development of new commissions for architecture and designers and the fostering of unique and alternative engagements with art and place. In this context, wealthy private individuals have promoted their public deeds through architectural commissions often attracting international media attention for the museum and its creator. The Museum of Old and New Art (MONA) in Australia continues to enjoy a national and international scrutiny that also extends to its founder David Walsh. MONA's large and distinct architectural design is home to Walsh's eclectic and curious collection of antiquities, cultural objects and modern and contemporary art. His engagement with the public and the public art museum sector – through exhibition collaborations and loans, financial and in-kind support – serves to further validate his own private collection and museum through his continued association with established institutions and art market professionals.[10] Furthermore, Walsh, and his international contemporaries, are actively situating their own museums within the public sphere of audience engagement and education and as major landmarks and cultural contributors to the reputations of their respective cities. This will be shown to mark a departure from earlier creators of private museums who sought to make significant public contributions that would benefit future generations, they were not intended to be a major civic contributor to their city's cultural development – this was largely seen to be the role of public institutions.

Iconic buildings, conversions and expansions such as Glenstone Museum (2018), Stiftung Nantesbuch (2017), The Centro Botín (2017), The Skulpturenhalle (2016), Langen Foundation (2004) and Museum Insel Hombroich (1996), and a number of other private museums are attracting attention for their unique approach to art, architecture and nature. In Germany, the private museum boom continues to gain momentum with new additions that include Museum Barberini (2017), The Feuerle Collection (2016) and additional exhibition spaces for the Julia Stoschek Collection (2016) and Museum Frieda Burda (2017) in Berlin. With the emergence of the Justin Art House Museum (JAHM) (2016) and The David Roche Foundation (2016) we have seen a refashioning of the house museum model in Australia. Between 2015 and early 2018, four private initiatives have emerged in the Netherlands even though this region is not known for their private museums: Museum No Hero (2018), Museum Voorlinden (2016), Modern Contemporary (Moco) Museum (2016) and Museum MORE (2015). This appears to go against the local tradition where ostentatious signs of wealth are usually frowned on in the Netherlands.

As newly founded private museums have mushroomed throughout much of the western world, it is difficult to generalise about their formation and character and to make assumptions about their founders and their nationality. As Director of the Kunsthaus Zürich Dr Christoph Becker, points out about searching for similarities:

> This is difficult to do – I think this is a good thing as there is no system behind it. It works off different aspects of wealth, publicity, politics, society, the situation within the city or the countryside. If there is interest within a community for a private or public space – this is good as it is competition between private individuals and public institutions. If it keeps people talking about culture, it is a great thing.[11]

The number of art collectors continues to follow an upward trajectory with greater media emphasis placed on the various art collectors that have emerged in the twenty-first century. To place today's private museums and collectors into a historical context we need to remember that museums began with private collectors. The emergence of the *Wunderkammer* ('chamber of marvels') and *Kunstkammer* ('chamber of art') in the mid-sixteenth century in Northern Europe came to be universally identified with the notion of the *cabinet of curiosities*. Cabinets or collectors' rooms housed collections of precious works of art, antiquities and relics, rare and exotic natural history articles and memorabilia, ethnographic and archaeologic objects and scientific instruments and models that reflected the collector's level of knowledge and perception of the world at the time.[12] As Patrick Mauriès explains, a long tradition of acquiring the unique object or art work was one aim of the sixteenth and seventeenth-century European collector.[13] The other was to exhibit them within a specific setting where the engagement of object and space would enhance the appearance and appreciation of both and introduce additional layers of meaning to the displayed objects.[14] These collectors ultimately influenced the type of museum spaces and buildings that would house their collections, not the public who later came to visit them.[15]

The notion of the state or national museum as we know it today did not exist to the same degree in the seventeenth century, as witnessed by the fact that some collections on display remained private.[16] It was not until the late eighteenth and nineteen century that newly established constituted monarchies sought to use the museum as a way to 'civilise and educate people'[17] recognising it was 'an important part of changing social values and practices'.[18] 'The public' aspect of the public museum in the late eighteenth and nineteenth century simply meant that the educated and elite members of society (largely male), alongside artists and scholars, were free to appreciate the works of art on display, so it was not entirely democratic by today's standards. As Jennifer Barrett points out 'the use of the museums by various social classes questioned the value of claims about the civilizing and educating role of museums for 'the masses'.[19] Thus, public museums were founded on the belief that museums and collections had a specific role and benefit that would serve society more broadly than if they were maintained as private collections for individuals to indulge in their personal pursuits. It was through private bequests that nations were able to amass valuable collections from individuals that would in turn be made available to the public.[20]

The nationalisation of the royal collection in the Musée du Louvre in Paris in 1793 would later serve as a template for other national public museums for years to come. Most newly formed public institutions did not possess the quality art collections and objects seen in the Louvre and therefore, relied on private individuals to help shape them and sometimes found them.[21] In doing so, private collectors and benefactors helped to build outstanding public museums, and also establish private collections of art that were in one way or another made publicly available: London's Dulwich Picture Gallery[22] and the National Gallery,[23] the Museum of Fine Arts in Boston, Metropolitan Museum of Art in New York[24] and Philadelphia Museum of Art amongst them.[25]

The late nineteenth-century the museum became a significant cultural symbol for the affluent middle class in the large capital cities seeking to accrue status through building art collections and architecturally designed buildings in which to house them. Museum building continued through the twentieth century in unprecedented numbers only to be interrupted by World War I and the political and economic events that occurred from 1929 until after World War II. Historian James Sheehan, asserts that art museums were regarded as 'indispensable sources of prestige and essential instruments for the spread of culture and enlightenment'.[26] Although he refers directly to the first 'Museum Age' of 1830 to 1880, this perception of museums' status and benefits has altered little over time and continues to serve as a significant motivation for wealthy business tycoons today.

During the 1980s and 1990s a significant number of public museums in the US and Europe refurbished or extended their museum buildings[27] or built new ones (in particular France and Germany)[28] to address a growing interest in the museum and what Ian Ritchie refers to as the 'commercialisation of art in the 1980s'.[29] These buildings are of remarkable architectural interest with their often-grandiose façades that are intended to be significant cultural landmarks within their respective cities.

The early-twentieth-century enthusiasm for art collecting and museum building is in many ways being replicated today, over one hundred years later, albeit, in more varied formats and more broadly across the globe. More recently, large public institutions like the Louvre, Guggenheim and the Tate Gallery have expanded their brands beyond their respective cities.[30] The cultural ambitions of the emerging Gulf nations is clearly expressed in the newly opened Louvre Abu Dhabi that drew immense international attention in late November 2017.

It will be shown that recent developments within the museum sector are driven by the need to publicly exhibit personal collections that have been amassed over relatively short periods of time. Private museums offer wealthy collectors alternative venues and methods of display that are seen to deviate from established exhibition practices of the public museum sector or even the intimate domestic settings of previous generations. Yet, often echoes of historical collecting patterns and traditions of benefaction can be found in these new approaches. This might suggest that the presumed demarcation between private interests and the public sphere when viewed in the context of today's private museum has become more hazy. This is complicated further as individual collectors seek to engage with public museums on various platforms, even though many also elect to construct their own private museums that are made publicly accessible within their own lifetimes. A state or nationally owned and operated museum is clearly understood to be public. However, a privately owned and funded museum that is made available to a general audience can also be seen to be public. One can attest that opening up private museums to everyone reasserts Jennifer Barrett's notion of the democratic ideal that is implied by 'the public'. By making private collections available to general audiences, collectors want to be seen to be democratic.

There is a steady blurring of the line between what is understood by society at large to be private and what is public. The distinction is not as clear as it was in the past when works entered the public realm upon the collector's death. As we shall see, the changing nature of the private museum, over the last one hundred years, has moved away from the conventional house museum to an institutional style of the house and 'stand-alone museum', and is thereby, deemed to be public by the community at large. As Dr Christoph Becker asserts:

> As long as it [the art collection] remains in your private home or it is in storage, it remains private, but if you go public things change. It is no longer you and the artwork – it is the public and the work of art. This changes the relationship between the individual and the work of art. The public takes away what you have built and consume it – it is no longer yours.[31]

In this sense, the evolving nature of cultural benefaction and the relationship between private and public raise a number of issues and difficulties that impact not only upon the public museum sector but also, privately founded and funded museums. This book investigates ways in which different trajectories spin off from the house museum. It examines their infiltration into the public sphere and how the individual private museums fare over time (the different formations of the house museum and its development from a house and domestic setting to one of exhibition space is discussed in Chapters 3 and 4). This discussion will lead into an analysis of the standalone museum and the various issues that can emerge upon the death of the original creator and the complex partnerships that are formed between private and public. As we shall see in Chapter 8, even preeminent institutions such as the Menil Collection in Houston can also confront problems upon the death of the founder. To secure the long-term future of their private institutions a number of wealthy German collectors (in their later years) have struck individual agreements with government officials that are a complex mix of gifts, part sales and long-term loans. This is discussed later in the book, noting that governments have found they must redirect funds away from the already struggling public museum sector to ensure that personal legacies and museums can endure in perpetuity.

A note on 'philanthropy', 'private' and 'public'

Before considering some of the more convoluted aspects of the private collector's museum it will be useful to clarify some of the implications of 'philanthropy' in the 'private' and 'public' domains. The dictionary definition of philanthropy is 'altruistic concern for human welfare and advancement, usually manifested by donations of money, property, or work to needy persons, by endowment of institutions of learning and hospitals, and by generosity to other socially useful purposes'.[32] Philanthropy involves donations for which no specific material benefit is intended. This understanding of philanthropy can easily be applied to the late John D. Rockefeller Jr. (1874–1960), who preferred to remain an anonymous benefactor with respect to many of his notable contributions to the Metropolitan Museum of Art in New York; it was the museum's board of directors who were keen to publicly disclose their patron's name.[33] In 1925, the museum formally announced the purchase of the property known as the Cloisters for $600,000 that was paid by Rockefeller and gifted to the Metropolitan Museum of Art. Just as Rockefeller declined several of the museum's offers to serve as a trustee, in 1930, he refused to have the new museum addition – the Cloisters – named in his honour.[34]

The relocation of the Cloisters to its existing picturesque location at Fort Tryon Park was made possible through the generous gifting of the park land to the city of New York by Rockefeller who also paid for the landscaping of sixty acres at a personal cost of around $13 million.[35] As the museum's benefactor, he funded the project and its new acquisitions, donated many works and set up the 'Gothic Fund' as an endowment for future purchases.[36] Besides giving the Metropolitan a new museum, Rockefeller made several unrestricted financial contributions to assist with the running costs and upkeep of the museum. Rockefeller's mode of philanthropy was collaborative. He sought little public recognition for his many gifts of works of art and donations of money that amounted to several millions of dollars from the mid-1920s through to the 1930s.[37] Similarly, he did not seek to exert power and influence over the museum as most of his dealings with them were low profile. It could be argued that Rockefeller assumed a traditional back-seat style of philanthropy.

When assessed within a museological framework, the term philanthropy can be complex and loosely applied. This is particularly so when complicated arrangements are struck between wealthy private collectors and public institutions; this might involve rigid clauses that insist on the permanent display of their personal collection, an agreement that might include long-term loans and donations of money or even an attempt to exert power and authority over the institution's decision-making process so as to secure the collector's legacy in perpetuity. In this instance, it could be argued that this is not philanthropy in the truest sense, it is perhaps something else.

The 100-year loan agreement between collector Donald Fisher's Foundation and the San Francisco Museum of Modern Art (SFMOMA) is an example of an alternative approach to the notion of 'philanthropy'. The contract signed in 2009 stipulates that 1,100 works from the Fisher Foundation will continue to be owned by the Foundation, however, the duty of care rests entirely on the museum. The collection was transferred to the new Fisher Wing at SFMOMA in May 2016. The underlying motivation behind such a prescriptive, and what might be perceived by many as a one-sided agreement, is to ensure the permanent display of the collection, for the next 100 years. While such an arrangement allows the museum to bolster its holdings of modern art, it limits their ability to attract new benefactors due to the permanent space allocated to the Fisher Collection. Furthermore, I would suggest that such an agreement is at odds with John D. Rockefeller Jr.'s approach to cultural benefaction and narrows the definition of philanthropy.

Nigel Baldwin's definition of philanthropy explains it as thus: 'Altruism at one end and enlightened self-interest at the other, and in between are concepts such as generosity, clarity, stewardship, patronage and endowment'.[38] Peter Frumkin likewise sees it as a civil duty when funds are contributed to private institutions or foundations for the benefit of the public.[39] Philanthropy, he suggests, can also be a way for givers to improve their public image or perhaps even a tarnished one that can be rebuilt by way of philanthropic deeds.[40] Frumkin elaborates further: 'In reality, the meaning of philanthropy is negotiated and defined every time donors and recipients are joined through philanthropy. Philanthropy translates the private expressive desires of donors into public action aimed at meeting needs'.[41]

Writer, journalist and politician (Canada's Minister of Foreign Affairs, 2017) Chrystia Freeland, suggests that amongst the 'super wealthy' elite 'the most coveted status symbol isn't a yacht, a racehorse, or a knighthood; it's a philanthropic foundation – and, more than that, one actively managed in ways that show its sponsor has big ideas for reshaping the world'.[42]

Assessing the application of the terms 'private' and 'public' in the context of the private museum, and in conjunction with 'philanthropy', can appear equally complex. The understanding of private is to be personal, individual, privately owned, undisclosed, even if also associated with the idea of private enterprise. Public on the other hand, implies state or nationally owned, shared, undisguised, accessible as well as referencing the people more generally – society as a whole. Jennifer Barrett discusses in great detail the notion of 'public' within a variety of museological formats. She argues that the term 'public' is 'slippery and evasive, paradoxically, despite the assumption that the meaning is accessible'.[43] Barrett suggests this inconsistency has much to do with the changing nature and continual referencing to the idea of democracy that is implied by the notion of 'the public'. A constant attempt to be egalitarian is one way the public museum defines itself, its role and the institutions it represents.[44] The term 'private' she adds is seen to not be 'public' and is 'to be with oneself, to be an individual, to be particular . . . it can relate to the private interests of the individual, or to a privatised market economy'.[45] Furthermore, Barrett implies 'private persons and their particular concerns are often presumed to be separate from the public realm'.[46]

This book will argue that contemporary collectors, are seeking to redefine and challenge existing boundaries of what constitutes cultural philanthropy. In doing so, I explore the different ways in which collectors manipulate and mould the notion of giving and what is deemed to be private and public in their attempt to fulfil their own personal ambitions. That is, I examine the ways 'philanthropy' can operate within a fixed framework and ask how wealthy collectors see their role in defining or prescribing the understanding of philanthropy through the formation of the private museum.

Being private

The growing number of private museums founded over the last two decades has been largely unprecedented. Significant investment in architecture combined with the formation of substantial art collections has occurred during this time frame because very wealthy collectors want to embrace new and innovative ways to communicate their personal and cultural narrative. It is also because they express a desire to innovate, to make a mark, and to be the best of their time by leveraging their personal ambitions more keenly. It is this aspect that is intended to set them apart from their contemporaries and, indeed, their predecessors.

The most recent data published by *Larry's List* (January 2016) suggests that around 317 private museums have been founded globally since the year

2000, while the *BMW Art Guide by Independent Collectors* (2016) notes 256 Collections.[47] According to *Larry's List*, the largest number of private museums that have been established over the last two decades are situated in Germany (42) and the United States (US) (43). The US represents 15 per cent of all private museums founded internationally, that is, 25 per cent of all global collectors are located in the US; although Germany has a lower percentage ratio (eight per cent of collectors worldwide), it has a disproportionally large number of private museums. This is despite Germany having around a third of the number of American collectors, that is, 250 compared with 768 American collectors.[48] My own study has examined around 68 private museums that have been founded during this time: that is, 26 private museums in Germany (38 per cent) and 21 in the US (31 per cent). Australia has six private museums (nine per cent) that have been founded since 2010, with three existing museums undergoing large expansion projects: The Museum of Old and New Art (MONA) opened their new James Turrell Wing in late December 2017, as well as undertaking a number of new works and commercial projects; the Lyon Housemuseum's new purpose-built Housemuseum Galleries opened in March 2019, and sits alongside the Lyon Housemuseum; and in March 2018, founder of the White Rabbit Gallery Judith Neilson, opened the new 'Dangrove' facility that comprises of storage, research and exhibition spaces.

Victoria Newhouse writes that private museums offer a 'welcome antidote to the seemingly unlimited space and to the depersonalisation of large public museums'.[49] Private museums, she argues, are not subject to the same ongoing financial and attendance pressures as public institutions and have the luxury of being selective and unconventional in determining the organisation in which exhibition displays are mounted.[50] At face value this might appear to be so, however, many collectors want the public to come and appreciate their art collections and museums, why else would they found them? While the funding of private museums is not contingent on visitor numbers, if they fail to attract significant audiences and interest, the museum's relevance, future and the collector's own reputations are equally at risk. It might be argued that the Museum Brandhorst has struggled to grow their audience despite their association with, and close proximity to, the esteemed Pinakothek der Moderne in Munich. The Broad in Los Angeles, on the other hand, places much emphasis on citing visitor numbers and reports them on a regular basis. Their web site proclaims that in over two years The Broad attracts over 800,000 visitors a year. Media reports and attention has focused on the museum's visitor numbers because they serve to validate and quantify the success or failure of any institution – private and public.

Newhouse also states that the presentation of the collection is key in many private museums, with little to distract the viewer from the art.[51] Again, I would counter this by adding that the static and predictable presentation of the Museum Brandhorst, and other private collections, has done little to inspire repeat visits to the museum. It would appear that a number of recent temporary exhibitions at the Museum Brandhorst drawing on the Pinakothek der Moderne's curatorial expertise is intended to reposition their exhibition programme in response to the declining visitor numbers. The exhibition entitled 'Creating Realities. Encounters between art and cinema' (16 April–31 May 2015) saw the collaboration between the Pinakothek der Moderne, Museum Brandhorst, the Goetz Collection and Kino der Kunst. The survey exhibition of American artist Seth Price (21 October 2015–8 April 2018) extended the Museum Brandhorst's collaboration to the Stedelijk Museum Amsterdam, thereby, deviating greatly from their earlier exhibition approach.

Private museums need to rise to the challenge and offer a different experience to that of public museums if they are to continue to attract audiences and remain relevant in the long-term. Furthermore, the operating of private museums requires a firm and ongoing financial commitment – the issue of sustainability is always top of mind, both during and after the founder's own lifetime. Senior Curator from the Fondation Beyeler Dr Ulf Küster, points out:

> The cost [of running a private museum] is very high – 75 per cent of what we spend we get back through entrance fees, the museum shop and restaurant. A cultural institution like this is constantly in the minus – it is very difficult to make money, if not impossible. If you make money, this is only possible with very successful exhibitions, as you always spend more than you earn …You should never establish a private museum unless you do it as Ernst Beyeler did – you should always fund it because running a museum is mostly privately funded. We get some contribution from the Riehen and the canton of Basel, but that is relatively less compared to the private contribution.[52]

The size and quality of one's personal collection is perceived to be prestigious and culturally advantageous within art and elite circles. As Don Thompson writes, expensive collections of art have today become synonymous with 'wealth and independent taste', not forgetting power and influence; thus, reinforcing art as the ideal status symbol for the twenty-first-century collector.[53] Despite the number of private museums that have been founded since 2000, maintaining them and their holdings intact, indefinitely, continues to be the biggest challenge facing many contemporary art collectors and benefactors. In Chapter 7 I will show that contemporary private collectors, in their later years, are looking at different ways to secure the future of their respective museums, beyond their own lifetime.

This fundamental concern will play out in one of three ways. One alternative is to include the support of third party individuals and their foundations; the second is to gift the museum and collection to the public. In either case, significant endowments will be required to assist financially challenged cities and public institutions in the running of these museums, if they are forthcoming, as such funding gestures will be at the expense of existing public museums, their publics and limited public resources. As Dr Küster, reminds us that

> in Bern, the Klee museum was financed by a wealthy individual, but now the funds are gone. This is what many feared would happen here [Fondation Beyeler] as well. Now the Canton of Bern has to take over the responsibility of the collection, the building and the staff. It is now part of the Kunstmuseum in Bern.[54]

The third alternative is simply to allow private museums to see out their time, however long that may take. In 2016, Switzerland's oldest collector's museum, the Oskar Reinhart 'Am Stadtgarten' (1951) in Winterthur, faced the prospect of closing its doors unless the city or the Canton of Zürich intervened as the foundation was close to bankruptcy.[55] The house museum Villa Flora (1995), also in Winterthur, closed its doors in 2014 as the family foundation could no longer afford to sustain the museum – and the city was, at the time, unwilling to fund it. Their trajectories are examined further in Chapter 4.

When considering the individual private museums within a broader museum context we need to assess their fiscal sustainability and how each museum will endure beyond the original founder's lifetime. The New York art-world attorney Barbara Hoffman, states that some collectors involve their heirs, however, the reality of 'ensuring continuity after a single dominant patron is no longer active remains a major challenge for private institutions'.[56] It must also be noted that the collector's heirs may not share a similar passion or have sufficient funds to ensure such a philanthropic initiative is perpetuated.[57] As former director of the Museum Oskar Reinhart 'Am Stadtgarten' Dr Marc Fehlmann, emphasised: 'You don't have to create a museum for every collection. Some of them have their time and then it's finished'.[58] Founding director of MONA Mark Fraser, expressed a similar opinion: 'Things should not always be done with perpetuity in mind. We assume museums are forever; museums are not permanent'.[59] In 2014, the Corcoran Gallery of Art in Washington, DC (1869–2014) closed its doors leaving its vast collection of art to the city's National Gallery of Art. After 17 years, the Essl Collection in Vienna also closed its doors in 2016. This prompts us to ask the question: why are we seeing such a shift towards private museums and how will so many of them endure the test of time?

Scope and structure

As I outline below, the book has been written in a series of in-depth contemporary case studies to allow the reader to understand the private collector's museums through the lens of history and how they have responded and endured over time. By using specific case studies, it draws attention to the individual aspects of collecting and demonstrates the various ways they have transitioned into the public sphere and their future trajectories. Earlier approaches to collecting and cultural benefaction and the relationship between private and public are also examined in some detail to emphasise similarities but also, differences and changes and how these play out within contemporary circumstances, different regions and changing economic times. It will be shown that there is not one superior model for establishing a private museum, and we cannot take for granted that museums will endure indefinitely, as even celebrated examples have been fiscally challenged by declining endowments and difficult economic periods. The numerous case studies reveal where difficulties have emerged and what the repercussions might be for the public museum sector facing shifts in private ambitions over time.

The scope of the study spans across Europe – predominantly Germany and Switzerland – the United States, England and Australia as they collect-ively draw on particular Western traditions: shared assumptions and cultural values, democratic conventions and similar legal and taxation principles that bind them together. Germany and other European nations have a long-standing tradition of private (princely courts) and public art museums and his-tory of culture that dates back to the second half of the eighteenth century to the twenty-first. As Sheehan writes, the collation of princely collections, their transition into the public sphere and their historical arrangements formed the intellectual, institutional and architectural basis upon which the German art museum would be established. As he points out, it was at this junction of princely and public that the art museum emerged, however, in Germany and in most parts of Europe, the museum building era did not materialise until the beginning of the revolutionary period of the nineteenth century.[60]

The opening of the first German museums in 1830 saw the construc-tion of art museums throughout central Europe. A number of non-princely patrons of the arts also helped to found public institutions by bequeathing their collections of art and fortunes to their respective cities: the wealthy Frankfurt merchant and collector Johann Friedrich Städel set up a civic foundation to establish The Städel Museum (1815); the *Germanisches Nationalmuseum* (1852) was founded through the persistence of Hans Freiherr von Aufsess and other civic-minded citizens; two independent benefactors formed the Wallraf-Richartz Museum in Cologne – Ferdinand Wallraf gifted his art collection to the city upon his death (1824) and local patron Johann Heinrich Richartz built the museum to house the collection (1861).[61] We can see that in many German cities, the driving force behind the creation of art museums came from local citizens, and a similar approach to patronage can still be observed today as a growing number of wealthy German collectors look to the private art museum as their preferred mode of benefaction. The Kunstmuseum in Zürich stems from similar foundations – established through a local art society in 1812 that gathered around the museum.

England provides a historical context for the development of public institutions and private (house) museums. Sir Hans Sloane's bequest in 1753 saw the foundation of the British Museum in 1759. His entire private collection was bequeathed to King George II for the nation on the proviso that a freely accessible museum was created and a payment of £20,000 given to his heirs. On 7 June 1753, an Act of Parliament was passed accepting Sloane's gift and thus it served to establish the British Museum. Similarly, the origins of the house museum can be traced back to the Private Act of Parliament in 1833 that saw Sir John Soane's Museum transition from house to museum in 1837, upon the death of the collector. Soane's quirky installations and collection continues to inspire contemporary collectors with many citing Sir John Soane's Museum as a major influence in creating their own private museums. In considering the influential role of earlier private benefactors and their personal collection, Chapter 2 examines the influential role of the Wallace Collection in prompting numerous American industrialist collectors (Henry Clay Frick amongst them) to create their own mansion museums at the turn of the twentieth century and assert their cultural credentials. The aristocratic associations and cultural capital connected with Continental Old Masters and British paintings allowed these newly minted industrialists to differentiate themselves. By drawing on European and English models of connoisseurship, collecting and culture more broadly they moulded them to reflect their own ambitions and in so doing, played a key role in simultaneously establishing many American (public) museums alongside their respective (private) collections. Their democratic and cultural aspirations helped to form a tradition of private giving – a complex hybrid of private and publicly operated and funded art museums that dominates the American cultural landscape to the present date and will be discussed further in Chapter 1. Australia conveniently borrows from all three Western museum models and philanthropic traditions.

The omission of Asia warrants a separate in-depth study as their collecting traditions have largely emerged in the twenty-first century and from an entrepreneurial rather than conventional model of philanthropy. The fast-growing number of art collectors continues to rise reflecting the number of art collectors that have emerged in China. The Chinese collector base began to emerge between 2001 and 2010, but more significantly, between 2010 and 2013. This is due to a broader economic context, the growth in newly wealthy individuals and the prestige associated with art collecting and museum building. Just as I have identified differences between collectors over time, there are also distinctions between Asian and Western models of collecting and philanthropy.

The book commences with an overview of the financial benefits that are often associated with making private collections publicly accessible. Allowing public access to private house and collection museums enables individual collectors and their foundations to receive various taxation benefits that would otherwise not be possible if they remained strictly private. Chapter 1 examines the many complex international taxation laws that generally promote and reward public-spiritedness with generous incentives, and places this within a historical framework. It seeks to contextualise American philanthropic conventions and taxation laws as a background to the contemporary case studies discussed in later chapters. Chapter 2 examines the shifts in private art collecting and cultural philanthropy in the twentieth and twenty-first centuries to emphasise how social and cultural prestige has led many super wealthy private collectors to establish their own museums. A new paradigm in philanthropy is shown to have arisen, which influences how private collectors are playing a key role in actively building their own public personae through their collections and philanthropic choices. In contrast to earlier modes of benefaction, a growing number of private art collections and collector-founded museums are open to their publics from the outset, and are generally established with the intention that they will be funded and operated as private institutions, indefinitely.

The house museum will be examined under two distinct categories: one focusing on the domestic aspects of the house, the other, on the exhibition space (in which cases the notion of the house is used mainly as a façade for the museum). This parallel development raises a number of questions: how is today's house museum evolving, what is the next step and how does its destiny play out over time? This discussion will lead into the 'stand-alone museum' (not a domestic house) and the various issues and difficulties that can emerge when high profile collectors seek to present their personal legacies on the contemporary global stage. Chapter 3 will examine how the personal aspects of living and experiencing art within an intimate and domestic environment are seen to be important characteristics of the house as museum. For instance, the Foundation E.G. Bührle Collection (1960–2015), became a house museum despite the collector never having lived in the house but the Lyon Housemuseum (2009) suggests a 'new type' of house museum that integrates domestic and public spaces seamlessly. This chapter will map out the similarities, differences and developments in the house museum over time and the difficulties that are emerging.

Chapter 4 will investigate why the transition of the house to museum resulted in a dramatic shift away from the domestic towards the house as museum and exhibition space. An in-depth study of The Oskar Reinhart Collection (1970), Glenstone Museum (2006) and the Julia Stoschek (2007) and Boros Collections (2008) will assess this journey over time. This will allow for a more nuanced reading of the different ways in which house museums have evolved and lead into the 'stand-alone' museum.

Chapter 5 sets out the complex destiny of the Museum Folkwang in Hagen, Germany (1902–1921) including the difficulties that dramatically altered the collector's fortune and the fate of his holdings and private museum. This chapter will show why the broader economic and political developments ensured Karl Ernst Osthaus was unable to financially secure the future of his collection and museum beyond his own lifetime. Upon his death his heirs sold the naming rights to the museum and collection to a private art consortium in nearby Essen who in turn reinstated the collection within the *Essener Kunstmuseum* renamed Museum Folkwang (1922). I discuss how this serves as a cautionary reminder for many contemporary collectors who are intent on securing the destiny of their private museums within their own lifetimes and how the Museum Folkwang set a precedent in the way private benefactors and the public museum sector have and continue to coexist within the German cultural landscape.

In examining the disproportionally large number of private museums that have emerged in Germany over the last two decades, Chapter 6 explores the repositioning of the nation's cultural landscape and the considerable reinvestment in the public museum sector between 1990 to the present day. If we analyse the public museum sector and the significant gaps that were identified within their holdings of modern and contemporary art, and the way in which key institutions went about addressing this concern, we may recognise how vulnerable many institutions were to the whims of individual wealthy collectors who sought to bolster public collections. While this mode of benefaction appeared to suit a number of collectors in the mid- to late-twentieth century, we can see that the rapid increase in museums, private wealth, the speculative art market and the predominance of the private museum presented wealthy collectors with alternatives beyond the public museum. This context will help to explain the growing popularity of private museums in spite of the difficult economic climate that is negatively impacting public museums and the cities charged with their stewardship. The recent partnerships between Museum Frieder Burda and the Staatliche Kunsthalle, Baden-Baden and Museum Brandhorst and the Pinakothek de Moderne, Munich (in Chapter 7), are explored to determine if they represent a new model between private and public museums.

Chapter 8 considers the creation of the Menil Collection in Houston (1987) which reinstated the single patron collection museum in the United States and much of Europe. Some of the key questions are: why did Dominique de Menil's engage the financial support of other Houstonians who helped to secure the museum's future during its greatest time of need? How did the Menil Collection's original character prevail despite attempts to formalise its administrative and curatorial structure following the passing of its charismatic patron and creator?

Finally, Chapter 9 draws attention to the successful self-made entrepreneur, Eli Broad who is attracted to the idea of creating a grand single-patron collection museum that distinguishes him from his peers. The Broad in Los Angeles will lead the investigation into contemporary monolithic museum design. The opening of The Broad, the media hyperbole, speculation and public reception has been largely unprecedented in Los Angeles. This chapter questions whether Broad's relationship with the Los Angeles County Museum of Art and Museum of Contemporary Art and entrepreneurial approach to philanthropy can be likened to a corporate takeover of the cultural sector in Los Angeles and asks if we are loosening our sense of public-spiritedness by succumbing to the dominant cultural ambitions of influential wealthy collectors?

Taken individually, the aim has been for each chapter to develop detailed overviews of particular stages in the evolution of the private museum model since the turn of the twentieth century, in order to inform our understanding of how the private collector's museum will play out in a contemporary context and how today's collectors go about redefining the notion of philanthropy. Reading across the chapters there emerges an underlying concern that private museums do not necessarily endure as long as public museums, owing to the large funds that are required to sustain them indefinitely. Thus, individual collectors are looking to the public sector to perpetuate their achievements as collectors and public museums are entering into complex and individually negotiated agreements.

The book concludes with some comments on maintaining personal collections and museums intact, indefinitely, and a few thoughts on how private museums benefit from a distinct character and curatorial approach and the degree of public-spiritedness that has prevailed in making private collections publicly accessible. In early 2017, La Maison Rouge, a private Parisian art space founded in 2004, announced that it would close its doors in 2018. When its founder Antoine de Galbert was asked why he decided to close the museum he responded accordingly: 'I think I can say that it takes courage to get involved in a venture like this. And I believe that courage is also needed to put an end to it'.[62]

Notes

1 Dr Tobia Bezzola, interview with the author.
2 Isabella Stewart Gardner (1840–1924), Henry Clay Frick (1849–1919), Henry Huntington (1850–1927) and Albert Barnes (1872–1951).
3 J.P. Morgan (1837–1913), Collis Huntington (1821–1900) and Henry Marquand (1819–1902).
4 William Corcoran (1798–1888), Henry Tate (1819–1899), Charles Lang Freer (1854–1919), William Walters (1819–1894) and Andrew W. Mellon (1855–1937).
5 Mrs. Henry C. Frick, Helen C. Frick, Childs Frick, George F. Baker Jr., J. Horace Harding, Walker D. Hines, Lewis Cass Ledyard, John D. Rockefeller Jr. and Horace Havemeyer.
6 Waiver dated May 14, 1920. Documents Relating to The Frick Collection, 'The Frick Collection' Incorporated 27 April 27 1920, New York, Printed for the Trustees 1923, VIII, Waiver, pp.27–29.
7 Duncan, Carol, *Civilizing Rituals: Inside Public Art Museums*, London and New York, Routledge, 1995, p.68.
8 Duncan, 1995, pp.69–70.
9 Newhouse, Victoria, *Towards a New Museum*, Expanded Edition 2006, New York, The Monacelli Press, 1998, p.279.

10 Donation to the Tasmania Museum and Art Gallery (TMAG) for the acquisition of the Colonial Huon pine furniture collection. The exhibition, *Theatre of the World* (23 June 2012–8 April 2013) at MONA included 300 works from TMAG. Picasso's *Weeping Woman* (1937) was on loan from the National Gallery of Victoria. Author's own visit to the exhibition on 14 July 2012. Also, *ABC News*, 'MONA to Hang Weeping Woman', Australian Broadcasting Commission.

11 Dr Christoph Becker, interview with the author.

12 Walker, Georgina, 'A New Role in Contemporary Art Collecting and Philanthropy: A Comparative Study of Private Collectors David Walsh & John Kaldor and Their Engagement with Private and Public Museums', M.A., The University of Melbourne, 2011, p.14.

13 Mauriès, Patrick, *Cabinets of Curiosities*, London, Thames & Hudson, 2002, p.50.

14 Walker, 2011, p.14; Mauriès, 2002, p.25.

15 Over time most collections that were displayed in private residences were eventually opened to the public: the Medici collection in Florence, Italy, opened as the Uffizi Gallery in the 1830s and the Borghese collection in Rome during the seventeenth century. Ritchie, Ian, 'An Architect's View of Recent Developments in European Museums', in *Towards the Museum of the Future: New European Perspectives*, edited by Roger Miles and Lauro Zavala, New York, Routledge, 1994, pp.8–9.

16 Duncan, 1995, p.24.

17 Barrett, Jennifer, *Museums and the Public Sphere*, West Sussex, Wiley-Blackwell, 2011, p.3.

18 Barrett, 2011, p.46.

19 Barrett, 2011, p.49. Also Weil, Stephen E. *Making Museums Matter*, Washington, Smithsonian Institution Press, 2002, pp.196–197.

20 Barrett, 2011, p.49.

21 The British Museum, London, was open to the public in 1759 through Sir Hans Soane's bequest (1660–1753). 71,000 objects were given to the museum upon his death in return for a £20,000 payment to his heirs. The British Museum, 'The Museum's Story', The British Museum.

22 Founded on the joint bequest of Noël Desenfans and Sir Francis Bourgeois in 1811 after refusing to gift it to the British Museum. Dulwich Picture Gallery, 'History of the Collection', Dulwich Picture Gallery.

23 Founded on the collection and bequest of the banker and German immigrant John Julius Angerstein in 1826. The National Gallery, 'History', The National Gallery.

24 The Metropolitan was founded in 1870 by a group of businessmen, collectors and philanthropists who sought to make art available to all Americans. The Metropolitan Museum of Art, 'History of the Museum', The Metropolitan Museum of Art.

25 Founded 10 May 1877, as the Pennsylvania Museum and School of Industrial Art with exhibits from the 1876 Centennial Exhibition and gifts from private donors.

26 Sheehan, James J., *Museums in the German Art World: From the End of the Old Regime to the Rise of Modernism*, Oxford and London, Oxford University Press, 2000, p.84.

27 The Louvre, Musée d'Orsay, Centre Georges Pompidou, the Jeu de Paume, the Palais de Tokyo in Paris; Museum of Modern Art, Barcelona; the Sainsbury

Wing at the National Gallery and the Sackler Galleries at the Royal Academy in London.

28 Many public museums in Germany underwent dramatic refurbishment, expansion, rebadging and mergers during the German Reunification process in 1990.

29 Ritchie, 1994, p.30.

30 Louvre Lens (2012); Louvre Abu Dhabi (2017); Guggenheim Bilboa (1997); Guggenheim Abu Dhabi (2020?); Guggenheim Helsinki (architect signed 2015 and rejected December 2016); British Museum Abu Dhabi (signed 2009 with deal under review 2018); Centre Pompidou-Metz (2010); Tate Liverpool (1988); Tate St Ives (1993) and the Victoria and Albert Museum, Dundee, Scotland (2017).

31 Dr Christoph Becker, interview with the author.

32 Dictionary reference.

33 Gross, Michael, *Rogues Gallery: The Secret Story of the Lust, Lies, Greed and Betrayals That Made the Metropolitan Museum of Art*, New York, Broadway Books, 2009, p.145.

34 Tomkins, Calvin, *Merchants and Masterpieces: The Story of the Metropolitan Museum of Art*, Revised and Updated ed., New York, Henry Holt and Company, 1989, p.253; Gross, 2009, p.130.

35 Tomkins, 1989, p.254; Gross, 2009, p.154.

36 Gross, 2009, p.145.

37 Gross, 2009, pp.145–147; Tomkins, 1989, p.253.

38 Baldwin, Nigel J., "Philanthropic' Support for the Arts: Views from the Corporate Sector', Doctor of Business Administration, Doctor of Business Administration, RMIT University, 2009, pp.16–17.

39 Frumkin, Peter, *Strategic Giving: The Art and Science of Philanthropy*, Chicago and London, The University of Chicago Press, 2006, p.17.

40 Frumkin, 2006, p.20.

41 Frumkin, 2006, p.21.

42 Freeland, Chrystia, *Plutocrats: The Rise of the New Global Super Rich*, London, Penguin Group, 2012, p.70.

43 Barrett, 2011, p.7.

44 Barrett, 2011, p.7.

45 Barrett, 2011, p.7.

46 Barrett, 2011, p.8.

47 Private museums founded: South Korea 45, China 26, Japan 11, Italy 19, France 10 and Spain 10. Bouchara, Claire, Bossier, Max, Howald, Christine, Liu, Shasha, Noe, Christoph, Woo, Kaisha, Xu, Cuiyun, Sunand, Yingxue and Ren, Wen, Private Art Museum Report, London, Larry's List and AMMA, 2016, pp.20, 22.

48 Bossier, Max, Noe, Christoph, Resch, Magnus and Steiner, Lasse, Art Collector Report, edited by Larry's List, Hong Kong, Modern Arts Publishing, 2014, pp.28, 51.

49 Newhouse, 1998, p. 273.

50 Newhouse, 1998, p.279.

51 Newhouse, 1998, p.274.

52 Dr Ulf Küster, interview with the author.

53 Thompson, Don, *The $12 Million Stuffed Shark: The Curious Economics of Contemporary Art*, New York, Palgrave Macmillan, 2008, p.13.

54 Dr Ulf Küster, interview with the author.
55 Dr Marc Fehlmann, interview with the author.
56 Kastner, Jeffrey, 'New Foundations', *Artforum International*, 48, no. 10 (2010), p.318.
57 Broad's two sons do not share his interests in art or enterprise and are not involved in his philanthropic foundations or business projects.
58 Dr Marc Fehlmann, interview with the author.
59 Mark Fraser, interview with the author.
60 Sheehan, 2000, p.42.
61 Sheehan, 2000, p.84.
62 Muñoz-Alonso, Lorena, 'La Maison Rouge, a Parisian Gem, Will Close in 2018', *artnet'news*, 12 January 2017.

Part I
Overview

1 Setting the foundation
Self-glorification is a small price to pay for philanthropy

The use of the term 'philanthropist' has become synonymous with many of today's wealthy and influential collectors. The word bestows status and prestige on the recipients and admiration from aspiring benefactors who might seek to enter this elite social sphere. Establishing notable cultural achievements, a growing art collection and even a private museum can help to improve a collector's esteem and public reputation in a way that their enterprising deeds cannot do. This is not a twenty-first-century phenomenon but one that dates back to the late nineteenth- and early-twentieth-century American industrialists, banking tycoons and railway magnates, who looked to improve their reputations and legacies through their cultural actions. Henry Clay Frick is one that readily comes to mind – we might consider Eli Broad to be his contemporary equivalent. By drawing similarities between today's collectors and their predecessors, we can observe that past collectors determined their philanthropic intentions towards the end of their life. Decisions about how their holdings would be dispersed upon their death were vital. Contemporary collectors however favour a more active approach to arts philanthropy. This is a significant development that has prompted a growing number of collectors to consider various formats of the private museum model above more traditional methods of benefaction. Opening up one's own museum to the public enables collectors to manage their public image. It also allows them to maintain authority over their holdings while securing generous tax benefits for themselves and their not-for-profit foundations and museums.

Traditionally, the options available to past collectors included: whether to sell their notable works of art at auction; bequeath them to their next of kin who inevitably sold them; give them away over time or gift them to a public museum; establish a private foundation and museum at considerable personal cost or allow their executors to determine the ultimate fate of the collection.[1] Frank Hermann argues the latter inevitably resulted in 'no philanthropy and certainly no self-glorification'.[2] Moreover, Hermann states that today's wealthy and successful businessmen and benefactors have been associated with a 'self-glorifying philanthropy' in pursuit of tax breaks rather than genuine altruistic pursuits. It is for this reason, he says, that serious art collecting is often seen to be synonymous with self-glorification.[3] There are other interesting aspects to Hermann's argument: for example, collectors often see their expansive holdings as a work of art in its own right and do not wish to see it disbanded over time, nor do they want it hidden in a public museum basement. The issue of estate tax is an additional complication that needs to be addressed upon the death of the collector.

By constructing one's own art museum, wealthy collectors can actively manage their holdings and public personae within the public realm and in their own lifetime, albeit at a greater price than gifting works to public institutions. Private museums allow their founders to take charge and address the dilemma of the shortage of exhibition space available for private collections to be on permanent display within public institutions. It can also be argued that the existence of private museums can deny public institutions future access to significant holdings that were once seen to benefit the museum.

This chapter examines how arts philanthropy affords benefactors public recognition and financial incentives in return for their generosity. Philanthropy can directly address the ongoing dilemma of public funding; however, it also raises a number of other concerns. In accepting donations of money or works of art public museums are expected to balance individual benefactors' expectations alongside their public responsibilities. More often than not, private bequests are usually accompanied by strict terms and conditions that are set out by the donors. Furthermore, tax incentives are seldom an immediate call to action and do not always prompt ongoing philanthropic giving within society. Governments also need to promote a sense of goodwill as changes to cultural and taxation policy alone might not bring about the paradigm shift required by governments.

It is generally accepted that most public museums throughout England, Europe and Australia have traditionally operated under the auspices of national, state or local government, irrespective of their private or public origins. Over time governments have assumed responsibility for basic funding, the appointment of boards of trustees and a degree of stewardship over the collections and exhibition programmes – the US is the exception to this rule.[4] In light of ongoing budgetary restraints throughout Europe, England and Australia, governments have, and continue to introduce taxation reforms to prompt wealthy individuals to increase their philanthropic contributions. There is a direct link between increased tax-paying and an increased desire for wealthy individuals to offset their earnings with tax benefits and philanthropic donations. Philanthropy is seen to reduce wealthy individuals' tax burden considerably.[5]

The 'American model' of philanthropy is seen to promote private philanthropic giving through generous tax inducements. Owing to the long-standing tradition of private philanthropy in the US and the complex relationship between private and public support, it is difficult to accurately distinguish between the two as they are often alike. The terms private and public when used in relation to American museums can often be complex and confusing.

Private individuals and donors have and continue to play a significant role in the formation of the private and public art museum in the US. It is, therefore, important to understand how philanthropy fits into the overall structure of American museums. This will be discussed in more detail shortly.

Fostering a culture of 'giving' – then and now

To better understand the complexity of the 'American model' of philanthropy, and its implications for collecting and museum building, we need to consider historical decisions, tax laws and different cultural traditions that have promoted private benefaction and established a culture of 'giving' in the US. During the late nineteenth century, American governments sought to incentivise wealthy industrialist collectors to transfer their holdings to the US, from Europe – especially England. The accumulation of expensive European art collections at the turn of the twentieth century was aided by the reduction, and eventual abolition, of import tariffs in the US. The Payne–Aldrich Tariff Act in 1909 saw import duties that were implemented in 1897 lowered by 20 per cent. What was even more significant was the abolition of import duties on European artworks that were more than 20 years old.[6] This not only encouraged wealthy American collectors to acquire important works of art but prompted those who kept them in storage abroad or in their European or English private properties, to bring them to America. Before 1909, American financier and banker, J. Pierpont Morgan (1837–1913) maintained works of art valued at $30,000,000 (approximately $719,000,000 in today's value) in London to avoid paying import taxes.

This positive tariff situation was confirmed in an interview conducted by the *San Francisco Examiner* on 27 March 1909, with renowned British art dealer Sir Joseph Duveen (1869–1939),[7] from the Duveen Brothers: 'At present, I have stored here [in London] millions of dollars' worth of art objects which Americans have purchased, but which they would not import owing to the tariff duties'.[8] By 3 October 1913, the import tariff rate would be further reduced to ten per cent under the implementation of the Underwood Tariff Act. Thus, it was not long before significant sums of money would be paid abroad to acquire notable paintings, sculptures, rare book collections and decorative objects that were ultimately destined for the American public. In this evolving cultural context, private collections soon provided the backbone of major public institutions that began to mushroom across the nation before and after the turn of the twentieth century.

The introduction of the Federal tax law in 1913 prompted the private sector to assist governments with the funding of social and cultural programmes. In return, charitable contributions were deducted to offset individual tax burdens. This continues to date as private foundations are established as tax-exempt entities. Unlike their European and British counterparts, American museums were not founded on elitist or enlightenment principles, instead they stemmed from a desire to make art available to all citizens – to make it accessible to every member of society, irrespective of their social standing. It was the initiatives and funding of civic-minded individuals, or groups of entrepreneurs, artists, collectors and philanthropists, that saw the formation of American public museums: amongst them, the Smithsonian Institution, Washington, DC (1846); the Metropolitan Museum of Art, New York (1870); the Museum of Fine Arts, Boston (1870); the Philadelphia Museum (1876); the Art Institute of Chicago (1883); the Brooklyn Museum (1897); the Dallas Museum of Art (1903); the Cleveland Museum of Art (1916); the Pasadena Arts Institute, California (1925); the Museum of Modern Art (1929) and the Whitney Museum, New York (1930); the Walters Art Museum, Baltimore (1834)[9] and the National Gallery of Art, Washington, DC (1937).

In conjunction with the founding of major public institutions, many wealthy benefactors also created large personal collections of art that were often displayed in private picture galleries within their lavishly appointed and decorated mansions. Over time many of these residences and collections were made publicly accessible upon the death of the collectors. The manner in which this took place varied greatly as individuals sought to immortalise their cultural contributions in perpetuity: Isabella Stewart Gardner and Dr Albert C. Barnes imposed strict guidelines, thereby preserving their original displays as a form of art in their own right; much of J. Pierpont Morgan's collection was sold and what remained was distributed between the Morgan Library and Art Gallery and the Metropolitan Museum of Art (New York) where his homely settings and holdings have been permanently installed; as founding director of the Phillips Collection, Duncan Phillips transitioned his collection into the public sphere within his own lifetime; Henry Huntington, along with his appointed board of trustees, actively participated in the founding of The Huntington Library, Art Gallery and Botanical Gardens; whilst Henry Clay Frick appointed others in his will to see through the passage from house to public museum, with few if any restrictions.

As the American 'public' art museum model was not founded by the state – but rather was created through the means of its citizens who went about purchasing the works to fill the museum walls – the art museum has operated largely independently of government.[10] For this reason, the American public has become accustomed to such a longstanding tradition of private governance and funding of public institutions. According to former director of the Art Institute of Chicago James Wood, public museums should be seen '. . . as expressions of individual talent and creativity protected by the Constitution from government control or manipulation. In contrast to European and virtually all other nation states, we have no Ministry of Culture . . .'.[11] Public institutions such as New York's Metropolitan Museum of Art and Museum of Modern Art (MoMA) and the Los Angeles County Museum of Art and Museum (LACMA), Museum of Contemporary Art (MOCA) and so forth, are mostly funded and governed through private means. As we shall see in Chapter 9, this can also present museums with a number of challenges.

It has been argued that fundamental American principles provided the framework for individual members of society to set up most of the public museums for the benefit of society as a whole: establishing their purpose, financing the buildings that were often situated on publicly gifted land, and compiling the holdings through private purchases and bequests.[12] Their existence was not formally acknowledged by the state but by the general public, as the late James Wood points out, through their 'use, support, and trust' in each museum. In return, government has provided generous income tax incentives to reward and encourage philanthropic gestures; and thus, American museums have remained privately funded and governed.[13] If art museums are to continue to flourish, to maintain their publics' confidence and uphold their democratic foundation, Wood argues they need to preserve their independence from the state's control and finances.[14] I would counter this argument by stating that while museums remain independent of governments, they are often at the behest of wealthy individual trustees and donors that can often exert influence over the museum's board of trustees and museum itself. Philanthropist and collector Eli Broad is one such example that will be discussed in Chapter 9. His complex relationship with LACMA and MOCA will be shown to have tested the museums' autonomy and their public role and responsibility, thereby prompting us to question Broad's 'philanthropic' spirit.

Public and private partnerships in the funding and governance of museums are an integral part of the American philanthropic tradition. Nonetheless, one needs to weigh up the degree of autonomy that is afforded to a museum with minimal government intervention and with the ongoing dilemma of fundraising to maintain fiscal independence by ensuring endowment funds are maintained at a sustainable level. As we shall see, this is the challenge facing many art museums – private and public – as the enormous scale of art museums has come to dominate their financial, exhibition, education and curatorial focus.

Other models of arts philanthropy

As a general rule, private foundations in the European Union are required to have a specific purpose that is seen to have a public focus and benefit. Economic activities that are unrelated to the foundation's specified activity can thus be taxed in some member states. In Germany, unrelated activities remain fully tax deductible providing the foundation's unrelated income does not exceed 35,000 Euros. Public benefit foundations in Germany enjoy a tax-free status with a minimum of 50,000 Euros required to set up a foundation, with a governing board appointed to manage it.[15] In September 2007, the German Parliament made adjustments to existing philanthropic tax laws that allowed for a further 20 per cent tax deduction on an annual taxable income with the option for individual benefactors to claim the full amount of up to $1 million Euros over ten years.[16]

In Germany, there are three types of not-for-profit organisation: Associations (*Verein*), Foundations (*Stiftung*) and Limited liability companies (*Gesellschaft met beschränkter Haftung*, or *GmbH*).[17] Association and private foundation qualify for tax-exempt status and Limited liability companies operate like a corporation while protecting the founder's personal assets as they cannot be held personally responsible for the organisation's debts or liabilities. While corporations can operate in perpetuity, Limited liability companies must be disbanded upon the death of the founder or if they are declared bankrupt. Non-profit organisations that exclusively and directly pursue a public benefit and philanthropic initiative are exempt of Inheritance, Corporate and Gift Tax while donations, endowments or gifts such as works of art can be deducted from the benefactors' taxable income. Their tax-exempt status is contingent on pursuing altruistic rather than profitable initiatives.

In 1999, the Australian Government commenced the implementation of significant tax reforms that encouraged corporate and private philanthropy through the introduction of the Cultural Gifts Program (CGP), Prescribed Private Funds (PPFs) and the forming of private foundations. In 2008, PPFs were converted to Private Ancillary Funds (PAFS). They allow companies, families and individuals to make donations that are tax deductible as the PAFS are granted deductible gift recipient (DGRs) status by the Australian Taxation Office (ATO).[18] The CGP and PAFs allow tax deductions to be made in multiple ways: first, charitable donations can be claimed in full. Second, cultural gifts bequeathed to public institutions that are granted charitable status by the ATO can be claimed at the current market value and depreciated over five years, without being subject to capital gains tax – irrespective of when they were purchased.[19] And third, a founder of a private museum is able to gift works of art along with their museum to the state or the nation, thereby making the bestowal fully tax deductible for its overall market value; likewise, if the gifted museum continues to be privately funded, the ongoing contributions are also fully tax deductible. For example, the privately founded and funded public museum, TarraWarra Museum of Art (TWMA), was established through the introduction of this initiative in 2003 and gifted to the State of Victoria by Marc and Eva Besen. They continue to fund the operating costs and acquisition of new works of art for the Museum.

In Australia, private museums that are opened to the public are usually set up as a company that is limited by guarantee; that is, to be overseen by a board of trustees and directors to manage the running and operating of the museum, its holdings and endowment fund according to the constitution that binds the organisation. The board appointed may include the founder, immediate family members and external professionals. TWMA was the first private bequest to be formed under the new provisions; established as a company limited by guarantee in October 2000. By sitting on the museum's board of directors, the original benefactors are able to exercise a degree of authority over what is effectively a public institution. This is distinct from one individual being the sole owner of the museum and its holdings. The museum in return is granted charitable gift status by the ATO so that it can enjoy a tax-exempt status, accept gifts and donations and allow members of the public to join the museum.

Under the CGP, benefactors are able to receive tax deductions up to the value of the donation when gifting property to the not-for-profit sector or cultural works to collecting institutions, which also includes privately funded museums.[20] TWMA has up until 2011, received over $63 million in donations through the CGP.[21] While the museum's original founders Eva and Marc Besen, continue to donate works of art to the museum, TWMA accepts works from other private collectors as well as artists. The founding and funding of TWMA was a direct consequence of the changes to Australian tax law. If future private collectors are to follow the Besens' example of philanthropy then it is critical for government to review current tax laws, in light of declining government funds, and to look at a broader range of inducements and approaches that are now necessary given this recent success. Without them, I would suggest a generosity of spirit alone will not result in a substantial philanthropic gift such as TWMA or the founding of other private museums in Australia.

Figure 1.1 Judith Neilson. Photo: David Roche. © Image Courtesy White Rabbit Collection.

Figure 1.2 Exterior view of White Rabbit Gallery. © Image Courtesy White Rabbit Collection.

Figure 1.3 Installation view showing Zhang Dali, *Chinese Offspring*, in 'Vile Bodies' exhibition, 2016, White Rabbit Gallery. Photo: David Roche. © Image Courtesy White Rabbit Collection.

Another example of the CGP in action is Judith Neilson's White Rabbit Gallery in Sydney (established in 2009). It was created to display her growing collection of 3000 works by 700 contemporary Chinese artists.[22] The Gallery is situated in the restored former Rolls-Royce building which has been gifted to the state of New South Wales. White Rabbit is a freely accessible private museum that costs around $4 million a year to run and is fully funded by Judith Neilson. More recently, Neilson has opened the 100,000-square-foot purpose-built state of the art Dangrove art storage facility in inner city Sydney (opened March 2018). As Neilson advised: 'Dangrove was built to store, care and nurture my private collection. It will be open to scholars by invitation only'.[23] Another of Neilson's projects is 'Phoenix' – the $41 million performance space, art gallery and sculpture garden that is an extension of Neilson's private residence and not a publicly accessible space.[24] Due to the variety of projects undertaken by individual collectors, it is important to clarify a couple of points: as White Rabbit Gallery and Dangrove have a public and education focus, they would be granted charitable gift status by the ATO; although Phoenix is essentially a private space it is not known if it operates as a not-for-profit entity.

Figure 1.4 Installation view showing Mia (Wen-Hsuan) Liu *Guggen' Dizzy*, and Shao Yinong and Muchen, *Fairy Tales in Red Times*, in 'Paradi$e Bitch' exhibition, 2015, White Rabbit Gallery. Photo: David Roche. © Image Courtesy White Rabbit Collection.

Also, in Australia, David Walsh's Museum of Old and New Art (MONA), located on the outskirts of Hobart, is registered as a 'for-profit' entity. His other businesses – Moorilla Estate wineries and restaurants, bars and the hotel on the same site – each contribute to the financial needs of the museum, thus MONA cannot be granted a charitable status as it is effectively part of a private business.[25] Walsh, however, is able to depreciate the works of art on display throughout the museum, hotel, restaurants or on loan to other institutions at the market value determined by the ATO as they are exhibited in public spaces.[26] It is important to note, that works that are in storage and not on public display are not eligible for a tax deduction as collecting works of art that are for private viewing, do not qualify for any tax benefit.

Figure 1.5 Interior view of 'The Void', on the lowest level of the Museum of Old and New Art (MONA). © Collection Museum of Old and New Art (MONA), Hobart.

The complexity of tax-funded philanthropy

The setting up of collector-founded museums and foundations as registered cultural institutions in the US can often be complex and challenge the notion of what is understood to be private and public and for-profit and non-profit. Glenstone Museum in Potomac, Maryland – a rural suburb of Washington, DC – has been registered as a private and non-profit organisation since 2006. It was established by science and technology billionaire collector Mitchell Rales. Through the Glenstone Foundation, Rales is able to maintain control and ownership of the art collection whilst being eligible for a number of benefits and tax deductions. Establishing a private operating foundation (Under Section 501 (c) (3) of the Internal Revenue Code) allows the collector to offset the cost associated with exhibiting, insuring, conserving and storing the collection. If the Foundation chooses to sell works from their holdings it is not subject to the 28 per cent capital gains tax that private individuals would incur. Similarly, if the foundation acquires new works of art it is not expected to pay sales tax in most states in the US, nor will the foundation be subject to an estate tax upon Rales' death.[27]

Such cultural initiatives are strictly controlled under Section 501 (c) (3) of the Internal Revenue Code, which also supports the founding of collector museums. To be granted tax-exempt status the institution cannot be set up for the benefit of individual interests, nor can its earnings and interests be seen to benefit any individual shareholder or persons. Any one individual seen to benefit economically from the organisation's transactions – directly or indirectly – may be taxed accordingly. Moreover, there is an annual requirement for the distribution of income by the foundation and constraints on 'self-dealing', that is, restrictions preventing individuals from making economic gains or pursuing their own economic interests ahead of the trust or shareholders.[28]

The complexity of such arrangements becomes clearly apparent in the case of Glenstone which consists of two buildings – the exhibition space that is open to the public and employs a curatorial team and security guards, and the other, which is the founder's private residence. Both properties are eligible for considerable tax deductions and benefits even though his home is not open to the public. According to the documentation provided by the IRS, Rales' private residence is set up to support 'the study, improvement and advancement of the arts', primarily as a lending library to other museums.[29] No further clarification of this role is provided as the two entities are maintained independently.

The merging of private and public, for-profit and not-for-profit becomes even more confusing as works of art registered under the trusteeship of the collection cannot be displayed in Rales' private residence, despite being part of the same estate, without getting into legal difficulties. What is more, tax documents pertaining to the private premises at Glenstone use the same mailing address as the owner's business headquarters. To complicate matters further, Angela Valdez's article in the *Washington City Paper*, notes that the works owned by the Glenstone Foundation – separate again from the two Glenstone buildings – cannot be placed on display at either of the two properties, as the long-standing foundation, according to tax records, has in the past invested and traded works of art.[30] It becomes clearly apparent that the managing of personal finances and philanthropic ones can be more hazy. With the opening of the Foundation's new Thomas Phifer-designed expansion and art pavilions (opened to the public on 4 October 2018) visitors are still required to schedule a visit in advance. While Glenstone promotes free access to the landscape, outdoor sculptures, the new exhibition Pavilions, and Glenstone more broadly, this is nevertheless, highly regulated and managed.

The various complex international tax laws ultimately influence the way that collector-founded museums and foundations are established, funded, structured and managed. In the case of the Fondation Beyeler in Riehen, Switzerland, it operates as two separate entities: Fondation Beyeler and the Beyeler Museum AG.[31] Beyeler Museum AG is a shareholder of the Fondation Beyeler and operates as a not-for-profit entity. The Fondation owns and operates the collection and the museum; the Beyeler Museum AG owns the retail operations connected to the museum. The museum staff are employed by the Beyeler Museum AG. The city of Riehen owns the grounds and the adjacent building that accommodates the museum's offices and restaurant; the lease agreement has been signed for 99 years.[32] This complex structure is perhaps unique to Switzerland and is a way for the Fondation to minimise its tax burden. The Fondation's board of trustees also manages the Beyeler Museum AG. The staff report to the director Sam Keller, and he in turn to the board of trustees and to the Fondation itself. They operate as two distinct entities. Senior Curator at the Fondation Beyeler Dr Ülf Küster, states that it is easier for sponsors and private benefactors to donate works of art and financially support a not-for-profit foundation than a foundation that is 'seen to be very rich'.[33]

The Kunsthaus Zürich is an institution that continues to benefit from individual and corporate benefactors due to its history and 'almost private' status. In 1812, it began to operate as a society of friends gathering at the museum and evolved by 1853 as a *Kunstverein* (art association) that functions more like a private museum than a public one. The museum receives around 40 per cent of its funding from the city and Canton of Zürich. The rest of the funding comes from retail initiatives and contributions from the Friends of the museum. 'It makes it easier than if you are stately funded' says director Dr Christoph Becker, explaining that collectors find it easier to bequeath works to the museum. He also points out that 'sometimes people find it a little more difficult to give something back for which they have already paid tax', concluding: 'We are almost a private institution'.[34] Art collections have moved from one generation to the next with many electing to gift them to the public says Becker: 'In Switzerland people can afford to simply give things away. If there is a museum at hand they are happy to give it to a local museum'.[35] It is important to note that Swiss benefactors gifting works to the museum are not entitled to tax benefits. 'There is a very small tax incentive' says Becker; 'it becomes more about donating works of art to institutions and the public. However, benefactors donating money to the museum are eligible for a tax benefit'.[36]

Conclusion

We can surmise that the formation of many private museums in the last two decades are directly or indirectly linked to generous tax incentives as they help to offset individual tax burdens and promote arts philanthropy. The various complex international tax laws ultimately influence the way that private museums and foundations are established, funded, structured and managed. The generosity and breadth of American, Australian, English and European tax laws is a factor in the promotion of private museums, the lending or gifting of artworks to public institutions and the contribution towards their new building additions. While the link between increased tax paying and a desire to minimise it with tax benefits and philanthropic donations cannot be ignored, it is important to recognise the degree of public-spritedness that has prevailed in making notable private collections publicly accessible from the outset. As we shall see, tax inducements are often insufficient to support private museums indefinitely, and it is for this reason that wealthy collectors are looking to new ways to perpetuate their cultural projects and passions.

Notes

1 Herrmann, Frank, 'Collecting Then and Now: The English and Some Other Collectors', *Journal of the History of Collections* 21, no. 2 (2009), p. 263.
2 Herrmann, 2009, p. 263.
3 Herrmann, 2009, p. 263.
4 Paroissien, Leon, 'Museum Governance and Funding: International Issues Requiring Local Analysis and Informed Solutions', in *Intercom: International Committee on Management Conference: New Roles and Missions for Museums*, Taiwan, 2006, p.4.
5 Carmen McElwain, Partner at Maddocks law firm and Associate; Daniel Slater, interview with the author.
6 Bennett, Shelley M., *The Art of Wealth: The Huntingtons in the Gilded Age*, San Marino, California, The Huntington Library, Art Collections and Botanical Gardens, 2013, p.176.
7 Duveen provided key American collectors – Henry Clay Frick, Andrew Mellon, Samuel H. Kress, Arabella Huntington and Henry E. Huntington – with access to European and British paintings, sculptures, decorative art objects and furnishings from 1879 through the early twentieth century.
8 Bennett, 2013, p.176.

9 Walters Art Gallery, along with 22,000 works was bequeathed to the city of Baltimore in 1931, upon the death of Henry Walters. The collection was collated by father and son William Thompson Walters and Henry Walters. In 2000, the museum was renamed Walters Art Museum.

10 The formation of many nineteenth- and early-twentieth-century American public museums depended on the initiatives and funding of civic-minded individuals or private collectives.

11 Wood, James N., 'The Authorities of the American Art Museum', in *Whose Muse? Art Museums and the Public Trust*, edited by James Cuno, New Jersey, Princeton University Press and Harvard University Art Museum, 2004, p.106.

12 Wood, 2004, p.107.

13 Wood, 2004, p.107.

14 Wood, 2004, pp.107–108.

15 European Foundation Centre. 'Comparative Highlights of Foundation Laws: The Operating Environment for Foundation in Europe', Belgium, European Foundation Centre, 2011, pp.9, 18.

16 European Foundation Centre, 2011, p.19.

17 Richter, Andreas, 'Philanthropy Impact: Germany', *Philanthropy Impact*, UK, 2011.

18 Meachen, Vanessa, 'A Guide to Giving for Australians', Philanthropy Australia, 'Prescribed Private Fund (PPF)', 2006, 2010, p.28.

19 Meachen, 2006, 2010, p.28. Also Carmen McElwain and Daniel Slater, interview with the author.

20 Mitchell, Harold, 'Building Support: Report of the Review of Private Sector Support for the Arts in Australia', Canberra, Australian Government, October 2011, p.19.

21 Mitchell, 2011, p.18.

22 The floating of Kerr Neilson's Platinum Asset Management business in 2007 made $2.8 billion, after tax. Hutchinson, Samantha, 'Is Judith Neilson Australia's Greatest Arts Patron?' *Financial Review*, 28 March 2015.

23 Judith Neilson, email correspondence with the author.

24 Judith Neilson, email correspondence with the author.

25 Mark Fraser, interview with the author.

26 Depreciated over 100 years or less for ephemeral works of art.

27 Valdez, Angela, 'A Very Private Collection', *Washington City Paper*, 6 June 2008, www.washingtoncitypaper.com/articles/35679/a-very-private-collection (accessed 3 April 2013).

28 Internal Revenue Service, 'Private Foundations', US Treasury, Treasury Inspector General for Tax Administration, US Gov.

29 Valdez, 'A Very Private Collection', *Washington City Paper*, 6 June 2008.

30 Valdez, 'A Very Private Collection', *Washington City Paper*, 6 June 2008.

31 AG is the abbreviated form for the German word *Aktiengesellschaft* – a company that is managed and owned by shareholders.

32 Dr Ulf Küster, interview with the author.

33 Dr Ulf Küster, interview with the author.

34 Dr Christoph Becker, interview with the author.

35 Dr Christoph Becker, interview with the author.

36 Dr Christoph Becker, interview with the author.

2 Private collecting

Collecting in the twentieth and twenty-first centuries

Today's influential private collectors leverage their art collections and cultural choices to advance their personal reputations within the public sphere. We need to remember that the desire to accrue social and cultural prestige has led many wealthy private collectors from the late-nineteenth century to the twenty-first to establish their own collection museums. As Rita Hatton and John Walker have advocated, the motivation to become a serious art collector is influenced by both the degree of authority and control obtained within an aspect of the visual arts, as well as the notable social prestige, cultural and economic value that is associated with it.[1] As a growing number of contemporary collectors are making their fortunes sooner than their predecessors they are redirecting their focus and fortunes towards art collecting and making their holdings publicly accessible by way of their own private museum. Access to global markets and personal wealth accrued through technological industries and manufacturing has created a new breed of very wealthy individuals that has been unheard of since the Industrial Revolution. Although earlier collectors are increasingly being recognised as playing an important role in actively building their own public personae through their collections and their philanthropic choices their posthumous methods of benefaction were clearly limited: to build their own house museum that would, in due course, be gifted to the public;[2] bequeath their vast art collections to an existing public institution[3] or donate their collection to help create a public museum.[4] Today, a majority of art collections and collector-founded museums are open to the public from the beginning and are generally set up with the intention that they will be funded and operated as private institutions, indefinitely.

Although Henry Clay Frick's mansion was built for the single purpose of being a 'gallery of art', it was not intended to be open to the public within the collector's lifetime. Little in the way of firm details and plans for the bequest was formally documented by Frick. Any direct correspondence with his attorney referred to 'that matter' and was not specifically discussed.[5] Frick's will – dated 24 June 1915 and probated 6 December 1919 – formally entrusted a board of trustees to see through the 'formation' and 'organisation' of 'The Frick Collection'.[6] He issued them with the authority to establish a board of trustees to organise such an institution, appoint directors and to oversee the conversion of the Frick residence into a public 'gallery of art'. The Frick Collection was thus formed by way of the 1920 Act of Incorporation.[7] Following the death of Mrs Adelaide Frick on 4 October 1931, the Committee on Organisation and Policy was formed to oversee the transformation of the Frick residence into the public sphere.[8] The Trustees agreed that the building's origins as a private residence should not be compromised. Therefore, only necessary modifications were made to accommodate members of the general public and operate as a public house museum.[9] The Frick residence was opened to the public, as a museum, in 1935 – 16 years after Frick's death. Just as Chicago architect Daniel H. Burnham boldly declared in his letter to Frick himself (1909): 'the building ought to distinguish your name forever'[10] and it has, albeit after the founder's death. As Russell W. Belk writes in *Collecting in a Consumer Society*:

> In a materialistic society, the quality and quantity of our possessions are broadly assumed to be an index of our successfulness in life in general. In addition, by competing for rare objects of value, we are able to demonstrate our relative prowess and the effects of superior knowledge, tenacity, monetary resources, cleverness or luck.[11]

The suggested prestige applied to *objets d'art* has long been part of European tradition: Belk asserts that anyone can buy trinkets, but not everyone can distinguish and acquire notable works of art. 'The latter objects were those sought by the bourgeois as "marker goods" with which to make status claims'.[12] This chapter will examine the dramatic cultural shifts that have taken place over the last century. It will take into account the cachet associated with making private collections and museums accessible to the public and the way that collectors continue to compete with their peers to assert their cultural prowess. The study of the Wallace Collection (1897) will be examined alongside the cultural aspirations of the newly wealthy American industrialist collectors to emphasise the symbolic value associated with collecting notable works of art and creating one's own private museum. The Museum of Old and New Art (MONA) in Australia (2011) will lead the study into the acceleration of the privatisation of art and culture in the twenty-first century and the way that private collectors and their museums are dramatically changing the existing cultural landscape. The examination of the development of the private museum over time provokes two questions: why do wealthy collectors look to the private museum as a preferred mode of benefaction and how do contemporary collectors differ from their predecessors? This chapter will tackle these questions and conclude by outlining a perspective on the notion of cultural philanthropy which will structure and guide the rest of this book.

Background: building America's cultural reputation

As America did not share Europe's established traditions and cultural heritage of art collecting they were denied access to any significant royal, cleric, aristocratic cabinet of curiosities and even public collections. Late-nineteenth-century Americans were forced to start their own, thereby emulating English and European traditions they keenly admired from afar. By the late 1870s, successful American industrialists, bankers, lawyers and railway magnates were keen to exercise their newly gained wealth. As W.G. Constable points out, they were not content to model themselves on the English aristocracy and wealthy European merchant princes; they intended to rival them by collecting not only the fashionable French contemporary works of art, but the same Old Master paintings the aristocracy had collected for generations.[13]

This is evidenced in the way that wealthy Americans soon realised that an exemplary fine art collection was an entry card into established circles of the social elite both at home and abroad. Their abundant wealth was not enough to earn them the cultural credentials that they were so desperate to acquire. It was art itself that would bestow them with the social status and prestige; hence, they pursued it with a vengeance as they sought to rid themselves of the uncultured and tasteless tag that was often applied to them by the European elite. Scholars Barbara Klose-Ullman and Manfred Holler point out, American collectors were keen to 'legitimise their immense wealth by spending some of it on art, thus demonstrating and legitimising their own importance and power'.[14] The immediate availability of wealth allowed these wealthy tycoons to act quicker than most established museums as art historian Anne Higonnet describes, and 'could find and afford just about anything they wanted'.[15] Hence, the number of works shipped from private English stately homes and European private collections reached a climax between 1909 and 1910, with the equivalent value of $106 million of art works exported to America.[16]

The aristocratic associations and cultural capital connected with Continental Old Masters and British paintings justified the exorbitant prices attached to them – they were difficult to obtain, scarce and expensive, thereby asserting their power and wealth more keenly. Such acquisitions were seen to be significant differentiators for the social climbing industrialists; art was seen as a tool for self-promotion, prestige and cultural sophistication amongst elite circles nationally and internationally.[17] It was the predominantly self-made upper middle class male industrialist and banking tycoons who played a pivotal role in establishing many American museums and their respective collections. Their democratic and philanthropic zeal may not always have been honourable and altruistic, as one could argue that they were driven to a great degree by personal, political and commercial ambitions.[18] However, there would have needed to be an element of public-spiritedness for this to take place. If not public minded per se then they must have felt an obligation to give back to society having come from humble beginnings and prospered.[19]

Their benevolent actions were not intended to acknowledge individual commercial achievements and social status gained by it, but rather, to honour themselves as distinguished art collectors and philanthropists. In fact, they hoped to extinguish any suggestion or connection between their business exploits and their fine art collecting pursuits. The two aspects of their lives were seen to be diametrically opposed; therefore, the act of collecting was seen to be key to their own self-image and public persona. Peter Frumkin notes that 'philanthropy can also be a way for givers to improve their public image or perhaps even a tarnished one that can be rebuilt by way of philanthropic deeds'.[20]

Henry Clay Frick (1849–1919) wanted little or no reference made to his business dealings as a pioneer in the Pittsburgh coke and steel industries or as a financier.[21] Frick's own declaration, 'I want this collection to be my monument' confirmed his desire to be remembered as a gentleman of fine taste and for his outstanding collection of European masterpieces.[22] Frick and his contemporaries collected with tremendous passion and purpose – to build a collection of paintings for future generations to appreciate

Figure 2.1 Henry Clay Frick, 1916. © Courtesy of The Frick Collection/Frick Art Reference Library Archives.

Figure 2.2 Frick Residence, Fifth Ave Façade, 1927. © Courtesy of The Frick Collection/Frick Art Reference Library Archives.

and a legacy for themselves. This is reinforced in Colin Bailey's overview of the Frick collection and mansion declaring that Frick revealed that buying paintings provided him with 'more real pleasure than anything I have ever engaged in, outside business'.[23]

Isabella Stewart Gardner (1840–1924) also sought to redefine her own social position through perceived cultural superiority. Despite marrying into an elite Bostonian family, she felt ostracised by Boston's conservative (male) members of high society, both as a woman and as an outsider (being a New Yorker).[24] In 1891, Gardner inherited $1.75 million upon her father's death. This allowed her to embrace Europe's illustrious art historical traditions that she greatly admired and in due course was able to pass them on as her own.[25] Gardner's long-time adviser Bernard Berenson (1865–1959) played an integral role in sourcing, advising and steering her collection along the way. Amassing a notable art collection enabled Gardner to create her very own private museum. This in turn bestowed upon her the respect and recognition she sought as a serious collector, in spite of her gender,[26] thereby, allowing her to develop and manage her own public persona by way of her art collection and museum.[27]

It would not be long before wealthy American collectors ensured America was no longer seen as 'a country without art' as art museums boomed across the country at a rapid rate.[28] The remarkable collections that began to be amassed so quickly by a select group of American tycoons from 1869 until World War II helped to place America on the international cultural map. The philanthropic ambitions of these pioneering individuals served to benefit not only personal ambitions, but also those in the general community. William Corcoran (1798–1888) founded the first private museum in America in 1869 the – Corcoran Gallery of Art in Washington, DC. The museum was completed after the Civil War and opened in 1874, long before Isabella Stewart Gardner's museum opened in 1903.[29] The museum endured for almost 150 years. However, as its ongoing financial difficulties could not be resolved, the board of trustees sought a court order to dissolve Corcoran's deed of gift. After protracted negotiations, America's oldest private museum was forced to shut down in 2014. The closure resulted in the transfer of the museum's entire holdings (17,000 works) to the National Gallery of Art in Washington, DC.[30]

The fate of the Corcoran Gallery of Art raises two key questions that this book seeks to examine in the later chapters: how can private museums endure when the original founders is no longer active and should they be allowed to simply see out their time?

In pursuit of cultural prestige: Wallace Collection, London (1897)

Visiting the Wallace Collection in London had a profound effect on Henry Clay Frick and the formation and gifting of The Frick Collection. In 1949, Helen Clay Frick wrote that her father 'resolved at once that, if he achieved success, he would form such a collection of paintings for the enjoyment of the people of his own country'.[31] The building of The Frick Collection in 1913–1914 draws on many aspects of the Wallace Collection's interior design aesthetic, art collection and decorative art objects.[32] The Wallace's grand staircase, Great Gallery and Oval Drawing Room can be seen in the Frick's own staircase, West Gallery and the Fragonard Room. Paintings by Rembrandt, Rubens, Titian, van Dyke, Fragonard, Boucher, Hals, Reynolds and Gainsborough featured prominently in Frick's collection as they did in Sir Richard Wallace's inherited holdings.

Sir Richard Wallace (1818–1890) was the illegitimate son of Richard Seymour Conway (1800–1870), the fourth Marquess of Hertford.[33] He was the primary beneficiary of his father's exemplary collection of art, decorative art collections, personal wealth and properties in both France and England. In 1871, the title of Baron was bestowed upon him by the British Government as an acknowledgement of his generosity both in Paris and London.[34] Notwithstanding their aristocratic lineage, the Hertford family was often criticised for being mean spirited and not living up to the responsibilities expected of their rank.[35] As Peter Howard points out, Wallace was 'the first member of the family to behave in an altruistic manner and to take seriously the responsibility associated with his wealth'.[36]

Figure 2.3 West Gallery, 1927. © Courtesy of The Frick Collection/Frick Art Reference Library Archives.

In 1872, Wallace decided to relocate his inherited art collection and decorative art objects from Paris to London as the Franco-Prussian War posed considerable risk for the collection's safety. His decision to make the Hertford collection available to the public, on a three-year loan to the Bethnal Green Museum in London, between 1872 and 1875, attracted favourable public response. No less than 977 paintings and 923 decorative art objects were displayed at Bethnal Green while Wallace undertook signifi-cant renovations of Hertford House.[37] He personally funded the exhibition that was organised by the South Kensington Museum – what is now known as the Victoria and Albert Museum. A loan of this size was unique as it was the single largest private collection that was lent to the museum for so long. The exhibition attracted more than 25,000 people on the first day.[38] Although it was the first time the collection was shown in London, a smaller selection of art was shown at the Manchester Art Treasures Exhibition in 1857, where a room was set up for the display of paintings, furniture, bronzes, ivories, miniatures and so forth.[39] The generosity of the loan was nonetheless unprecedented. Wallace's philanthropic actions drew favourable public recognition and commendation for him personally and his impressive family collection which would have been socially advantageous for Wallace.

Figure 2.4 Great Gallery, John Thomson Gallery XVI, Looking West, 1897.
© Wallace Collection.

According to Suzanne Gaynor, Wallace's aspirations to be part of elite
society was largely attained through art: lending works to Bethnal Green,
the *Old Masters Exhibition* and the National Portrait Gallery was key to
building his credentials.[40] Wallace himself contributed some 40 paintings
to the Wallace Collection – predominantly Dutch and eighteenth- and
nineteenth-century French schools that were acquired in 1872. This further
supports Wallace's aspirations to be part of the landed gentry, as can be
seen in his choice of painters such as Thomas Lawrence and Edwin (Henry)
Landseer – Queen Victoria's favourite artist. The acquisition of Landseer's
painting 'The Arab Tent' (c.1865–1866) from the Prince of Wales after 1874,
demonstrates this very clearly as does Lawrence's 'King George IV' (1822)
and Clarkson (Frederick) Stanfield's 1833 'Orford'.[41] In the tradition of an
English gentleman, a country estate and having friends in the highest circles
of society was paramount.

Wallace's father, the fourth Marquess, had become a serious collector
upon the death of his own father – Francis Charles Seymour Conway
(1777–1842), the third Marquess of Hertford. With an annual income of
£250,000 at his disposal he was free to buy whatever he wanted.[42] The

Figure 2.5 Great Gallery, John Thomson Gallery XVI, East, 1897. © Wallace Collection.

fourth Marquess is largely credited with the formation and character of the Wallace Collection acquiring the notable Old Master paintings, the eighteenth-century paintings and decorative arts objects.[43] According to R.A. Cecil, the Hertford and Wallace Collection of eighteenth-century sculpture was considered one of the most important private collections at the time of Lady Wallace's death (in 1897).[44] The fourth Marquess once wrote: 'my collection is the result of my life'.[45] This is reminiscent of Frick's own aspirational declaration: 'I want this collection to be my monument'.[46] I might suggest that a great many contemporary collectors have constructed their own art collections and museums with similar aspirations in mind. Australian collector David Walsh and the Museum of Old and New Art immediately comes to mind.

Museum of Old and New Art (MONA), Hobart, Tasmania (2011)

The Museum of Old and New Art (MONA) belongs to a new group of private museums that has emerged in the twenty-first century and indicates an acceleration of the privatisation of art and culture. MONA prescribes to an individualised approach to the collector's museum and its engagement

Figure 2.6 David Walsh. © Collection Museum of Old and New Art (MONA), Hobart.

with the public at large. At one level, it is typical of most private collection museums where the combination of architecture and art fosters a unique and alternative engagement with art and place. MONA reflects the personal ambition and passion of its creator – mathematical *wunderkind*, professional gambler and entrepreneur – David Walsh, while making a significant contribution to Australia's cultural landscape. On the other hand, Walsh is 'atypical' as he has demonstrated an active disregard for traditional art historical niceties, and didactic texts in favour of an aesthetic, sensorial and distinctive curatorial approach that allows visitors to be guided by their own curiosity rather than more traditional exhibits. It is important to point out that Walsh clearly states that his museum is not an altruistic gesture, but an opportunity to show off the 'stuff' he has accumulated and to ensure that visitors have fun and enjoy themselves:[47] 'I'm not trying to bestow wisdom' he says, 'it's about subversion, but it's not too serious'.[48] In spite of such claims, the museum is freely accessible to all Tasmanian residents with only interstate and overseas visitors expected to pay the $28 admission fee.

Despite the museum's location in the working-class suburb of Glenorchy, MONA has managed to attract more than two million visitors since its opening in 2011. In so doing, it has propelled the island state of Tasmania on to the international cultural map. To appreciate Walsh's extremely innovative brand of museum fashioning it is important to also consider the unique set of drivers that informs Walsh's cultural (not philanthropic) ambitions and the active promotion of MONA.

Seven years have passed since MONA's opening and Walsh continues to invigorate local and global audiences with the unveiling of the new James Turrell wing. MONA's new 750-square-metre wing entitled *Pharos*, opened in December 2017. Named after The Pharos of Alexandria, the lighthouse built for Ptolemy I Soter around 280BC, MONA's purpose-built gallery houses four of James Turrell's newly acquired site specific light installations alongside works by Jean Tinguely, Nam June Paik, Randy Polumbo, Charles Ross and Richard Wilson. Walsh elaborates further on the museum's web site but does so with some irony through the voice of his two-year-old daughter Sunday Walsh:

> Pharos was a lighthouse in Alexandria. One of the original Wonders of the World. Its seems to me Daddy is a bit up himself naming the new bit of MONA after a Wonder of the World, but we'll leave that aside.[49]

Walsh's self-mocking approach has become characteristic of MONA's desire to be in the vanguard of museum practice, but without needing to take one's self too seriously. This is an important aspect and hence MONA's appeal to traditional and non-traditional museum visitors who continue to make their pilgrimage to Hobart.

MONA's immediate success and the public's unexpected curiosity with Walsh's un-museum museum has since prompted a number of Australian public institutions to rethink their curatorial and exhibition approaches. It is important to note that at the time of MONA's opening a number of them cited MONA as one of the reasons for their declining visitor numbers, despite the 600- to 1000-kilometre distance and sea straight that separates Tasmania from the Australian mainland.[50] As Newhouse points out, public art museums can struggle to reposition themselves in the current evolving global arts landscape and can be perceived to be the antithesis of the new privately founded museums, which are seen to be brimming with excitement and originality.[51] This is the general perception of Walsh's MONA that has not diminished over the last seven years. MONA's radically innovative approach can be attributed to Walsh's willingness to be unlike every other private or public museum. Provocative works of art and exhibitions are often used to attract media attention and trigger public debate. Furthermore, the curatorial team inject an element of inquisitiveness and wonderment to their displays by drawing on earlier models of collecting and the notion of the *Wunderkammer*.

MONA's departure from the established museological concept of the 'white cube' emerged from the MONA team's concerns on how best to display Walsh's disparate collection. The 'white cube' is an international standard that emerged for the display of modern art in the early twentieth century where paintings are hung in a linear manner within stark contemplative galleries with little to distract the visitor from the art itself. This mode of presentation has dominated curatorial practices since Alfred Barr's embrace of it at the Museum of Modern Art (MoMA), New York, during the 1930s.[52] French museum director and curator Jean-Hubert Martin's exhibition 'Artempo: Where Time Becomes Art' at the Palazzo Fortuny, Venice (9 June–5 November 2007), reinforced MONA's decision to adopt a more distinctive curatorial approach that would be representative of Walsh's personal taste and idiosyncratic collection. As MONA's founding director Mark Fraser, explained: 'While the "Artempo" exhibition helped persuade some "white cube" advocates in the MONA team that the course we were on was sound it was not the foundation or the rationale for it'.[53] Fraser asserts that MONA's chosen curatorial displays allow them the flexibility to move exhibits without disrupting the overall presentation, thereby, allowing for more frequent rehanging and greater curatorial innovation than a conventional white cube display format. He maintains it is less likely to draw attention to collection gaps and anomalies.[54] The use of subdued and dramatic spot lighting effects on objects further enhances MONA's distinctive character creating a theatrical museum space that challenges the preconceived 'notion of a museum and what it should look like'.[55]

This last point deserves further attention as many private collectors want to be seen to generate discussion around their respective holdings, their

Figure 2.7 Interior view of a walkway on level B1 of the Museum of Old and New Art (MONA). © Collection Museum of Old and New Art (MONA), Hobart.

Figure 2.8 Interior view of the Museum of Old and New Art (MONA). © Collection
Museum of Old and New Art (MONA), Hobart.

aesthetic arrangements and curatorial juxtapositions. Ian Ritchie suggests
that contemporary museums (in general) are moving away from the idea
of the museum as educator and place of study to one 'of provocation and
debate'.[56] This is evidenced by MONA's curatorial approach and the desire
to subvert established museological principles. This defiance may also be
seen as an expression of individual subjectivity as private collectors seek to
adopt an alternative engagement between art and audience that is intended
to be personal above all else. As Fraser points out, 'Private museums remind
us that the art cannot be treated objectively'.[57]

Conclusion

Despite the many years that have passed one thing has remained the same –
the desire for the newly formed upper middle classes to acquire cultural
capital and social prestige through the collecting and appreciation of art.
This is clearly apparent when considering that Henry Clay Frick looked
to American collector Benjamin Altman's (1840–1913) picture gallery and
the Walters Art Gallery in Baltimore along with the Wallace Collection
in London when constructing his very own picture gallery and mansion
museum. The Wallace Collection represented the ultimate aristocratic house
museum for Frick and other American collectors of his time. As Higonnet
writes, their desire to appropriate an aristocratic and high society lifestyle is

evident as they went out of their way to buy it, refine it and stamp their own signature to it as if it was theirs all along.[58]

David Walsh has devoted around $208 million to build a collection and a privately funded and operated (for-profit) museum to engage and share with the public. MONA has in a short time earned a global reputation by offering an alternative exhibition program and the many varied ancillary events to offer a point of difference from most other museums – private and public. It is for this reason that visitors continue to make their journey to the most southern point of Australia to take in the MONA experience and Walsh's unconventional and engaging ways of supporting contemporary art practice and art and culture more broadly. MONA's intuitive and spectacular presentation has done much to reinvigorate the art museum on the Australian and international cultural landscape, just as Walsh had hoped to do. His desire to democratise the appreciation and access to art museums is one thing, but to make them fun and entertaining is key to this maverick collector.

Notes

1   Walker, Rita and Hatton, John A., *Supercollector: A Critique of Charles Saatchi*, 4th ed., Surrey, Institute of Artology, 2010, p.347.
2   Isabella Stewart Gardner (1840–1924), Henry Clay Frick (1849–1919), Henry Huntington (1850–1927) and Albert Barnes (1872–1951).
3   J.P. Morgan (1837–1913), Collis Huntington (1821–1900) and Henry Marquand (1819–1902).
4   William Corcoran (1798–1888), Henry Tate (1819–1899), Charles Lang Freer (1854–1919), William Walters (1819–1894) and Andrew W. Mellon (1855–1937).
5   Documents Relating to The Frick Collection, Incorporated 27 April 1920, p.7. The Frick Collection/Frick Art Reference Library Archives, New York.
6   Mrs Henry C. Frick, Helen C. Frick, Childs Frick, George F. Baker Jr, J. Horace Harding, Walker D. Hines, Lewis Cass Ledyard, John D. Rockefeller Jr and Horace Havemeyer.
7   Corporate seal affixed as 12 April 1921. Documents Relating to The Frick Collection, Incorporated 27 April 1920. Printed for the Trustees, 1923, p.19 and Conveyance by the trustees to the Frick Collection and Acceptance, p.26. The Frick Collection/Frick Art Reference Library Archives, New York.
8   Description of Rooms, and Historical Note, 1936, n.p. The Frick Collection/Frick Art Reference Library Archives, New York.
9   The Frick Collection/Frick Art Reference Library Archives, New York, 1936, n.p.
10 Bailey, Colin B., *Building the Frick Collection: An Introduction to the House and Its Collection*, New York, Scala Publishers, 2006, p.25.
11 Belk, Russell W., *Collecting in a Consumer Society*, London and New York, Routledge, 1995, p.87.
12 Belk, 1995, p.41.
13 Constable, W.G., *Art Collecting in the United States of America: An Outline of a History*, London, Edinburgh, Thomas Nelson and Sons, 1964, p.1.

14 Klose-Ullman, Barbara and Holler, Manfred J., 'Art Goes America', *Journal of Economic Issues* XLIV, no. 1 (March 2010), p.92.

15 Higonnet, Anne, *A Museum of One's Own: Private Collecting, Public Gift*, Pittsburgh and New York, Periscope Publishing, 2009, p.xiv.

16 Klose-Ullman and Holler, 2010, p.92.

17 Rovers, Eva, 'Introduction: The Art Collector – between Philanthropy and Self-Glorification', *Journal of the History of Collections* 21, no. 2 (2009), p.158.

18 Duncan, Carol, *Civilizing Rituals: Inside Public Art Museums*, London and New York, Routledge, 1995, p.54.

19 Constable, 1964, p.98.

20 Frumkin, Peter, *Strategic Giving: The Art and Science of Philanthropy*, Chicago and London, The University of Chicago Press, 2006, p.20.

21 Duncan, 1995, p.83.

22 Quodbach, Esmée, '"I want this collection to be my monument" Henry Clay Frick and the Formation of the Frick Collection', *Journal of the History of Collections* 21, no. 2 (2009), p.238.

23 Bailey, 2006, p.14.

24 Higonnet, 2009, p.13.

25 Higonnet, Anne, 'Self-Portrait as a Museum', *Anthropology and Aesthetes* Autumn, no. 52 (1997), p.80.

26 Matthews, Rosemary, 'Collectors and Why They Collect: Isabella Stewart Gardner and Her Museum of Art', *Journal of the History of Collections* 21, no. 2 (2009), p.187.

27 German-Dutch collector Helene Kröller-Müller used her private art collection and museum to reassert her position within high society – to earn the respect as an accomplished (woman) collector in her own right. Rovers, Eva, 'Monument to an Industrialist's Wife: Helene Kröller-Müller's Motives for Collecting', *Journal of the History of Collections* 21, no. 2 (2009), pp.241–252.

28 Klose-Ullman and Holler, 2010, p.90.

29 Others preferred to bequeath their collections to the newly formed Metropolitan Museum of Art, New York, that was founded in 1870 and opened 1872. Alternatively, many used their collections to found new public institutions such as the Freer Gallery at the Smithsonian. Charles Lang Freer bequeathed his collection and founded the Smithsonian museum – Freer Gallery of Art opened in 1923. Andrew W. Mellon donated his art collection along with $10 million for the construction of Washington's National Gallery in 1937. Walters Art Gallery in Baltimore was founded by Henry Walters (son of William) and opened as a public museum in 1934. New York's Guggenheim Museum was established by Soloman R. Guggenheim in 1939 as the Museum of Non-Objective Painting. The museum assumed its current name in 1952.

30 Montgomery, David and Judkis, Maura, 'Judge Approves Corcoran Gallery of Art Plan to Partner with National Gallery, GWU', *The Washington Post*, 18 August 2014.

31 Helen Clay Frick, Quodbach, Esmée, 'I want this collection to be my monument' Henry Clay Frick and the Formation of the Frick Collection, *Journal of the History of Collections* 21, no. 2 (2009), p.231.

32 The date of Frick's initial visit – be it 1880 or 1905 – remains unclear as there is little evidence to support the anecdotal references pertaining to his 1880 trip

to the Wallace Collection. Refer to Harvey, G., *Henry Clay Frick. The Man*, New York, 1928, p.332; Quodbach, 2009, p.238.

33 Wallace was born Richard Jackson to Mrs Agnes Jackson. At the age of 24, he changed his name to Wallace – which was his mother's maiden name – for reasons that are not clearly understood. Refer to Howard, Peter, *Sir Richard Wallace: The English Millionaire of Paris and the Hertford British Hospital*, Glasgow, The Grimsay Press, 2009, pp.63, 67.

34 Wallace inherited his father's estate and fortune which included the apartment in Paris, Chateau du Bagatelle, the estates in Ireland and the Hertford collection of Dutch and Old Master paintings, eighteenth-century French paintings, decorative arts and nineteenth-century works. Wallace was made a baronet in recognition of his benevolent gestures towards the English poor in Paris, during the Franco-Prussian War. The French Government awarded him the Cross of Commander of the Legion of Honour for his contributions to the fine arts. Refer to Howard, 2009, pp.5, 57–59. Spielman, M.H., *The Wallace Collection in Hertford House*, London, Paris, New York and Melbourne, Cassell and Company, 1900, p.10.

35 Howard, 2009, pp.59–61.

36 Howard, 2009, p.75.

37 Lasic, Barbara, '"Splendid Patriotism" Richard Wallace and the Construction of the Wallace Collection', *Journal of the History of Collections* 21, no. 2 (2009), pp.173–174.

38 Howard, 2009, p.105.

39 Spielman, 1900, p.10.

40 Gaynor, Suzanne, 'Sir Richard Wallace and His Own Collection', *Antique Collector*, no. April (1983), p.53.

41 Gaynor, 1983, p.53.

42 Ingamells, John (ed.), *Wallace Collection the Hertford Mawson Letters: The 4th Marquess of Hertford to His Agent Samuel Mawson*, London, The Trustees of the Wallace Collection, Manchester Square, 1981, p.10; Spielman, 1900, p.7.

43 Warren, Jeremy, 'The 4th Marquess of Hertford's Early Years as a Collector', *The Burlington Magazine*, no. August (2008), p.544.

44 Cecil, R.A., 'French Eighteenth-Century Sculpture formerly in the Hertford-Wallace Collection', *Apollo Magazine*, June 1965, p.449.

45 Private correspondence between Lord Hertford and his London agent, Samuel Mawson, during the years 1848 and 1861. Warren, 2008, p.544.

46 Quodbach, Esmée, '"I Want This Collection to Be My Monument" Henry Clay Frick and the Formation of the Frick Collection', *Journal of the History of Collections* 21, no. 2 (2009), p.238.

47 Walker, Georgina, 'A Twenty-First-Century Wunderkammer: Museum of Old and New Art (MONA), Hobart, Tasmania, Australia'. *The International Journal of the Inclusive Museum* 9, no. 2 (2016), p.10; David Walsh as cited in Hume, Marion 'Wild At Art', *Wmagazine.com*, 2011.

48 Walker, 2016, p.10; David Walsh as cited in Bevan, Robert, 'Tasmania's Cheekiest Devil', *The Guardian*, 19 December 2010.

49 Museum of Old and New Art website.

50 Munro, Peter, 'For Art's Sake, the Gallery Confronts Its New Challenges', *The Sydney Morning Herald*, 5 February 2012.

51 Newhouse, Victoria, *Towards a New Museum*, Expanded Edition 2006, New York, The Monacelli Press, 1998, p.273.

52 Barr's visit to the Museum Folkwang in Essen, in 1927, greatly influenced his curatorial practice. Staniszewski, Mary Anne, *The Power of Display: A History of Exhibition Installations at the Museum of Modern Art*, Cambridge, MA, MIT Press, 1998, p.64.

53 Mark Fraser, correspondence with the author.

54 Mark Fraser, correspondence with the author.

55 Walker, 2016, p.10; David Walsh as cited in Rulz, Christine, 'A "Subversive Disneyland" at the End of the World', *The Art Newspaper* 19, no. 215 (2010), p.30.

56 Ritchie, Ian, 'An Architect's View of Recent Developments in European Museums', in *Towards the Museum of the Future: New European Perspectives*, edited by Roger Miles and Lauro Zavala, New York, Routledge, 1994, p.12.

57 Mark Fraser, correspondence with the author.

58 Higonnet, 2009, p.xiv.

Part II

The private collector's museum

3   Where house and art museum converge

As a rule, early-twentieth-century house museums incorporated a more personal approach to the display of art, differing from the comprehensive methods adopted by museums at the time. Art historian Anne Higonnet writes: 'a typical collector's museum embeds its objects in total environments: concatenations of materials, colours, textures and surfaces of interiors and gardens. By preserving their entire collections in perpetuity, founders put the possession of art on display'.[1] According to Higonnet the waters start to muddy a little when a notable art collection is involved within the house, in which case, the question arises whether the art becomes the distinguishing feature, and not the house itself.[2] This chapter will examine how the personal aspects of living and experiencing art within an intimate and domestic environment are seen to be important characteristics of the house as museum. For instance, the Foundation E.G. Bührle Collection (1960–2015), became a house museum despite the collector never having lived in the house but the Lyon Housemuseum (2009) suggests a 'new type' of house museum that integrates domestic and public spaces seamlessly. This chapter will map out the similarities, differences and developments in the house museum over time and the difficulties that are emerging.

Quasi-museum and residence: Foundation E.G. Bührle Collection, Zürich (1960–2015)

Overview

The examination of the German-born Emil Georg Bührle (1890–1956) and the Foundation E.G. Bührle Collection is a unique example of how a house became a house museum despite the collector never having lived in it, thereby, challenging our understanding of what a house museum should be. The converted villa at 172 Zollikerstrasse in Zürich sat alongside Bührle's own home and was purchased to store his art collection. The villa was not intended to be a museum; it was a personal space where Bührle could look at his pictures – a quasi picture gallery – to which he withdrew late at night, alone and occasionally with invited guests and friends, looking at the many

Figure 3.1 Emil Bührle and his Collection. Foundation E.G. Bührle, Zürich, The LIFE
Picture Collection. Photo: Dimitri Kessel (June 1954). © Getty Images.

paintings that surrounded him. The house became a house museum by default. In 1990, the collector's grandson Christian Bührle, refers to the villa's supposed domesticity: 'Its extensive gardens and distinctive furnishings give it the feel of a private home where the visitor finds a collection bearing the imprint of Bührle's personality'.[3] Although the villa was transformed to look like a house museum, in reality it was largely unfurnished and akin to a museum storeroom than a house museum.

In a deed of gift dated 24 February 1960, 168 paintings and 30 sculptures were permanently gifted to the newly formed Foundation E.G. Bührle Collection on the proviso that they would be made publicly available and placed on display within the original villa that housed them.[4] It was Bührle's longtime friend and confidant Arthur Kauffmann to whom the Bührle family turned and asked to select the works that would ultimately form the basis of the Foundation, and establish the collector's public legacy upon his sudden death in 1956.[5] The villa was thus converted into a museum by 1960. The family and the Foundation replaced Bührle's random and personal way of ordering his pictures with one that is more art historical in its presentation. In 2013, the Foundation E.G. Bührle announced their decision to close the house museum and after 55 years the museum closed its doors in 2015. As of 2020, the E.G. Bührle Collection can be viewed in the new David Chipperfield Architects wing at the Kunsthaus Zürich where the Collection will occupy around 20 per cent of the extension and ten per cent of the institutional wing where a number of works are currently on permanent loan.[6] The Collection's complex trajectory highlights a number of challenges identified with private museums: long-term financial commitment and whether future generations are willing or able to sustain them indefinitely and the redefining of the collector's own narrative and relationship with the villa and his art collection.

It has been difficult to create an accurate picture of the collector and his impressive art collection as information about Emil Bührle is tightly controlled. The few publications that do exist have been compiled by the Foundation E.G. Bührle Collection. Earlier sources often provide brief biographical or information pertaining to the exhibition of Bührle's holdings (after his passing) or journalistic publications that cobbled together material pertaining to his complex business dealings. James Stourton's *Great Collectors of our time: art collecting since 1945* (2007) provides a more insightful introduction to Bührle's collecting interests and behaviours, however, there are significant gaps in the Bührle narrative. The limited material pertaining to an important, yet lesser known twentieth-century collector, needs to be more keenly addressed. Due to the often-controversial nature of Bührle's business dealings the Foundation received my requests with some scepticism: why was I so keen to present the Bührle Foundation as an example of a house museum and why did I want to write about Bührle? It was through my discussions with the director of the Kunsthaus Zürich Dr Christoph Becker and other Swiss museum directors – Dr Tobia Bezzola and Dr Marc Fehlmann – that I was able to gain a better understanding

Figure 3.2 Exterior view of the Foundation E.G. Bührle, Zürich, 2014. Photo: Georgina Walker.

of Bührle – the man behind the collection and his quasi-house museum. Visiting the Foundation E.G. Bührle Collection in 2014 was also crucial to this study. This chapter will provide a clearer understanding of the formation of the house as museum and Bührle's patterns of collecting alongside his complicated personal narrative and the way that this has played out over time. It is my intention to deviate from the linear and more general interpretations of Bührle as the overly energetic businessman who collected art feverishly during difficult political times.

Background

Bührle was born into a middle-class family in the southwest German town of Pforzheim in the state of Baden-Württemberg. He was educated at the Universities of Freiburg in Baden-Württemberg and Munich where he studied literature and art history and became a highly respected medieval art historian. His appreciation of Medieval art is evidenced by the number of works, beautiful sculptures and a few paintings seen within the collection. Bührle's visit to Berlin's Nationalgalerie in 1913, was his first introduction to the many French artists he would spend much of his free time and available finances pursuing in decades to come.

It would be many years before Bührle was able to realise his ambition as an art collector as the lack of personal funds prevented him from buying works of art as did the commencement of World War I. He went on to serve in the Prussian cavalry regiment for the duration of the war, having fought in France, Russia and Rumania. Around the 1920s he decided to pursue a career as an industrialist joining a machine-tool factory in the German city of Magdeburg.[7] After serving his four-year apprenticeship in Magdeburg, Bührle was sent to manage the company's debt-ridden Swiss subsidiary, located in the suburbs of Zürich – Ateliers de Construction – that traded under the name of *Schweizerische Werkzeugmaschinenfabrik Erlikon* (S.W.O.). The company's severe financial losses after the war meant that Bührle was given the responsibility of reversing the company's financial woes. His steadfast business acumen saw the young Bührle increase the company's production with the introduction of armaments and machine-tools, despite being instructed to reduce the company's manufacturing capacity.

Over time he would not only improve the company's fortunes, but also increase his shareholdings within the firm to become the director, then the main shareholder, and eventually the owner of S.W.O. (later renamed Oerlikon E. Bührle & Co.). His military experience and entrepreneurial skills enabled him to build prototypes of air-defence and anti-tank weapons becoming a significant supplier of armaments to the British and German armies, selling anti-tank guns, anti-aircraft cannon and a variety of other weapons and ammunition.[8] The Royal British Navy and United States Navy used Oerlikon anti-aircraft guns and the Germans used anti-aircraft cannon to destroy several aircrafts belonging to the allied forces.[9] Thus, the company expanded from employing 150 people in 1924 to 3,000 in 1940, with this number growing to 6,600 during and after World War II.[10] Due to his commercial success Bührle never returned to his native Germany becoming a Swiss citizen in 1937.

Bührle's financial situation improved dramatically in the lead up to World War II as Germany began its rearmament campaign under the direction of the newly appointed Chancellor of Germany Adolf Hitler in 1933. This tense political landscape meant that both Germany and other European countries looked to re-arm themselves placing increased demand on military equipment and instruments of warfare, with Bührle prospering financially from such adverse political conditions.[11] His many business ventures and successes finally allowed Bührle the opportunity to pursue his long held desire to collect art.[12] Whilst some sources suggest that Bührle's collection expanded rapidly between the years 1946 and 1956, British art historian Douglas Cooper argues that it was most likely during the years 1938–1956, that much of the collection was formed.[13] This is also confirmed on the Foundation E.G. Bührle Collection web site that clearly states that around 100 paintings were acquired during the war years.[14] As we shall see Bührle's business dealings made it particularly difficult for him and his art collection to be openly accepted in Switzerland within his own lifetime, and even today.[15]

Building the collection

The years 1937–1938 and the purchase of Cézanne's 'Montagne Sainte-Victoire' (1904–1906) signalled a significant shift in Bührle's collecting and the type of paintings he would focus on in the decade ahead; it was also the first expensive work of art to enter his possession. The painting was purchased from the established art dealer Siegfried Rosengart in Lucerne, for a sum of 100,000 pounds.[16] This would set the bar high for works to come as Rosengart himself remarked to Bührle upon the successful conclusion of negotiations: 'The expensive part of this picture, Herr Bührle, is not the amount you are paying for it but the consequence that from now on you can only buy pictures of this quality'.[17] Indeed he was correct, as Bührle took heed of Rosengart's advice; in the same year he acquired van Gogh's 'L'olivette' (Olive Orchard) series, Manet's 'La rue Mosnier aux drapeaux' (Rue Mosnier with Flags) (1878) and an early landscape painting by Gauguin from Rosengart's gallery. Between the years 1938 and 1948 Cooper argues that Bührle went on to buy eight paintings by Monet, six by van Gogh, three by Cézanne, two each by Corot, Courbet, Manet, Degas and Utrillo and one each by Sisley and Pissarro. Over time he would acquire around 20 paintings by Manet – an extraordinary feat at the time. He later expanded his collection to include works by Delacroix, Daumier, the Nabis, Neo-Impressionists and artists that included Braque, Derain and Vlaminck.[18] Bührle's holdings were impressive given that he was building a private collection at a time when most of the significant works of art by the artists he collected had already made their way into public museums.[19] What is more, Cooper notes that international art dealers were running short of quality works of art and the competition from his American contemporaries was intense.[20] Despite this, or in spite of this, Cooper adds that Bührle demonstrated how 'a man with money, knowledge, taste and the will to buy the best could still find what he wanted' even after the difficult war years.[21]

With little time to visit dealers in New York, Paris and London, Bührle would combine his buying sprees with business trips where he often bought up to ten paintings at any one time. In 1952, on a single visit to Paul Rosenberg's art gallery in Paris, he bought works by Cézanne, Courbet, Daumier, Degas, Ingres, Monet, Manet, Renoir, Sisley and Pissarro.[22] As Bührle's fortune mounted Cooper points out that he continued to expand his collection buying 15 paintings in 1951 and 18 in 1952.[23] In 1953, a further 25 paintings were added to the collection that spanned more broadly into earlier centuries in an attempt to 'round out the scope of his collection' by incorporating paintings by Tiepolo, Guardi, Canaletto and Fragonard. Many of these Old Master paintings originated from well-known English stately homes and collections.[24] Moreover, during the 1950s, Bührle was amassing Antique and Gothic sculptures, and towards the last few years of his life he also collected twentieth-century artists such as Picasso, Braque,

Gris, Chagall, Modigliani, Matisse, Marc and Kokoschka.[25] Thus, in less than 20 years Bührle amassed an incredibly diverse art collection.[26]

One cannot discount the fact that Bührle stock piled works of art as his business prospered, most notably during the difficult war years. Masterpieces within Bührle's holdings came under intense public and legal scrutiny immediately after World War II. From the 100 paintings that Bührle acquired during the war years, 15 of those became the focus of postwar investigations and law suits; an inquiry that Cooper undertook at the direction of the Allied forces, with the Swiss Federal Court in Lausanne in 1948–1949 challenging the provenance of these paintings.[27] Moreover, Bührle was accused of dealing directly with the Nazi regime, supplying Germany with armaments despite Switzerland's neutral position, with surviving German Jews questioning his relationship with Hermann Goering.[28] Cooper's investigation concluded that 13 paintings from Bührle's collection – from a total of 77 seized in Switzerland – had been illegally obtained by the Germans in occupied France and sent to Switzerland.[29]

Many of these paintings were traced back to French art dealer Paul Rosenberg's holdings. Having fled Paris during the war years, Rosenberg was forced to resettle in America, and it was from New York that he began legal proceedings against Bührle – questioning Bührle's ownership of select paintings that were unlawfully taken from his gallery.[30] The outcome of these proceedings, and others, enabled Bührle to repurchase nine of the 13 works from the original owners and returned four of them. All transactions were finalised by February 1951, with Bührle declared the rightful owner of the works in question acknowledging that he acquired the works in good faith.[31] Coincidently, Rosenberg would come to supply Bührle with many of his key paintings in years to come. Bührle soon recognised the importance of being made aware of the painting's correct provenance. In 1948, he employed the young art historian Walter Drack, as his curator to help manage his holdings, record their provenance, exhibition history and any literature pertaining to works within the collection.[32] Today, much of the collection is well documented, however, the Kunsthaus Zürich has observed that a couple of works exhibited at the museum have incomplete documentation and this has been noted in detail on their records.[33]

It is difficult to obtain a clear insight into Bührle the collector and benefactor as his business initiatives, at times, overshadow his cultural achievements. I would argue that unlike some of his contemporaries – Oskar Reinhart for example – Bührle did not harness any specific long-term cultural aspirations, other than to publicly display his art collection at the Kunsthaus Zürich. Even so, Bührle demonstrated a degree of uncertainty in publicly displaying his art collection, declaring that his collection was never complete and thus not ready for public viewing.[34] This is in complete contrast to many of today's collectors who are perhaps a little too quick to share their collections with the general public. The desire to own as many quality works of art as possible, and to have them at his disposal, was an important aspect of Bührle's collecting and self-image. By his own admission, they provided him with a degree of companionship.[35] For Bührle, art and the collecting of it implied a degree of refinement, education and good taste that became clearly apparent on his first visit to Berlin's Nationalgalerie in 1913.

The villa

Bührle's collection was informally hung in the villa's empty rooms, in corridors, alongside the staircase, or stacked along the floor placed against walls and doorways. Suffice to say that Bührle arranged his pictures according to his own order, which was above all, personal. Collecting was a private pursuit and he had little interest in sharing his paintings and sculptures with a broader audience, within his own lifetime; hence, he was less interested in the aesthetic display of his paintings with many of them randomly placed or hung throughout the villa; to have the paintings in his possession was all that mattered to Bührle. As Bührle himself disclosed:

> I was ceaselessly determined . . . to gather such paintings around me; Monet's enchantment has held me in thrall and I wanted to have Cézanne, Degas, Manet, Renoir, close to me on my own walls. And I have succeeded, for now they are here.[36]

Bührle would guide his visitors from one painting to the next without uttering a word, contemplating and enjoying the paintings' presence and beauty. Former director of the Kunsthaus Zürich René Wehrli, recalled:

> [H]e would get up, take a bunch of keys and invite one to go through the unlit garden, climb up a flight of stairs and enter an apartment bare of furniture where the masterpieces were ranged along the walls, as if a museum storeroom.[37]

For Bührle the undecorated rooms and their neutral walls provided a private space for reflection says Wehrli, not necessarily for their display; the collector did not consider it necessary to engage in any form of discussion or seek to analyse the works within his holdings; the act of viewing was simply one of meditation and diversion for Bührle.[38]

The first opportunity to display much of the Bührle Collection, beyond the confines of his private home and adjoining villa emerged in 1956. The inaugural exhibition at Kunsthaus Zürich was to correspond with the opening of the museum's new exhibition wing in 1958, that Bührle himself had funded. He would not live to attend the opening or to see the public display of his much-loved art collection as he died suddenly of a heart attack in November 1956, aged 66. Thus, the exhibition at the Kunsthaus Zürich was in memory of the benefactor with 237 paintings, mediaeval sculptures and 18 works of ancient art prominently displayed within the museum's new addition.[39] Director of the Kunsthaus Zürich and member of the E.G.

Bührle Foundation's board Dr Christoph Becker, advises that Bührle always wanted his collection to go to the museum:

> In the 1950s, he had plans to build a new wing at the museum to house his collection. It was originally intended to house the Bührle Collection. The museum switched it to what we now have – the Exhibition Hall. The family set up the Foundation and installed the collection there.[40]

The Exhibition Hall was intended to house the collection, Bührle's unexpected death however altered these plans. Former director of the Oskar Reinhart Museum Dr Marc Fehlmann notes:

> Although Emil Bührle would have given his collection to the Kunsthaus Zürich, it would not have been appropriate at the time. In the 1950s, nobody would have accepted the gift from a person who worked with the Nazi regime. They wanted to keep it away . . . even so, it is an amazing collection.[41]

Other exhibitions soon followed with the Bührle Collection exhibited at the Charlottenburg Palace, Berlin (1958), Haus der Kunst, Munich (1958–1959), Royal Scottish Academy, Edinburgh (1961) and the National Gallery, London (1961).[42]

The posthumous bequest

Time did not allow Bührle the opportunity to plan a suitable future for his personal art collection, however, one thing is certain, he wanted to preserve his holdings. Bührle had no desire to bequeath his collection to a museum as he feared it would be broken up and dispersed across various curatorial departments within the museum, and thus, compromise the 'collection's unique character'.[43] Shortly before his death Bührle did consider establishing a foundation as a way to maintain the collection as one, indefinitely, whilst making it publicly accessible upon his passing. Without a will, Bührle's heirs – his wife Charlotte Bührle-Schalk, daughter Hortense Anda-Bührle and son Dr Dieter Bührle – honoured his wishes and established the Foundation E.G. Bührle Collection to manage part of his 520 works that included paintings, works on paper and sculptures.[44]

A rare glimpse at Bührle's personal arrangement at 172 Zollikerstrasse can be seen in the photograph taken by Dimitri Kessel in 1954 – as part of a feature for LIFE magazine (refer to Figure 3.1). Bührle is seated directly in front of Degas' 'Madame Camus at the Piano' (1869). This dense arrangement is a far cry from the way the works have been displayed following Bührle's death. The many rooms within the villa have been arranged in art historical, nationalistic and thematic groupings. 'Madame Camus at the Piano' hangs in the Portrait Room on the ground floor. Even though the villa was never intended as a house museum, it was nevertheless fashioned to look like one. The Collection's financial needs were met by the Foundation E.G. Bührle and the collector's immediate family. Operating as a private institution, access to the Bührle, until early 2015, was strictly by appointment with the house museum open to the public on the first Sunday of each month. Even so, the Foundation E.G. Bührle's transition from private to public was, and still remains unclear.

I would suggest that converting the villa into a museum may have also contributed to this ambiguity as it changed the relationship between the house, the collection and the collector. This is because it was never intended to be a house museum, rather it evolved into one reluctantly upon Bührle's passing. Furniture, furnishings and decorative objects were installed into what was essentially a quasi-picture gallery that was devoid of any signs of domesticity. Perhaps, Bührle's heirs were left with little choice when considering his future legacy? Harking back to the collector's grandson Christian Bührle's description of the villa it suggests an inaccurate depiction of the house and the collector's relationship to it: 'Its extensive gardens and distinctive furnishings give it the feel of a private home where the visitor finds a collection bearing the imprint of Bührle's personality'.[45] This confusion continues to date as it was made clear to me that the villa is not a house museum as the collector never saw the museum or lived in the house. If one is to present a critical perspective of the largely unknown (outside of Switzerland) Emil Bührle narrative and the important collection that was amassed over a short period of time, to separate the collector from the villa would be misleading. It played a crucial role in the collector's own lifetime and the formation and appreciation of the collection itself – hence, I would argue that the two are inextricably linked.

Public access, although a clear stipulation of the formation of the Foundation was limited and tightly controlled as is much of the information pertaining to the house museum and collector. One reason for their rigid public access policy can be attributed to the February 2008 robbery where four masterpieces valued around $160 million were stolen from the Foundation E.G. Bührle Collection at gunpoint, half an hour before the museum closed. The armed robbery would certainly have influenced Bührle's next of kin and their decision to relocate the collection from the intimate setting of the house museum into a more public space. Of the four paintings that were stolen, Cezanne's 'Boy in a Red Waistcoat' (c.1888–1890) and Degas' 'Ludovic Lepic and his Daughters' (c.1871) were recovered within a week; however, van Gogh's 'Blossoming Chestnut Branches' (1890) and Monet's 'Poppies Near Vétheuil' (c.1879) were not recovered until 2012.[46] At the time of the robbery the main security at the Bührle Collection was a single security guard and the alarmed glass that surrounded the respective paintings; this level of security was clearly insufficient to protect the artworks displayed throughout the house. Risk Management professional Bill Coffin, notes that private museum owners today are faced with the difficult decision to employ obtrusive security guards that can often interfere with the public's engagement with the works of art on display, or simply to choose to trust the public.[47] This is an important factor that may have prompted Dr Dieter Bührle and Hortense Anda-Bührle's decision to commit to a long-term loan agreement with the Kunsthaus Zürich.

Relocating the house museum

As of 2020, the Collection will relocate to the new modern and contemporary art wing at the Kunsthaus Zürich.[48] On 28 May 2012, the *Zürcher Kunstgesellschaft* and the Foundation E.G. Bührle Collection signed an agreement to make 166 paintings and 25 sculptures available on long-term loan to the Kunsthaus Zürich until 2034.[49] The Collection will be on permanent display as one, and will sit alongside the museum's own holdings, within the Bührle family funded wing. During this time the Kunsthaus will serve as the custodian of the Bührle collection where it will be secure, permanently displayed, conserved and researched whilst allowing the works to be enjoyed by a broader general audience at no additional cost to the Foundation or the family, beyond a contribution to the financing of the new museum wing.

The Kunsthaus currently has several works on permanent loan from the collection. Dr Christoph Becker asserts that the museum does not feel restricted by this long-term arrangement as it has the autonomy to change the display of the Bührle holdings, move them around and to lend them to other institutions. As Becker points out:

> There is a lot of flexibility in the agreement struck with the Foundation. This is an advantageous position for both the museum and the Foundation. It was a long way to get them to the Kunsthaus and to a public institution. The name Bührle sounds a bell in Switzerland due to his past and to the history of the country. So, it was a difficult task to bring Bührle to a public institution – both from a political position and the fact that the collection is a precious one and can be better shown in a public museum than it can currently. From a political point of view, it still remains a big issue despite the time that has lapsed. If you don't talk about it, things don't get raked up. They worsen actually.[50]

Dr Becker hopes the collection will remain at the Kunsthaus Zürich after 2034, and believes it is unlikely that the collection will be removed from the museum.[51] This optimistic outlook has much to do with the museum's close and longstanding relationship with the Foundation Bührle (Becker is on the Board of the Foundation Bührle and a staff member from the Foundation works at the Kunsthaus Zürich). The Foundation operates as an independent body at the Kunsthaus, in much the same way as other Foundations, such as the Giacometti Foundation.[52]

In considering the future of their father's collection and the transition to the Kunsthaus, I would suggest that Dr Dieter Bührle at the age of 90

Figure 3.3 Extension Kunsthaus Zürich. View of the new main entrance, across Heimplatz from the intersection Zeltweg and Rämistrasse. Non-binding rendering 2015. © David Chipperfield Architects.

(1921–2012) and Hortense Anda-Bührle (1926–2014) in her 87th year, took into account three significant factors: first, at the very late stage of their own life they sought to find a suitable home for Bührle's collection that would ensure it remains publicly accessible whilst avoiding its dispersal upon their own passing. Second, the permanent display of the Bührle art collection at the Kunsthaus finally establishes the collector's legacy as an important art collector and philanthropist in Switzerland. And third, the relocation allays their long-term concerns around the security, insurance and the ongoing expense associated with making a private museum available to the public. Dr Becker adds that the Foundation's poor financial predicament and their inability to ensure the security and safety of the collection and villa have forced the Bührle family to look at alternative options to provide for a secure future for the collection; he points out that 'there is no money in the Foundation'.[53] The pressure placed on the Foundation after the security breach in 2008 restricted public access to 12 days a year, thereby making it difficult to increase visitor numbers to help offset the cost associated with such an initiative.[54]

The relocation of the Bührle holdings to the Kunsthaus Zürich nevertheless raises the following question: how will Bührle's personality and the collection's unique character be maintained in a museum context beyond the confines of the original villa that housed it for more than seven decades? The new David Chipperfield Architects wing sets out a 'house of rooms' where individually sized exhibition spaces will help to create a more intimate engagement with the works that are of domestic proportions. This method of display is consistent with the Kunsthaus' current curatorial position and the original Karl Moser designed building. As Dr Becker elaborates:

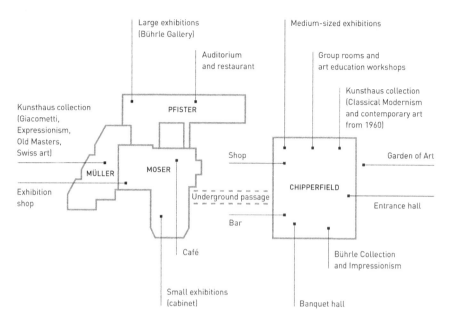

Large exhibitions
(Bührle Gallery)

Medium-sized exhibitions

Auditorium
and restaurant

Group rooms and
art education workshops

Kunsthaus collection
(Giacometti,
Expressionism,
Old Masters,
Swiss art)

PFISTER

Kunsthaus collection
(Classical Modernism
and contemporary art
from 1960)

Shop

Garden of Art

MÜLLER

MOSER

Exhibition
shop

Underground passage

CHIPPERFIELD

Entrance hall

Bar

Café

Banquet hall

Small exhibitions
(cabinet)

Bührle Collection
and Impressionism

Figure 3.4 Extension Kunsthaus Zürich. Allocation of key content and offerings to the buildings. © Kunsthaus Zürich.

Figure 3.5 Extension Kunsthaus Zürich. Gallery with overhead light for the Bührle Collection. Non-binding rendering 2017. © David Chipperfield Architects.

The Bührle holdings will continue to look like a private collection as the smaller rooms will create a sense of intimacy without trying to recreate aspects of the current installation. The Kunsthaus has many small rooms within the overall museum, so this will be in keeping with the rest of the building to accommodate smaller art works. When they come [to the museum] they will have their own rooms. It is not just a large wing, it is within the extension on the second floor.[55]

This leaves us with one final question – will the Bührle house museum continue to exist as a house museum without the works of art that were once hung or casually placed against its walls and that ultimately defined it? The villa's fate is not yet known; as Dr Becker points out, the Bührle family and Foundation will decide on its future in due course – it is after all a private matter.[56]

'Private lived-in collections'

'A new type of building': Lyon Housemuseum, Melbourne (2009)

In 1939, the expatriate American art collector Peggy Guggenheim (1898–1979), considered the possibility of opening her own museum of modern art in London. She canvassed the idea with her friend, art critic and curator Herbert Read, with the intention that he would be the director. She went about methodically formulating a list of artists that she needed to include with Read's assistance.[57] During 1939–1940, Guggenheim went about acquiring the many works that were intended to form the basis of her new museum. Her plans were nevertheless halted as she was forced to flee Paris fearing German occupation. Upon moving to Italy, Guggenheim made the eighteenth-century Palazzo Venier dei Leoni on Venice's Grand Canal her home in 1948; by 1949 she transformed it into a museum – the Peggy Guggenheim Collection. Hence, the palazzo was both a private home and a 'public' museum during the collector's own lifetime. By 1951, the converted palazzo was opened to the public three afternoons a week and continued to be accessible to visitors for some thirty years. Guggenheim's house museum was openly democratic with no restrictions in place, and has remained so to date. Exhibitions were held in the sculpture garden, in the converted cellar, the servants' quarters and laundry that were redesigned as art galleries. Guggenheim's unique arrangement of the house as museum and 'lived-in collection' provided the intellectual stimulation for Corbett Lyon who pondered the idea for some 20 years before embarking on his own house museum.

Corbett Lyon's (born 1955) purpose-built Housemuseum provides an interesting link to earlier models of the house museum but also a counterpoint to the current trend of the house as exhibition space. In 2009, Lyon constructed the Lyon Housemuseum and what he describes as a 'new type of building' and house museum where domestic and public merge seamlessly.[58] The Housemuseum is designed to be both house and museum. At face value it appears to draw on earlier examples of the house museum, however, upon closer scrutiny we can appreciate that this is an experimental approach to living with permanent displays of art. Lyon aims to personalise the experience for the visiting public and to promote contemporary Australian art in an environment that combines positive aspects of the home and museum. As the architect, patron and collector, Lyon wanted to create a new 'architectural hybrid' that could sit alongside the Peggy Guggenheim Collection and the quirky nuances of Sir John Soane's Museum in London.

Corbett and Yueji Lyon's decision to incorporate living spaces and the display of contemporary art appears to be sympathetic to the needs of the Lyon family and the visiting public. Individual rooms merge seamlessly without the need to stipulate a clear separation of space that defines other contemporary case studies discussed in the following chapter. Lyon's sketches and

Figure 3.6 Corbett and Yueji Lyon. Photo: Nils Koenning. © Image courtesy Lyon Housemuseum.

Figure 3.7 Exterior view of the front façade of the Lyon Housemuseum. Photo: John Gollings. © Image courtesy Lyon Housemuseum.

design thinking emphasise the physical aspects of the house along with the exploration of how specific design points and spatial components consider the viewpoint of the users of the building itself. The element of surprise and curiosity plays a key role in his thought process and in setting out the visitor experience. This is not surprising if we consider the influence of Sir John Soane's Museum and the way that objects are exhibited throughout numbers 12 and 13 Lincoln's Inn Fields where the engagement of object and space enhance the appearance and appreciation of both. As Lyon elaborates:

> How might they [the visitor] experience these layered, flowing spaces in the building? How would their experience unfold? . . . These drawings explored the framing of a particular viewpoint or artwork and how space and artwork could be made to work together to create a sense of anticipation and discovery for the viewer.[59]

Lyon's vision for the Housemuseum was that it be 'experimental and speculative' exploring alternative perspectives about living with art while also challenging the notion of private and public space and what a twenty-first-century house museum might be: 'What does a contemporary "house museum" look like? Like a house? Or like a museum? Or something which has attributes of both? What might people experience living in and visiting such a building?'[60] He considered the relationship between the private and public spaces of a home and whether the 'public' museum component should be an extension to the private spaces (just as Oskar Reinhart commissioned

Figure 3.8 Interior view of the Lyon Housemuseum. Photo: John Gollings. © Image courtesy Lyon Housemuseum.

Figure 3.9 Installation view of the Lyon Housemuseum. Photo: John Gollings. © Image courtesy Lyon Housemuseum.

Figure 3.10 Courtyard view of the Lyon Housemuseum. Photo: John Gollings. ©
Image courtesy Lyon Housemuseum.

architect Maurice Turrettini to design a picture gallery to be built alongside the villa 'Am Römerholz'); or whether they should be segregated with
a penthouse apartment installed on the top of the museums (as epitomised
by Christian Boros and Julia Stoschek in Chapter 4). The third option was
to create a purpose-built structure that blended the two types. As Lyon
explained:

> A concurrent series of sketches explored the interweaving of the two
> programs in plan, one public and one private, with house and museum
> cohabitation in this new, single building . . . the term 'housemuseum'
> was invented to describe the newly created hybrid type.[61]

The Lyon Housemuseum is designed around a series of internal architectural boxes that each contain private and public spaces. A two-storey white
cube space at the front of the house and a large black cube towards the back
serve to support the series of spaces that are integrated within the overall
plan. A large enclosed room, akin to a central courtyard envelops the many
internal spaces that are juxtaposed throughout the building. Within this,
seven are categorised as public areas and are located throughout various
areas of the two-level building making it difficult to distinguish between the
two. Upon entering the house visitors are immediately introduced to both
the domestic and public spaces: kitchen and family living rooms sit alongside

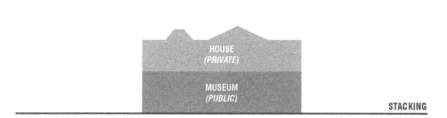

Figure 3.11 Sketches exploring design strategies to combine the two programmes and types. © Image courtesy Lyon Housemuseum.

Figure 3.12 Sketches infusing and juxtaposing public and private – the '*housemuseum*'. © Image courtesy Lyon Housemuseum.

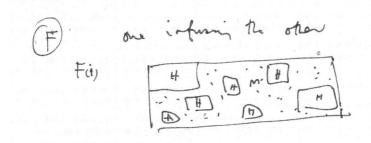

Figure 3.13 Sketches exploring the interweaving of house and museum elements. © Image courtesy Lyon Housemuseum.

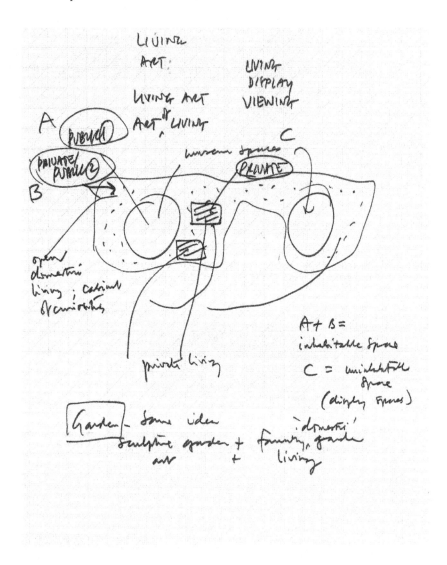

Figure 3.13 (Cont.)

the museum-style white cube that is placed in the centre of the lower level; the music room, adjacent gallery and the black box at the far end of the house are more clearly defined as public. As the Housemuseum has been created with the public in mind, the central section of the second level is strictly off limits as it contains private bedrooms and study areas that can be easily cordoned off. The long rectangular windows along the narrow corridor and dining room on the upper level allow visitors to voyeuristically look into the

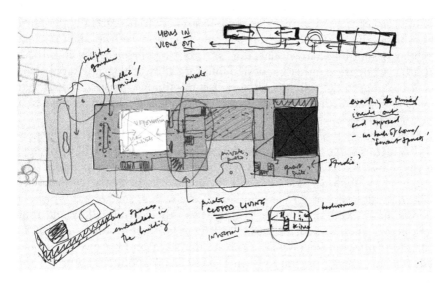

Figure 3.14 Sketches of the white cube and black box cube spaces anchoring the plan with domestic and museum spaces flowing between them. © Image courtesy Lyon Housemuseum.

white cube and across the entire house getting a sweeping glance at aspects of the Lyon family's Australian contemporary art collection.

With the exception of two works of art all other spaces in the house were created without the consideration of specific works of art: the permanent display of Howard Arkley's 17 painted panels entitled 'Fabricated Rooms' (1997–1999) can be viewed in the upstairs dining room; and Brook Andrew's animated neon and wall painting installation work 'You've always wanted to be black (white friend)' (2006) is installed in the lower level music room. Visits to the Lyon Housemuseum must be pre-booked via their web site with guided tours designated throughout the year; this ranges from around three to five tours per month that are conducted by both Yueji and Corbett Lyon.

Housemuseum Galleries (2019)

In March 2019, the Lyon Housemuseum welcomed its sibling – the new stand-alone Housemuseum Galleries (HM Galleries). Situated alongside the Housemuseum it is also designed by Lyon – as evidenced by his meticulous attention to detail and experimental approach to thinking through his architectural projects. The two buildings share complimentary architectural forms as can be seen in the way that they are spatially arranged around a series of enclosed, box-like spaces that are surrounded with an open internal court. The Housemuseum's dark grey zinc cladding compliments the new building which is clad in Australian bluestone with 12,000 projecting pieces of pale grey bluestone that are carefully designed into the building's façade to create a three-dimensional effect. Their distinct angular design lines, street elevation and roof profile elegantly link them together while the contrasting design interiors allows their individual character to come to the fore: the Housemuseum's timber veneered panels that are overprinted with small texts are set alongside the white cube spaces at the HM Galleries.

Developed by the Lyon Foundation (that was formed in 2012), the new HM Galleries will operate as a not-for-profit art museum. It will be opened to the public six days a week and will host three exhibitions per year. The inaugural exhibition, 'ENTER', will feature works from the Lyon family collection alongside newly commissioned art works; the second will be a monographic exhibition that will span across the central gallery and four peripheral galleries; and the third, will focus on architecture and design. The Housemuseum operates as a private initiative, and for the time being, will remain a separate entity. When I asked Lyon about the future of the Housemuseum and the ongoing funding of HM Galleries he advised that it is his intention to gift the Housemuseum to the Lyon Foundation making the two museums accessible to the public as a single public entity. They have been designed with this in mind – a shared entry point has been integrated into the new building that will (in the near future) allow visitors to move freely between the two buildings. That being so, without the Lyon family in the house, the Housemuseum will function as a museum where the house is merely a façade for the exhibition space. It is unclear at this early stage exactly how both entities will be funded in the long-term, whether

Figure 3.15 Interior view of the front façade Left, Housemuseum Galleries. © Image courtesy Lyon Housemuseum.

Figure 3.16 Interior view of the Café, Housemuseum Galleries. © Image courtesy Lyon Housemuseum.

the Foundation will continue to fund both museums indefinitely or if Lyon would prefer to gift them to the state of Victoria – only time will tell.

Sphere of influence

Corbett Lyon has also spurred other collectors to reconsider the house museum model. In 2012, Charles and Leah Justin visited the Lyon Housemuseum and were greatly influenced by this model along with other international examples of the house museum. In April 2016, they established the Justin Art House Museum (JAHM) in the Melbourne suburb of Prahran. One of the principal challenges for the Justins was how to differentiate JAHM from other house museums. As expressed in their own words: we want 'to provide a very personal and intimate experience to our visitors, to make them feel like guests in our home, but also to be intellectually stimulated, like attending a soirée'.[62] It is no coincidence that their exhibitions are often thematic and loosely based around contemporary issues – social, religious, cultural and political – so as to promote a platform for critical debate and public discourse.

Situated within an existing remodelled residential apartment block, JAHM occupies three levels of the corner building. Their residence is partly clad in Tunni Kraus' art work, 'Striped wall to external gallery façade' (2013/2014) and serves to differentiate JAHM from its neighbours. The brief for their architect daughter Elisa Justin, was not clear cut: they needed a space for two people that could also accommodate up to 70 visitors. They settled on a model that would incorporate a separate gallery space for exhibitions (located on the second level) and allow them the flexibility to display their art collection throughout the apartment. Unlike the Lyon Housemuseum's purpose-built structure that blends the two types – that is, an extension to private spaces versus the segregated apartment – JAHM sits somewhere in between. It has been designed to flexibly shift between the two models where private and public spaces become a little opaque in the way that they can be utilised and in the way that some spaces can be multi-faceted in their function. Their car garage, for instance, can double up as a black box projection space. This flexibility in the space allows them to adapt to the needs of the individual exhibitions while also preserving their domestic environment and the scale of it when it is just the two of them.[63]

The Justins personally conduct guided interactive tours of the collection and encourage visitors to walk through every part of the three-level apartment. They have attracted between 4,000 and 5,000 visitors to date.[64] The collection comprises of around 250 works of art (largely abstract art with a focus on digital and video works). They host three exhibitions a year: invite guest curators to reinterpret their own collection; display works from other Australian private collections (Susan Taylor and Peter Jones); and invite international and local artists to create new and site-specific works (three German artists: Lars Breuer, Sebastian Freytag, Guido Münch). JAHM has created its own path and model that has quickly attracted attention and a keen following to the numerous public events, lecture series and changing exhibition programs and guided tours.

Figure 3.17 Charles and Leah Justin, 2017. © Image courtesy Justin Art House Museum.

Figure 3.18 Exterior view of the Justin Art House Museum. Photo: Andrew Wuttke. © Image courtesy Justin Art House Museum.

Figure 3.19 Installation view of the Justin Art House Museum, 2017. Photo: Jaime Diaz-Berro. © Image courtesy Justin Art House Museum and Justin Architecture.

Conclusion

As Emil Bührle was not afforded the time to determine the future of his holdings, his heirs sought to perpetuate his legacy by exhibiting a significant part of his art collection in the villa that served to house them. In doing so, they did not wish to draw attention to Bührle the successful entrepreneur, but to Bührle the connoisseur and collector of fine art. Just as Helen Clay Frick spent much of her life defending her father's name so too have Bührle's heirs and his Foundation. Yet, they and others will be remembered for their important art collections that have been made publicly available upon their passing.

The case studies in this chapter have drawn our attention to the importance of viewing and experiencing art in the personal and intimate environment of the collector's private residence. It raised concerns about the ongoing financial commitment required to support such an initiative and ensuring the safety of the works of art can prove equally challenging over time. I have also raised concerns about the difficulty in recreating an intimate engagement with the Bührle's art works once they are confined to a large public museum. As I have noted, the Kunsthaus Zürich appears to be the most logical home for Bührle's holdings as the collector and his family maintained a long-standing association with the museum as is evidenced by the numerous acts of benefaction (gifted works of art and two exhibition wings). Dr Christoph Becker's determination to eventually return the collection to the museum, albeit 62 years later, and against a number of obstacles, has certainly paid off for the museum and their visitors. While the public will have the privilege of viewing Bührle's masterpieces at the Kunsthaus Zürich I am nonetheless grateful to have had the opportunity to experience them within Emil Bührle's quasi-picture gallery at 172 Zollikerstrasse. It was here that I realised that Bührle the business man was not feverishly buying works of art for the sake of it, but rather as a former art historian he attempted to build a comprehensive collection of masterpieces that spanned across various eras.

Corbett Lyon has on the other hand started his journey towards the future with the construction of the new HM Galleries that will contribute to the evolution of the Housemuseum and reinforce Lyon's broader cultural vision to create an important art hub in the leafy suburban neighbourhood of Kew. His purpose-built twenty-first-century house museum elegantly integrates family living with the display of contemporary Australian art along with a curious public in mind. In doing so, he has redefined what is understood to be a house museum and what it should look like and how it should function. With this in mind, Lyon's cultural ambitions will in due course see the Housemuseum transition into a museum. The following chapter will examine the contemporary house museum as exhibition space.

Notes

1 Higonnet, Anne, *A Museum of One's Own: Private Collecting, Public Gift*, Pittsburgh and New York, Periscope Publishing, 2009, p.81.
2 Higonnet, 2009, pp.19–20.
3 Bührle, Christian, Foundation Emil G. Bührle Collection, *The Passionate Eye: Impressionist and Other Master Paintings from the E.G. Bührle Collection*, edited by The Foundation Emil G. Bührle Collection, Zurich and Munich, Artemis Verlag, 1990, p.37.
4 Bührle, Foundation Emil G. Bührle Collection, 1990, p.35.
5 Stourton, James, *Great Collectors of Our Time: Art Collecting Since 1945*, London, Scala Publications 2007, p.193.
6 Dr Christoph Becker, interview with the author.
7 Cooper, Douglas, 'Emil G. Bührle and His Collection', in Masterpieces of French Painting from the Bührle Collection, edited by The Arts Council of Great Britain, Exhibition at The National Gallery – London, 29 September to 5 November, London, The Arts Council of Great Britain, 1961, n.p.; also Hahnloser-Ingold, Margrit, 'Emil Georg Bührle – A Student of Art History Turned Industrialist and Art Collector', in *The Foundation Emil G. Bührle Collection*, 1990, pp.19–21. Bührle married Charlotte Schalk in 1920, the daughter of a well-known banker in Magdeburg which further enhanced his career. Hahnloser-Ingold, 1990, p.19.
8 Cabanne, Pierre, *The Great Collectors*, London, Cassell, 1961, pp.126–131; also, Davison, Phil. "Dieter Bührle: Controversial Arms Dealer." *The Independent*, 18 December, 2012, n.p.
9 Davison, Phil. 'Dieter Buhrle: Controversial Arms Dealer'. *The Independent*, 18 December 2012, n.p.
10 Cabanne, 1961, pp.128–129.
11 Cooper, 1961, n.p.
12 Bührle's company expanded to include textiles, welding and airplane industries, high vacuum thin film and coating technology and interests in the hotel business. Hahnloser-Ingold, 1990, p.21.
13 Hahnloser-Ingold, 1990, p.20; Stourton, 2007, p.189; Cooper, 1961, n.p.
14 Foundation E.G. Bührle website, 'Emil Georg Bührle 1890–1956, Entrepreneur and Art Collector, 1939–1945: Second World War'.
15 Dr Christoph Becker, interview with the author.
16 Father of Angela Rosengart – founder of the Rosengart Collection in Lucerne.
17 Rosengart, Angela (ed.), *The Rosengart Collection*, Munich, London, Berlin and New York, Prestel Verlag, 2002, p. 21.
18 Cooper, 1961, n.p.
19 Bührle owned 20 Manet paintings which was remarkable at the time. Dr Christoph Becker, interview with the author.
20 Cooper, 1961, n.p.
21 Cooper, 1961, n.p.
22 Stourton, 2007, p.189.
23 Cooper, 1961, n.p.
24 Cooper, 1961, n.p.
25 Cooper, 1961, n.p.
26 Includes 45 Cézanne paintings, 3 self-portraits and 49 Renoir paintings. Author's own visit to the E.G. Bührle Collection, Zürich, 5 January 2014.

27 Cooper, 1961, n.p.
28 Davison, 2012, n.p.
29 The authors challenge the due diligence undertaken by the Bührle Foundation and the Kunsthaus Zürich; the two institutions have thus publicly contest these allegations. Buomberger, Thomas, *Schwarzbuch Bührle: Raubkunst Für Das Kunsthaus Zürich?*, edited by Guido Magnaguagno Zürich, Zurich, Rotpunktverlag, 2015.
30 Refer to Hickley, Catherine, *The Munich Art Hoard: Hitler's Dealer and His Secret Legacy*, London, Thames & Hudson, 2015.
31 Cooper, 1961, n.p.; Stourton, 2007, p.189; Kunsthaus Zürich's website, Van Gogh, Cézanne, Monet – the Bührle Collection Visits the Kunsthaus Zürich 12 February to 16 May 2010', Kunsthaus Zürich.
32 Refer to exhibition document Kunsthaus Zürich, Background Information: 'Van Gogh, Cézanne, Monet – The Bührle Collection Visits the Kunsthaus Zürich' 12 February to 16 May 2010, Media Release 2010.
33 Kunsthaus Zürich, 2010, n.p. Also refer to provenance of all works that can be found on the Foundation E.G. Bührle Collection website.
34 Hahnloser-Ingold, 1990, p.25.
35 E.G. Bührle. Cabanne, 1961, p.135.
36 Bührle, Emile, Foundation Emil G. Bührle Collection, 1990, p.26.
37 Hahnloser-Ingold, 1990, pp.17–18.
38 Hahnloser-Ingold, 1990, p.18.
39 Anda-Bührle, Hortense, Foundation Emil G. Bührle Collection, 1990, p.13.
40 Dr Christoph Becker, interview with the author.
41 Dr Marc Fehlman, interview with the author.
42 Anda-Bührle, Foundation Emil G. Bührle Collection, 1990, p.13.
43 Bührle, Foundation Emil G. Bührle Collection, 1990, p.35.
44 Stourton, 2007, p.193.
45 Bührle, Foundation Emil G. Bührle Collection, 1990, p.37.
46 Dewey, Diane, 'Emil Bührle's Modernist Art Collection Dazzles Zürich: Impressionism to Picasso', *Artes Magazine* (2010), n.p.; Sturcke, James, '£84m Paintings Stolen in "Spectacular" Swiss Raid', *The Guardian*, 12 February 2008, n.p.; Coffin, Bill, 'The Great Swiss Art Robbery', *Risk Management* 55, no. 4 (2008), p.18. Also Foundation E.G. Bührle Collection website, 'The Museum: From 1960: Foundation E.G. Bührle Collection'.
47 Coffin, 2008, p.18.
48 It is designed by architect David Chipperfield Architects, at a cost of CHF 200 million ($213 million). The new wing will also include works from Swiss collector Hubert Looser's collection that will be on permanent loan; he is considering gifting the collection to the Kunsthaus. Hickley, Catherine, 'Swiss Magnate Looser Spends Fortune on Art, Gives It Away', *Bloomberg.com*.
49 Permanent loans cannot exceed 25 years as the loan, legally, becomes a gift. After 20 years such agreements are usually renegotiated. Dr Christoph Becker, interview with the author. Also, Kunsthaus Zürich website, 'Kunsthaus Extension'.
50 Dr Christoph Becker, interview with the author.
51 Permanent loans cannot exceed 25 years. If they do exceed 25 years it is not legally binding and would then be considered a gift, not a loan. After 20 years such agreements are often renegotiated. After 25 years they are considered a gift.
52 Dr Christoph Becker, interview with the author.

53 Dr Christoph Becker, interview with the author.

54 Dr Christoph Becker, interview with the author.

55 Dr Christoph Becker, interview with the author.

56 Dr Christoph Becker, interview with the author.

57 The war did not prevent Guggenheim from pursuing and collecting the works by artists she befriended and those suggested to her by Herbert Read. Shenker, Israel, 'Peggy Guggenheim Is Dead at 81; Known for Her Modern Art Collection', *New York Times*, 24 December 1979.

58 Lyon,Corbett, 'Collecting Contemporary Art & the Contemporary House Museum with Corbett Lyon' at The Johnston Collection Study Day 2013, The Fine Art of Collecting – A Matter of Taste, Saturday, 12 October 2013.

59 Corbett Lyon, interview with the author and access to Lyon's unpublished material.

60 Corbett Lyon, interview with the author and access to Lyon's unpublished material.

61 Corbett Lyon, interview with the author and access to Lyon's unpublished material.

62 Charles and Leah Justin, correspondence with the author.

63 Charles and Leah Justin, correspondence with the author.

64 Charles and Leah Justin, correspondence with the author.

4 Subverting the notion of the house museum

The house museum's embellished mode of display was seen to be too personal and unprofessional for many twentieth-century collectors and benefactors. Dr Albert C. Barnes (1872–1951), collector and founder of the Barnes Foundation in Philadelphia, embraced a studious and professional approach to collecting and to the display of his disparate holdings of nineteenth- and twentieth-century French paintings, African art and Old Master paintings, wrought-iron and Native American objects. They were exhibited in the purpose-built picture gallery that was designed by Paul Philippe Cret (in 1925) to sit alongside his home at Merion and curated and managed by his staff from the outset. The foundation gallery and the private living areas were connected by a corridor, thereby keeping the private and public spaces completely separate.

Similarly, Hertford House incorporated four purpose-built galleries to display Sir Richard Wallace's private art collection and decorative objects. These galleries were made publicly available in Wallace's own lifetime but were tightly controlled to protect his privacy and to ensure the collection remained secure. Those allowed access to the collection included scholars and artists and the cultured elite within his immediate social circle, who advised of their intent to view his paintings and art objects. Access was granted strictly by 'visitor's card' that he sent ahead of their tour of the collection.[1] Barnes also maintained strict control over who gained access to his paintings in the 1930s: those who were critical of him and his avant-garde collection, and people he had taken a dislike to were simply denied entry into the foundation gallery – such was his admission policy.[2]

This chapter will investigate why the transition of the house to museum resulted in a dramatic shift away from the domestic towards the house as museum and exhibition space (in which case the notion of the house is used mainly as a façade for the museum). This will be shown in three parts to chart the departure from the domestic towards one that focuses primarily on the exhibition space and in so doing, subverts the concept of the house museum in a way that the museum itself becomes the defining aspect of the house: I. The Oskar Reinhart Collection's (1970) transition from a private residence to house museum saw the removal of the collector's identity along with most of the domestic elements with little to suggest that it existed as a private home. II. Glenstone Museum (2006) expands on the notion of the 'collection house' as it is essentially an exhibition space that is completely detached from the collector's private residence but is situated within the same compound. III. The Julia Stoschek (2007) and Boros Collections (2008) include a separate penthouse apartment above the exhibition space signalling a significant departure from the domestic towards one that focuses primarily on the exhibition space. This will allow for a different reading of the ways in which these trajectories spin off the house museum and lead into the 'stand-alone museum' (not a domestic house) and the various issues and difficulties that can emerge when high profile collectors seek to present their personal legacies on the contemporary global stage.

Figure 4.1 Oskar Reinhart (on right) during the rehanging of the collection, assisted by his Chauffeur Albert Fritschi, c.1955. Photo: Albert Gnant, 1955. © Archive Collection Oskar Reinhart 'Am Römerholz', Winterthur.

The transition from villa to public museum: the Oskar Reinhart Collection 'Am Römerholz', Winterthur, Switzerland (1970)

Overview

Villa 'Am Römerholz' was created to house and display Oskar Reinhart's (1885–1965) collection of European and Old Master paintings while acknowledging his sense of fine taste. The villa and its holdings were officially bequeathed to the Swiss Confederation in 1958. The remodelling phase took place upon Reinhart's passing with the villa opening to the public as the Oskar Reinhart Collection 'Am Römerholz' in 1970. During this period of transition, it evolved from a private residence to a public museum – personal aspects of Reinhart's home and references to the collector himself were largely removed.[3] What furniture remains serves to demonstrate the fashionable interior displays that were admired by the wealthy elite during the 1950s and 1960s; that is, the tasteful installations of select French furniture and decorative objects placed alongside old masterpieces with little in the way of ornamentation. Works of art, decorative art objects and furniture are elegantly and economically displayed within Reinhart's individual rooms that hint of their previous existence as a former private home.

The removal of domestic references within the villa might appear to be in keeping with a more traditional trajectory from private to public, however, there is little to suggest that Reinhart the man even existed. The Huntington Library, Art Collection and Botanical Gardens in San Marino has adopted a similar approach, yet portraits of Henry and Arabella Huntington adorn the lobby of their former residence to establish a point of departure for contemporary audiences. Establishing two sets of significant holdings for two distinct institutions (within his own lifetime) seems to indicate Reinhart's highly visible and aspirational approach to benefaction, so why have his beneficiaries erased his visual image and thus rewritten his narrative?

Oskar Reinhart came from a wealthy merchant family in Winterthur. The nineteenth-century industrial developments transformed Winterthur into the second largest city in the Canton of Zürich, and by the early twentieth century it became a thriving city for the arts. This was because a growing number of merchant collectors and benefactors used their personal wealth and influence to promote the arts and their benefits within the community.[4] Oskar Reinhart's father, Theodore Reinhart, was the head of the merchant trading firm Gebrüder Volkart (Volkart Brothers). At the time, the Reinhart family was placed in the top twenty wealthiest families in Switzerland and were influential patrons in their home town of Winterthur.[5] Theodore Reinhart supported many Swiss artists and served as an important role model for his four sons: the eldest son Georg collected works of the European avant-garde and Asian art; Hans a poet, supported and promoted literature and the theatre; Werner's interests lay in music and he supported important composers that included Stravinsky, Schönberg, Webern, Berg, Hindemith and Strauss along with several Swiss composers and musicians; and the youngest Oskar, was an art collector like his father and older brother.[6] Collecting became a life-long interest that dominated much of Oskar Reinhart's adult life.

Two collections – two foundations

Alongside his personal collection at Villa 'Am Römerholz', Reinhart also formed a collection of 500 German, Austrian and Swiss paintings and sculptures dating from the late-eighteenth to mid-twentieth centuries, along with 7,000 prints from the fifteenth to the twentieth centuries. With the intention of perpetuating his collection he established the Oskar Reinhart Foundation in 1940, to allow it to remain in Winterthur. He founded the Museum Oskar Reinhart 'Am Stadtgarten' which opened to the public in 1951 and is the oldest collection museum in Switzerland.[7] Recognising that the city could not afford to sustain two museums he decided to bequeath the Villa 'Am Römerholz' to the Swiss Confederation and the Museum Oskar Reinhart to the city of Winterthur. Over time this proved to be an accurate assessment as the museum's future, was more recently in doubt.

In 1941, the Oskar Reinhart Foundation's endowment comprised CHF 100,000. At the time of Reinhart's death his estate contributed a further CHF 2.5 million to the Foundation. According to former director of the Oskar Reinhart Museum 'Am Stadtgarten', Winterthur, Dr Marc Fehlmann, the Foundation was expected to run out of money in 2016: 'after 65 years the museum came close to bankruptcy'.[8] The Foundation was forced to consider a number of options as the Canton of Zürich and city of Winterthur were for some time unwilling to financially assist the museum in its time of need: the decision to close down the museum, reduce opening hours, sell works from the museum's holdings or tour the collection to raise the much needed funds were options that were considered.

At around the same time, the neighbouring house museum Villa Flora (built in 1846), suffered a similar fate as the Oskar Reinhart Museum 'Am Stadtgarten'. It was the home of the collecting couple Arthur (1870–1936) and Hedy Hahnloser (1873–1952). By 1980, the Hahnloser/Jaeggli Foundation was established by the Hahnlosers' heirs and in 1995 opened Villa Flora to the public. As the Foundation could no longer afford to run the museum and the city was reluctant to financially assist with the much-needed refurbishment of the building, Villa Flora was forced to close in 2014.[9] Since the closure, over 100 works from the Hahnloser Collection have toured a great number of European museums. It is currently on display at the Kunstmuseum Bern as a long-term loan. More recently, the city of Winterthur changed their original decision to assist with Villa Flora's preservation and it is hoped that the collection will in due course move back to its original location. The decision is part of the city's broader plan to merge the Museum Oskar Reinhart 'Am Stadtgarten' and the Villa Flora along with the former Kunstmuseum that was founded in 1848 by the *Kunstverein* Winterthur. The Hahnlosers and Oskar Reinhart's brother Georg, were founding members of the *Kunstverein* and supported the museum financially and through donations of art. In early 2018, the three institutions were renamed Kunst Museum Winterthur. As Oskar Reinhart's endowment has largely supported the museum's operating costs until 2016 it is reasonable to expect the city of Winterthur to assist the museum in its greatest time of need. This might appear to counter my argument in Chapter 7 where I state that governments should not redirect funds away from the public sector to financially support private museums. In this context, however, it is important to acknowledge that Winterthur relied on the Reinhart and Hahnloser families' patronage and contributions to develop the city's cultural institutions and art collections and thus such historical efforts cannot be ignored – without the museums they helped to establish there may be little reason to attract contemporary visitors to Winterthur. As a national house museum, the Oskar Reinhart Collection 'Am Römerholz' is financially secure.

Creating a collection with the house in mind

Villa 'Am Römerholz' is an important aspect of the Reinhart narrative as the collection was formed with the house in mind. So why has the Swiss Confederation's Department of Museums and Collections elected to erase Reinhart's presence from the villa by removing all personal aspects of the house, choosing instead to adopt a more institutional approach to the house museum? From the public's point of view, he exists in name only; we do not sense Oskar Reinhart's presence as the creator and founder of the collection and villa. Instead, the authorities have created a mythologised perspective of Reinhart as the discerning (yet absent) connoisseur. To better understand why this may be so we need to consider Reinhart's collecting patterns and ambitions, personal circumstances and his philanthropic actions. The Collection 'Am Römerholz' and the Oskar Reinhart Museum revealed two opposing perspectives of Reinhart the collector. The Collection 'Am Römerholz' and their publications adopt a hagiographical representation of Reinhart as a discerning collector, art connoisseur and philanthropist.[10]

In complete contrast, the Oskar Reinhart Museum's former director Dr Marc Fehlmann, expressed a less sympathetic point of view, suggesting that Reinhart became less discerning over time due to his deteriorating financial position.[11] Because of the opposing points of view the Oskar Reinhart Museum conducted their own research to present a more accurate perspective of the Reinhart narrative. This however proved difficult as the Reinhart family removed most of his personal correspondence from 'Am Römerholz' at the time of Reinhart's death.[12] Recognising that the Villa 'Am Römerholz' and the Oskar Reinhart Museum are inevitably linked as they were formed simultaneously and for different reasons, my study, however, will critically evaluate the villa's transition from a private residence to a public museum.

Figure 4.2 The gallery of paintings built as an extension to the villa 'Am Römerholz' 1924/1925 and the villa, c.1915, both by architect Maurice Turretini. © Archive Collection Oskar Reinhart 'Am Römerholz', Winterthur.

Villa 'Am Römerholz' was intended to house the paintings Reinhart planned to acquire over the coming decades. Upon visiting the villa Reinhart felt that the house was ill-equipped for the display of paintings. Despite his initial reservations he purchased the 1915 house that was built by the Genevan-based architect Maurice Turrettini, and by 1924, he moved in. It was not long after this that Reinhart commissioned Turrettini to design a picture gallery to be built alongside the villa. It was completed in August 1925.[13] 'Am Römerholz' accommodated Reinhart's collection of Old Master paintings, French Impressionist and Post-Impressionist paintings, sculpture and works on paper.

He was conservative by nature as was his art collection. As Dr Fehlmann explains:

> There is little in the way of nudity. There is nothing erotic – even his Cézannes were considered to be tame as was the Picasso painting [from the blue period]. He did not choose anything that was seen to be daring.[14]

Dr Fehlmann suggests that Reinhart did not want to attract unwanted attention through the subject-matter of his paintings due to the insecurity about his presumed homosexuality. This was an important consideration at the time especially with the Reinhart family's standing within conservative Winterthur and their immense personal wealth.[15]

Reinhart's pattern of collecting and display is formal and conventional in its approach: he balanced the shades and colours of the pictures so as to present an overall harmonious arrangement. He did not adhere to a nationalistic presentation of his collection at the villa 'Am Römerholz', choosing to hang his French and German paintings alongside one another. The few detailed notes and records that have been left behind indicate that although he often rearranged works they generally adhered to a similar aesthetic – according to colour and subject-matter – demonstrating his interest in visual and artistic relationships between the works rather than their art historical connections. Today, many of the paintings are displayed in a visually harmonious linear hang with little in the way of period detail to distract the viewer from the art work.

Villa 'Am Römerholz' is situated at the top of the hill and overlooks the entire city of Winterthur. The villa itself is of elegant proportions. It is surrounded by a long drive way, formal manicured lawns and hedges with rambling gardens extending beyond the house. The entry lobby is almost monastic in appearance with only a front desk and book shelf placed to one side of the spiralling staircase that leads to the second level. The individual

Figure 4.3 The gallery of paintings built as an extension to the villa 'Am Römerholz', 2014. Photo: Georgina Walker.

Figure 4.4 Exterior view of the villa 'Am Römerholz', 2014. Collection Oskar Reinhart 'Am Römerholz', Winterthur. Photo: Georgina Walker.

spaces are of modest proportion with most of them facing the manicured lawns and vista towards Winterthur. Aristide Maillol's life-size sculpture 'La Méditerranéa' (1905–1907) and Renoir's 1913 painting 'After the Bath' adorn the first room and lead visitors into the Tapestry, Renaissance, Rococo, Ante and Daumier rooms.

The picture gallery was built to the side of the original house. The rear aspect includes a conservatory that leads into the three new galleries that display smaller paintings and works on paper. Reinhart extended the picture gallery adding two additional spaces – first the one to the right and then the other at the rear of the main gallery. The proportions of Reinhart's picture gallery accommodate the domestic scale of the paintings well. The tall marble fireplace takes pride of place with Renoir's 1864 still life 'Lily and Greenhouse Plants' that continues to hang handsomely above it. The gallery was previously furnished with large couches around the fireplace, clusters of tables and chairs positioned from various vantage points to appreciate the many paintings on display. Today, three white leather benches are carefully positioned so not to disrupt the unadorned contemplative space that has replaced Reinhart's homelier decor. Although the gallery was not opened to the public during Reinhart's lifetime, I would suggest it was created with the public in mind as he always intended to bequeath the villa to the state.

Figure 4.5 The big hall in the gallery of paintings, c.1950. © Archive Collection Oskar Reinhart 'Am Römerholz', Winterthur.

Perpetuating one's own legacy

The beginning of the war in 1939 had major ramifications for Reinhart and his collecting as did his falling out with his brother Georg (who was at the helm of the family firm). Reinhard's excommunication from the family and dramatic salary reduction meant that his collecting and life-style was dramatically impacted and could no longer afford the purchase of expensive paintings. It is claimed, the reason for their fall out was due to Reinhart's extravagant spending and concerns about his intimate private life.[16] The Reinhart family perceived their corporation and the company's assets were under threat by the Third Reich, should Reinhart's private life be exposed. The corporation's headquarters were moved to New York and the entire family (except Oskar Reinhart) was moved to Lake Geneva as Switzerland feared being invaded by Germany during 1938 and 1939.[17] Dr Fehlmann suggests that Reinhart's intimate private life placed him under constant pressure from his conservative family. As the family removed all of Reinhart's personal papers upon his death, it is difficult to ascertain the exact cause of their concerns.

Much of the literature produced by villa 'Am Römerholz' suggests that Reinhart's 'retirement' from the family firm meant that he was free to pursue his passion for art and collecting. They do recognise that his capacity to purchase quality works of art from this point on deteriorated slowly.[18] Reinhart no longer had the means to continue buying 'high quality' paintings. Although the Collection 'Am Römerholz' supports this claim by stating that Reinhart's departure from the Volkart Brothers made him 'dependent on investments and [Reinhart] had to limit outlays for pictures' they quickly add that the restricted hanging space in the house compelled Reinhart to be more selective in his acquisitions and 'sharpen his eye as a connoisseur'.[19] The exact circumstances are unknown, yet we can assume that both the difficult war years and Reinhart's worsening financial situation may have contributed to his collecting patterns. Even so, the Collection 'Am Römerholz' does at times present an idealised account of the collector by constructing a narrative that can be neatly presented to the general public.

The war years did prompt Reinhart to formalise his will and future plans for villa 'Am Römerholz' and his collection. On 10 October 1940, he set up a foundation that allowed him to bequeath his collection to the municipality, despite his earlier plans to gift his Old German masterpieces to the Museum Oskar Reinhart 'Am Stadtgarten' along with the more recent works of German art that occupied much of the Foundations' holdings.[20] The signing of Reinhart's testamentary gift in 1944, allowed 'Am Römerholz' to be officially bequeathed to the nation upon his death; by March 1956 the donation to the Swiss Confederation was finalised.[21] The will stipulated that works within the collection could not be loaned, sold or gifted as Reinhart believed that the aesthetic value of the collection could be better appreciated when viewed as one.[22] Such stipulations appear consistent with earlier benefactors (Isabella Stewart Gardner, Albert Barnes, Sir John Soane and Lady Wallace) who viewed their collections as a work of art in their own right.

We cannot be sure if villa 'Am Römerholz' was intended to be a personal expression of Reinhart's taste and a lasting token of the value he placed on art as the collection often appears formulaic and detached. The approach adopted by the villa 'Am Römerholz' can appear distant with the focus strictly on the art collection. This can be attributed to the transformation process that sought to erase the personal history of the house and its creator in favour of a more stylised approach. Several rooms at 'Am Römerholz' were lost and others rearranged to ensure the villa could satisfactorily adapt to its new role as a public institution. As a result, historical aspects of the house, its personal attributes and original installations of the collection and interior displays were compromised. The removal of private documents at the time of Reinhart's death further undermines our understanding of the collector and his true motivations. Despite the many claims and the interpretation of limited information, we cannot ignore Reinhart's public-spiritedness as seen in his gifting of the two museums and their vast holdings, which continue to be publicly accessible in Winterthur.

Collection house or museum?

Overview

Isabella Stewart Gardner, Henry Huntington and Henry Clay Frick constructed their own aristocratic domestic environments with fine art, decorative art objects and period furniture which were installed within the lavishly decorated interiors. They carefully planned their own destiny through their respective creations and it was only a matter of time before these collection houses would become museums for the people. They were founded essentially as a museum for the display of notable art collections and second, as a private house; that is, a museum built to look like a house, but not to function primarily as a domestic residence. This quasi-domesticity was seen as a façade as the collectors set about deliberately creating a domestic environment with the installations of living and dining-rooms, libraries, bedrooms, parlours, halls and even bathrooms and kitchens to create what Anne Higonnet calls the appearance of a home: 'The effect is only an effect' she says, as private records suggest that these collectors initiated the construction of their 'homes' once they decided to found and create what would in due course become public museums, despite their private origins.[23] This passage from private home to a publicly accessible art museum generally began to take place upon the founder's death by way of their indenture. Thus, the distinction between private and public was clearly articulated, as was their transition into the public sphere.

That being so, Gardner challenged philanthropic protocol by making Fenway Court available to the public within her own lifetime.[24] Museums were not meant to be lived in; the notion of living in what was considered to be a 'museum' was a contradiction in terms and Gardner dared to question established perceptions of both house and museum at the turn of the twentieth century. Although public access was encouraged it was tightly controlled by Gardner who constantly changed the conditions of entry to suit herself. She would issue two hundred tickets a day for twenty days of the year at one dollar each to members of the public wishing to visit Fenway Court.[25] Gardner also staged regular recital concerts, charity events for the social Boston elite and an inaugural reception for the opening of the museum in January 1903. Despite this, the law challenged Gardner's rules of entry and understanding of 'public' access, arguing that whilst she was free to control the number of visitors and to charge a fee, the museum was required to be open at regular times to allow the public to choose when they wanted to visit the museum.[26]

This condition underpinned the notion of what was understood to be a public museum in 1903, and as she failed to comply with the law she was subject to various taxes. In Gardner's attempt to revoke the tariff duties imposed upon her, she argued that the collection was housed within a museum that was opened to the public through the promotion of art education. It was thus countered that Fenway Court could not be a museum with Gardner still living in the house.[27] The revenue department's understanding of public and museum in this case differed greatly from that of Gardner's. This degree of ambiguity continues today as individual collectors question and (re)define what is clearly understood to be private and public and what is a house and museum. Mitchell Rales' contemporary collection house (Glenstone Museum) faced similar challenges that have provoked the public to question his understanding of public access.

Glenstone Museum, Potomac, Maryland (2006)

Billionaire industrialist collector and founder of Glenstone Museum Mitchell Rales (born 1956), has constructed a collection house that is principally an exhibition space, despite sitting alongside his private home.[28] The building was designed by the late Charles Gwathmey.[29] It is situated 25 kilometres from downtown Washington DC and was intended to be open to the public from the outset. Glenstone is completely detached from Rales' private living space, which remains strictly private. Public access to the 150-acre private landscaped residential enclosure is securely guarded, as is the collector's privacy. The blending of art, architecture and landscape underpins the concept behind Glenstone's formation. The recent expansion project includes a stand-alone museum with galleries spanning 50,000-square-feet, nine exhibition pavilions, a new visitor entrance, parking, a library, a bookstore, storage facility, two cafés and around 230-acre landscaped meadows. This has transformed Glenstone from a collection house to the largest private museum in the United States.

Until recently, visitors were required to attend docent-led tours that were restricted to 12 persons and spanned one hour. Visitors can now move freely around the galleries but are still required to schedule their visit ahead of time. The 22,000-square-foot exhibition space, designed by Charles Gwathmey, displays a smattering of Rales' 800-strong holdings at any one time. Art works from the collection include paintings, sculptures, photographs, installations, paper and multimedia works. The building occupies a single level and comprises nine galleries. The Entry Pavilion doubles up as a sculpture gallery that opens out onto the terrace, pond and outdoor sculpture garden. At the time of my visit, we were not permitted to deviate from the prescribed tour of the galleries or walk onto the terrace to view the sculptures; however, modifications to these rules have been introduced as Glenstone prepared to open its new pavilions to the public on 4 October 2018.

Rales' entry to art collecting in the 1990s coincided with the adverse economic period at the time, thereby taking advantage of the dramatic decline in the art market, art prices and the availability of quality art works. His holdings have and continue to be strategically compiled and researched by Rales himself, his curator and art dealer wife Emily Wei, and art advisers who have helped to guide the collection. Rales and Wei are not likely to give in to impulsive urges when considering expensive works of art as they adopt a more considered approach that is methodical, above all else. Gaps within the collection are identified, the relevant works located and private collectors approached in pursuit of securing new acquisitions as the Rales seldom buy works at art auctions or art fairs.[30] It is difficult to ascertain the depth and breadth of Rales' collection as this information is not publicly available. The only insight into his holdings can be gauged from the broad list of blue chip artists available on Glenstone's website and installation shots of past and current exhibitions and works on loan. The focus appears to be on American and European postwar art through to contemporary.

Private or public?

Although the collection house was always intended to be publicly accessible, Rales has challenged the notion of 'public' and 'accessibility' to the extent that many would argue that Glenstone has been far from being publicly accessible. This is indeed a point that has been under investigation by the US Senate Finance Committee and the IRS commissioner. Glenstone is amongst eleven private museums that have been under investigation so as to determine if the generous tax incentives given to them offsets their public agenda in much the same way that the IRS questioned Gardner's understanding of 'art education'.[31] I would also draw attention to the limited number of exhibitions hosted at Glenstone: that is, a total of five exhibitions between September 2006 and January 2018. The early exhibitions were on show for two to three years – this is a particularly long time, even for private museums. This also suggests that Glenstone was simply not open to the public for a great deal of this time. It was not until the 'Peter Fischli David Weiss' exhibition (May 2013–December 2014) that the duration of the exhibitions was reduced to a year. This shift coincided with Glenstone's expansion strategy and the need to seek local approval for their ambitious plans. This will be discussed in a little more detail shortly.

Returning to the issue of public access, the number of people who have managed to get a glimpse into the reclusive collector's collection house in the first seven years varies; however, most of the sources seem to suggest that 10,000 people visited Glenstone during this time. This is no mean feat as admission has in the past been particularly stringent – more so than most other private collections. Anyone seeking to write or publish their comments or thoughts on the collection were asked to advise them ahead of their visit and to request their permission; even so, the media, social networkers and bloggers and scholars were usually denied access. Those who managed to visit the heavily controlled exclusive compound have been issued with very strict instructions and ushered around the gallery rooms.

My own experience was not dissimilar to the few reviews I have been able to access. Upon gaining entry into the secured compound, the security guard provided strict instructions ensuring I did not stop the vehicle to view the large sculptures that were displayed along the driveway. On arrival, the docent met our party of three at the pavilion's entrance and led us through the Peter Fischli and David Weiss exhibition (May 2013–December 2014). The welcome was friendly, however, the information provided about the collectors and individual installations was at times a little sparse. The time allowed in the individual galleries was restricted to around ten minutes and the visit was surprisingly short – a little less than one hour – considering the drive to Glenstone was under an hour from Washington DC. The system of vetting is one thing, but once inside the collection visitors are directed on how to engage with the individual works on display. This is achieved by restricting the time spent in front of the individual works, the limited information shared about the art collection and Glenstone itself, despite the Foundation's educative focus as set out on their website. The Rales' private residence and pool house could be seen from the exhibition pavilion, but little reference was made to then. Once the tour was completed I was asked to make my way out through the secure gate without stopping along the way. The overall experience was enjoyable and professional, but impersonal if not a little tense.

Portuguese blogger Gisela Gueiros, described Glenstone as 'inhospitable and brilliant', a 'magical, incredible and sinister place'.[32] I concur with Gueiros' comment that the controlled environment and the lack of information shared with visitors detracted from the overall experience. Angela Valdez from the *Washington City Paper* suggests Gueiros' post went largely unnoticed by Glenstone because it was written in Portuguese. Other commentary that did manage to get published was retracted promptly from circulation. Furthermore, Valdez's own requests for a visit and guided tour of the collection were rejected on numerous occasions as Rales does not grant visits to the media: 'As a private museum, it is necessary for us to maintain the privacy of the owners', advised Glenstone's curatorial assistant Cicie Sattarnilasskorm.[33] Given Glenstone's tax-exempt status, the founder is not obliged to grant unconditional public access. Providing the Glenstone Foundation continues to make works available through loans or donations of money to not-for-profit institutions, its tax-exempt position is not compromised.

Creating a private-public museum

In contrast to Rales' reclusive style he was forced to increase his public profile upon declaring his intentions to expand Glenstone with the construction of the new $125 million project designed by New York architect Tom Phifer. Much of these plans depended on the Montgomery County Planning Department's willingness to grant Rales permission to connect on to the local sewer system. This was granted even though local residents and politicians vetoed the plans for environmental reasons as the 3,000-foot sewer was seen to interfere and place at risk the local stream. Such restrictions are in place to ensure the area is not overpopulated by insisting that septic tanks can only be used. The expansion at Glenstone has forced Rales into the public realm in his quest to gain local and political support for his museum venture. The promotion of his new project can be attributed to the less rigid stipulations imposed on potential visitors over the last two to three years; this helps to boost Rales' overall image through a more public-spirited approach that includes improved public relations and access.

It is hoped that more of Rales' collection will be on display with Glenstone's new museum and pavilions that opened in October 2018. Glenstone estimates that around 100,000 people will visit every year. The 125,000-square-foot museum will overshadow the existing buildings on the current and adjoining compound that Rales has acquired and will include a number of interconnecting buildings for the permanent display of single artists' works and a larger space for temporary exhibitions; furthermore, the existing building will also stage a series of temporary exhibitions. Rales' focus is not simply on the construction of a new museum, but also the upgrading of the existing landscape and entrance that will include 5,000 native trees to be planted on site, a flowering water garden and a new Japanese cedar entrance structure.

The notion of an 'open house' can be seen as democratic as it is made available to a general audience while the collector continues to live in the house or the property; however, they can also be labelled as 'unwelcoming and exclusionary', as in the case of Glenstone.[34] Taking the time to visit Glenstone is worthwhile and the entire estate, art, exhibitions and architecture impressive. I would have welcomed more information about the museum and its collection so as to enhance my overall experience. Likewise, I would have appreciated the opportunity to walk freely around the galleries and look at the various outdoor sculptures that are placed within the estate. The degree of public access is at the collector's discretion and not part of a public charter, providing they adhere to the terms of their tax-exempt or charitable status. Even though art collecting has been taken out of the context of the private realm it is still very much a private affair, as Christian Boros reminds us: 'You have to remember that this is a private collection, not a museum. It's an incredibly subjective endeavour'.[35] Even so, a private collection that is publicly accessible differs little in most peoples' understanding of a museum that is also open to the public. This is supported by Dr Christoph Becker who draws our attention to the changing relationship between the individual and their artworks:

> The minute you go public things change. It is no longer about you and the work – it is more about the public and the art work. The public takes away what you have built and consumes it. It is no longer yours.[36]

Even so, contemporary private collectors can be seen to challenge the notion of the museum and what is deemed to be private and public under the guise of public-spiritedness, just as Gardner sought to do in 1903.

The segregation of private and public: Julia Stoschek Collection, Düsseldorf (2007) and Boros Collection, Berlin, Germany (2008)

Overview

The Stoschek and Boros Collections function as both house and exhibition space for collectors Julia Stoschek and Christian Boros. To accommodate public access to their collections they have set distinct parameters between private (living areas) and public (art galleries). This can be seen to expand on the precedent set by Sir Richard Wallace and Albert C. Barnes who instigated the separation between private and public spaces within their own residences. Wallace chose to cordon off aspects of Hertford House to maintain a degree of privacy and to provide a secure environment for his collection. Barnes, on the other hand, employed professional curatorial staff to manage the collection, thus it was necessary to maintain a distinction between his living and gallery spaces; that being so, only a long corridor separated the two. It could be argued that the approach adopted by the Stoschek and Boros Collections appear to challenge our understanding of a house museum as the notion of the house within the museum is becoming more difficult to distinguish. The emphasis has thus shifted away from the house to the exhibition space with the house or penthouse apartment playing a secondary role.

The Julia Stoschek Collection was founded in Düsseldorf under the auspices of the Julia Stoschek Foundation in 2007 as a permanent living and exhibition space. The four-level factory was built in 1907 and was converted to include a rooftop terrace and apartment on the top level, alongside the many galleries that span across three levels.[37] The Julia Stoschek Collection was opened to the public on 17 June 2007 and is accessible every Sunday between 11.00 am and 6.00 pm – free of charge. The Boros Collection was founded in 2008 by the advertising and communications agency owner and contemporary art collector Christian Boros and his wife Karen Lohmann.[38] The collection is installed within the World War II Friedrichstrasse Imperial Railway Bunker (*Reichsbahnbunker Friedrichstrasse*). It was built in 1942 and is situated in the former East Berlin Mitte district. The five-level windowless bunker was converted to serve as both a permanent art space for the Boros' collection that comprises of 800 art works and as a family home. The Boros family live in the 500-square-metre rooftop penthouse apartment that remains strictly private.

A house museum with an exhibition space attached: Julia Stoschek Collection

The Berlin-based architectural firm Kuehn Malvezzi was commissioned to reconfigure the disused factory into an exhibition space and private

Figure 4.6 Photograph of Julia Stoschek. Photo: Sirin Simsek. © Julia Stoschek
Collection.

residence for collector Julia Stoschek (born 1975). The building is dis-
cretely camouflaged within Düsseldorf's affluent suburban neighbourhood
of Schanzenstraße. It was originally constructed as a theatre equipment and
props manufacturing plant, however, over time it was used as an airship
engine testing site, a manufacturing plant for a variety of products that
included lighting equipment, medical corsets and women's undergarments
and military apparatus during World War II, and later as a factory for frames
and skirting boards. The architects created an internal layer, or shell, which
can be adjusted to control the day light within the various gallery spaces that
are situated within the 1000-square-metres of large metal external windows
that surround the building's perimeter. Furthermore, they redesigned the
individual spaces, roof top terrace and apartment and incorporated a small
cinema in the basement.

Above the second level the architects incorporated an open-plan penthouse
apartment and roof-top terrace that overlooks the city of Düsseldorf. The
all-white apartment reflects the white cube approach adopted throughout
most of the Julia Stoschek Collection. Despite the focus on time-based media
and installation art – ranging from the 1960s to the present day – black

Figure 4.7 Exterior view of the building in Düsseldorf. Photo: Ulrich Schwarz. © Julia Stoschek Collection.

boxes are seldom used; instead pristine white and pale grey museum walls prevail throughout the many rooms that appear within this large industrial building. The apartment is seamlessly integrated within the overall building with little to suggest a private residence exists within the converted building. The only hint is the roped off staircase that leads to Stoschek's private residence on level two.

The Julia Stoschek Collection adopts an innovative approach to their exhibition designs by integrating the highest quality technologically advanced digital, audio and visual projections into their exhibits.[39] To commemorate their 10th anniversary they invited British artist Ed Atkins, to curate the exhibition 'Generation Loss'. Atkins curatorial debut incorporated a different and innovative exhibition approach. He narrowed the focus to single channel video works that could be displayed in pairs and chose to separate them with glass. He selected 49 works from Stoschek's 750-strong holdings (that includes 250 artists) and choreographed the works in pairs. With the individual artists' approval, the edited video works were shown on large screens that were arranged in sequential order so that a number of screens could be viewed simultaneously. Acoustic glass separates the works aurally without disrupting the visual impact of the exhibition. The permanent walls within the first two levels of the Julia Stoschek Collection's nineteenth-century picture frame building were thus removed to accommodate the glass fixtures.[40]

Figure 4.8 Installation view of the exhibition *Generation Loss*, Julia Stoschek Collection, Düsseldorf, 2017. Photo: Simon Vogel. © Julia Stoschek Collection.

The exhibition format has evolved at the Julia Stoschek Collection along with the space itself. The above exhibition is a case in point. The designers and architects have allowed for a degree of flexibility when considering the layout and dimension of the individual galleries. My earlier visits revealed a different space to the current configuration: the many open alcoves and corridors within the central part of the building revealed various installations scattered across the two levels. Furthermore, the juxtaposition of individually configured galleries and the variety of projections – oversized, fixed and even floating screens – enhance the level of audience engagement that avoids a monotonous display of video and film works. The design and configuration of the internal spaces has allowed the curatorial team the flexibility to review the way they work with and exhibit the artists they collect without compromising visitors' ability to move freely from one installation to the next. Such curatorial innovation comes at a financial cost to the institution thereby making it difficult for public museums to compete due to the investment required in rapidly changing technology to not only show new media works but to stay abreast of the developments. Therefore, the Julia Stoschek Collection's focus on new media and video works can offer audiences an alternative platform and way to engage with the art on show;

Figure 4.9 Installation view of the exhibition *Number Twelve Hello Boys*, Julia
        Stoschek Collection, Düsseldorf, 2016. Photo: Simon Vogel. © Julia
        Stoschek Collection.

it also allows them to distinguish themselves from their public counterparts,
thereby, complimenting the existing cultural landscape rather than com-
peting with it.

The Collection's director Monika Kerkmann, explains that their initial
aim was to increase the public profile of the Julia Stoschek Collection by
presenting a variety of works upon making it accessible to a general audience.
Over time the emphasis has shifted from conventional group exhibitions
towards more solo shows and other experimental exhibition formats (more
specifically from 2011 onwards). New York's 2010 Performa (the performance biennial) held at the Museum of Modern Art P.S.1 (MoMA P.S.1) also
had a profound influence over the Julia Stoschek Collection's curatorial
focus and was the beginning of an important collaboration between the two
institutions. It was through the advice of then director of MoMA P.S.1 and
MoMA's Chief Curator at Large Klaus Biesenbach, that the Julia Stoschek
Collection hosted the exhibition '100 years: A History of Performance Art'
in Düsseldorf. Although they incorporated documentation and works from
the collection to support the show, it was the first exhibition that drew
on works beyond their own holdings. In conjunction with this show, the
Julia Stoschek Collection hosted a Performance program that incorporated
different performances almost every two weeks. This triggered a new way
of thinking about the diversity of contemporary art practice, ephemeral art
forms and the artistic developments since the 1960s and how best to present them.[41] Other collaborations soon followed with exhibitions at the

Figure 4.10 Exterior view of the Bunker, Boros Collection, Berlin. Photo: © NOSHE.
Image courtesy Boros Collection.

Deichtorhallen, Hamburg (2010), the ZKM I Karlsruhe (2014) and Tel Aviv
Museum of Art (2015).[42] Partnerships with notable institutions would lend
an imprimatur to individual collectors and their personal museums, even
situate them within elite global circles.

Boros Collection

Christian Boros (born 1964) began collecting the works of emerging artists
during the 1990s. His focus is on compiling a collection that features a
broad selection of artists and media. Boros does not employ a curatorial
team and relies solely on the many artists represented in his collection to
effectively install and curate the art on show; even so, he has a team of
26 including the director and assistant director.[43] The focus thus shifts
from the curation of the collection to the communication of it through the

62-bilingual docent-led tours that are conducted over four days each week. The Boros' first exhibition (2008–2012) attracted 120,000 visitors with over 7,000 guided tours conducted during this time. Exhibition #2 (2012–2016) saw 200,000 people undertake 9,000 guided tours at the Bunker. The cost of the tour is 15 Euro per person. This might appear to offer some financial assistance to the operation of the Collection, however, it is rarely sufficient to cover the costs associated with making private collections accessible to the public. As we shall see in the following chapters, running private museums is fiscally demanding and difficult to maintain beyond the original creator's lifetime.

The Boros Collection states that the four-year duration of the individual exhibitions allows a greater number of visitors to see each show, I would suggest that four years is an unusually long time for any single exhibition. As we have seen, this has also been the case with Glenstone Museum. Most private museums rotate their exhibitions more frequently to attract repeat visitors and to stimulate public interest – the duration of the Julia Stoschek Collection's exhibitions range from four, nine and 12 months. The absence of curatorial staff at the Boros Collection is an important point of departure as most private collectors employ a curatorial team; even so, I do wish to emphasise the active partnership between the artists represented in the Boros Collection and the collector can be seen to be mutually beneficial as artists can also influence the display of their artwork and contribute to the overall discourse on contemporary art practice.

The Bunker

Berlin's appeal as the international centre for contemporary art was an important aspect in determining where the Boros Collection would be situated. The city's affordability and availability of cheaper real estate has benefitted both artists and collectors. Berlin's interesting history and personality and what Boros calls a 'mix of imperfection and curiosity' were all important characteristics that influenced his final decision.[44] The Bunker is classified as a listed building in the city of Berlin. It was designed and built in 1942 by architect Karl Bonatz, at the request of the Third Reich. It was built as an air-raid shelter for local residents under the supervision of Albert Speer, General Building Inspector for the Reich Capital. The exterior of the building is designed in such a way that each side is identical to the next, with a total of eight entrances installed allowing easy access into the Bunker. The scars of war are evident on the façade of the building with bullet holes left as a brutal reminder of the city's history.

Upon buying the Bunker in 2003, Boros undertook a significant overhaul of the building. The redevelopment took five years to complete. It was led by the Berlin-based architect Jens Casper and his architectural firm Realarchitektur. It comprises 3,000 square metres of exhibition space where the 120 rooms were converted to a total of 80. The individual spaces contain some site-specific works (even room specific) installations commissioned specifically for the Bunker. By restoring the Bunker and making it publicly accessible, Boros has also heightened the historical and cultural profile of the building as a significant landmark for the city of Berlin.

More recently, German collector and art dealer Désiré Feuerle acquired and remodelled the former 1941 telecommunication bunker in Berlin Kreuzberg, to display his collection of international contemporary art alongside his Imperial Chinese furniture and Southeast Asian sculptures. The Feuerle Collection opened in November 2016, after a lengthy intervention by British architect John Pawson (who also sought the advice of Jens Casper and Realarchitektur). Members of the public can visit The Feuerle Collection by prior arrangement: four one-hour docent-led tours are conducted between Friday and Sunday each week at a cost of 18 Euros.

Figure 4.11 Installation view of the work by Justin Matherly at the Boros Collection, Berlin. Photo: © NOSHE. Image courtesy Boros Collection.

It is important to note that Feuerle has also integrated a private residence in the far end of the building.

Part of the remodelling of the Boros Collection's bunker included a new addition – the Boros family's 1,000-square-metre private penthouse apartment on the top level. Even though the building operates as both residence and museum, the defining aspect of Boros' overall project is the building, its historic architecture and raw exhibition galleries that display the many contemporary works from his holdings.[45] Even though the exhibition spaces are accessible to the public by prior arrangement – the apartment, however, remains private. The distinction between the private and public aspects of the Boros are clearly articulated and evidence of its existence as a house museum can often go unnoticed. The safety restrictions imposed on the building by Berlin's fire department allude to the building's role as a house museum. They stipulate that docent-led groups of no more than 12 persons can visit the Collection as it is officially registered as a private residence.[46]

The architectural design of the new rooftop structure echoes the Bunker's sharp angles and form and does little to disrupt the overall character and integrity of the building. The use of concrete throughout the apartment's interior spaces is juxtaposed with that of the Bunker's concrete exterior and interior. The old and new are smoothly integrated with the new addition constantly referencing the original one. The heavy concrete walls, interior design and installation of works of art with everyday objects and furniture echo the Bunker's interior design-led installations. Some of the art works within the Boros are generally interchangeable with those often seen hanging throughout the apartment. The works installed within the living spaces are of domestic proportions and tastefully arranged throughout their private spaces. Thus, the connection between the two cannot be ignored. Boros' apartment draws on distinct aspects of the Boros Collection and the notion of the house is far less obvious as it is largely informed through the Bunker.

It can be said that the Boros may appear un-museum in the way that exposed ducts, pipes, graffiti and crudely painted concrete walls remain intact. This can be seen to depart from the conventional white cube exhibition space that has become commonplace throughout many modern and contemporary museums and exhibition spaces. On my fourth visit to the Boros Collection (January 2019) I was surprised to see a greater number of the galleries painted white while others incorporated a combination of white painted walls and raw ceilings or vice versa. Artist might be reluctant to display their art in a space that can indirectly overshadow the presentation of the artworks; the white walls are seen to provide a more acceptable model for the display of art. Even so, I would suggest that the rawness and brutality of the interiors is worn as a badge of honour and allows the collector to create a prominent space to engage with contemporary audiences. 'This building is a landmark, a part of German history', Boros says, 'It's not the Brandenburg Gate, but it has seen Berlin change a lot over the last half century'.[47]

Figure 4.12 Christian and Karen Boros, Boros Collection, Berlin. Photo: © Wolfgang Stahr. Image courtesy Boros Collection.

Figure 4.13 Installation view of the work by Katja Novitskova at the Boros Collection, Berlin. Photo: © NOSHE. Image courtesy Boros Collection.

Figure 4.14 Installation view of the work by Michel Majerus at the Boros Collection, Berlin. Photo: © NOSHE. Image courtesy Boros Collection.

Christian Boros recognises that his art collection has the capacity to not only alter the internal spaces of the building, but also the perceptions of Berlin and Germany more broadly as international dignitaries and members of the public visit in great numbers. The architectural and historical aspects of the Bunker play a central role, as does the city of Berlin, in presenting Boros' private contemporary art collection and positioning his cultural initiatives. The two present a snapshot of not only the city's recent past, but also Germany's invasions, aspirations of victory, bombings, defeat, pain and redevelopment are all evident: 'The Bunker represents every phase that Berlin has experienced since 1940' says Boros.[48] Many want to take a closer look at how the current generation of Germans have dealt with what Boros calls the 'fascist legacy' and acknowledges that it is impossible to ignore or deny the reason for the building's existence.[49] Just as the building's architectural and historical significance cannot be ignored or viewed in isolation of the city's past, the art collector and the Bunker have become inextricably linked as the two have become synonymous since the opening of the Boros Collection.

Subverting the house museum

Both Boros and Julia Stoschek actively participate in the art and museum world and the social lifestyle that is often associated with collecting contemporary art – exhibition openings, biennales, art fairs and engaging with key public institutions. Little information appears to indicate whether Boros actively seeks the approval or has established ongoing relationships with key public museums. In complete contrast, his relationships with other private collectors and art gallerists appears well documented. Boros' focus seems to be on promoting the Boros Collection and 'hosting' exhibitions and guided tours of the Bunker. Until more recently, the collection has only been displayed at the Boros, not in other private or public institutions. Around 40 works from the Boros Collection have been on show at the Langen Foundation, Neuss, Germany, entitled 'Olafur Eliasson Works from the Boros Collection 1994–2015' (18 April–18 October 2015). This is the first exhibition from Boros' holdings to be staged outside the Bunker.

Julia Stoschek, on the other hand, has attracted the attention of the private, public, commercial and alternative art sectors. In 2013, highlights of the Julia Stoschek Collection were shown at Art Cologne – 'Das Bildermuseum Brennt [The Museum burns pictures]'.[50] It was not the first time a private collection had been exhibited at the art fair, but it was the first time the Julia Stoschek Collection was shown in the commercial sphere.[51] Likewise, the exhibition at the Deichtorhallen in Hamburg's centre for contemporary art and photography was the first time that the collection was shown in a museum context.[52] Some 50 artists from the Collection were displayed across 2000-square-metres of museum space featuring key video, sculptural and photographic works. As previously mentioned, the collaboration with New York's P.S.1 Contemporary Art Centre and the international performance biennale Performa was the first major engagement with public institutions with the exhibition travelling from Düsseldorf to New York.[53] Within the first year of opening the Collection to the public, Julia Stoschek collaborated with artist Andreas Gursky and the private Ukraine collector Victor Pinchuk, and his contemporary Art Centre in Kiev, as part of the Ukraine's German cultural festival.[54]

In June 2016, the Julia Stoschek Collection Berlin was founded to support the Collection in Düsseldorf. It is located in the late 1960s former Czech Cultural Centre in Berlin's Mitte district at Leipzig Strasse. In doing so, the Julia Stoschek Collection becomes the first private collection in Germany to have two publicly accessible sites that are open concurrently in both Düsseldorf and Berlin. The Museum Frieder Burda (refer to Chapter 8) also has two locations that are open to the public – Baden Baden and the new exhibition and project space – Salon Berlin (2017). The Julia Stoschek Collection's director Monika Kerkmann claims that it has long been an ambition of Julia Stoschek's to set up a second location in Berlin. When they had the chance to rent the former Czech Cultural Centre building they took the opportunity, albeit temporarily. After a trial period of six months they decided to make it a permanent arrangement (signing a five-year contract). The building has been remodelled (modestly) to accommodate the exhibiting of the collection while still maintaining the original character of the building. One of the principle motivations for the move to Berlin was to situate themselves closer to the contemporary art scene as nearly 80 per cent of the artists they collect live and work in the city. They also felt that it was important to introduce the Julia Stoschek Collection to a larger audience.[55] It was not long before the Julia Stoschek Collection faced some criticism from Berlin's established art world as it was considered unseemly to emblazon the Stoschek name upon the building's façade. Apparently, Berliners are far more modest and resist such bold demonstrative gestures. Kerkmann responded as thus: 'When the critics in Berlin asked why we were exposing ourselves in this manner – we thought, why not? We are reflecting contemporaneity – we have to think a little differently'.[56]

Figure 4.15 Exterior view of the building in Berlin. Photo: Robert Hamacher. © Julia Stoschek Collection.

Despite their differing approach Stoschek and Boros share a willingness to make their private spaces available to a general audience. Both adopt an active approach to patronage and are committed to enhancing the public's engagement with contemporary art practice and the promotion of art and culture more broadly. In doing so, they shift the emphasis away from the domestic towards one that focuses primarily on the exhibition space. This departs from earlier collectors and their subtle approach to restricting public access to certain areas of their respective house museums. Although Sir Richard Wallace and Albert C. Barnes instigated the separation between private and public spaces within their respective residences, the understanding of what constitutes a house museum, nevertheless, remained in-tact and easily understood despite Wallace and Barnes' modifications. I would suggest that Boros and Stoschek subvert the concept of the house museum in a way that the museum itself becomes the defining aspect of the house. Whilst the collection house paid homage to the notion of the house, in conjunction with the museum, here the removal of the house from the museum renders the house museum almost invisible, if not redundant.

Conclusion

The case studies in this chapter have drawn our attention to the absence of the domestic space within the respective house museums and what is understood to be private and public. The remodelling of Oskar Reinhart's villa into a public museum in the late 1960s not only triggered a changing approach to the established model of the house museum but a repositioning of the benefactor's public legacy. Upon making house museums publicly accessible today's collectors are actively positioning themselves within the public arena; cultivating significant relationships with artists, private, public and commercial art and museum sectors in a way that further enhances and acknowledges their cultural contributions and credentials. Blatant self-promotion would be viewed as abhorrent and this is avoided at all cost; instead the notion of collaborative relationships between artists and collectors, collectors and collectors, museum and art world professionals and collectors, architects and designers and collectors and members of the public and collectors are seen to be a more attractive platform to stage one's own narrative and persona in the public realm.

The following chapter takes up the discussion about the various trajectories that spin off from the house museum. Where do we go from the house museum; what is the next step and how do their fortunes fair over time?

Notes

1   Lasic, Barbara, '"Splendid Patriotism:" Richard Wallace and the Construction of the Wallace Collection', *Journal of the History of Collections* 21, no. 2 (2009), pp.175–176.

2 Anderson, John, *Art Held Hostage: The Battle over the Barnes Collection*, New York & London, W.W. Norton., 2003, pp.38–40.

3 Dr Marc Fehlmann, interview with the author.

4 Refer to Hahnloser, Villa Flora Winterthur Sammlung, 'Villa Flora Winterthur Sammlung Hahnloser', Villa Flora Winterthur Sammlung Hahnloser.

5 Dr Marc Fehlmann, interview with the author.

6 Zelger, Franz, 'Images of a Golden Age of Connoisseurship – Oskar Reinhart and His Concept of Collecting', in *Casper David Friedrich to Ferdinand Hodler: A Romantic Tradition Nineteenth-Century Paintings and Drawings from the Oskar Reinhart Foundation, Winterthur*, edited by Peter Wegmann, Frankfurt am Main and Leipzig, Insel Verlag, 1993, p.19.

7 The Alte Gymnasium (the old boys gymnasium and the adjoining library in the centre of town) were remodelled to accommodate the Museum Oskar Reinhart. The collection's focus is on German, Swiss and Austrian paintings from the end of the eighteenth century to the mid-twentieth century and works on paper from the fifteenth to the twentieth centuries.

8 Oskar Reinhart Foundation gifted the Museum Stiftung Oskar Reinhart to the city of Winterthur and until recently continued to fund their operation costs and exhibition program. Dr Marc Fehlmann, interview with the author.

9 Dr Marc Fehlmann, interview with the author.

10 The author's correspondence to the director of The Oskar Reinhart Collection 'Am Römerholz' Dr. Mariantonia Reinhard-Felice was not acknowledged.

11 Dr Marc Fehlmann, interview with the author.

12 Appointed in May 2012.

13 Reinhard-Felice, Mariantonia (ed.), *The Villa 'Am Römerholz' – Oskar Reinhart Collection 'Am Römerholz' Winterthur – Complete Catalogue*, Winterthur, Schwabe Basle, 2005, p.58.

14 Dr Marc Fehlmann, interview with the author.

15 Dr Marc Fehlmann, interview with the author.

16 Dr Marc Fehlmann, interview with the author.

17 Dr Marc Fehlmann, interview with the author.

18 Reinhard-Felice, 2005, p.58.

19 Reinhard-Felice, 2005, p.61.

20 Reinhart recognised that the city of Winterthur could not afford to operate two museums. Dr Marc Fehlmann, interview with the author.

21 Reinhard-Felice, 2005, pp.80–81.

22 Reinhard-Felice, 2005, p.89. As applied to the Oskar Reinhart Museum's deed of gift.

23 Higonnet, Anne, *A Museum of One's Own: Private Collecting, Public Gift*, Pittsburgh and New York, Periscope Publishing, 2009, p.xii.

24 Gardner's palazzo was known as Fenway Court within her lifetime. It was renamed the Isabella Stewart Gardner Museum after her death in 1924, as a permanent memorial to herself.

25 Higonnet, 2009, p.176.

26 Higonnet, 2009, p.176.

27 Higonnet, 2009, p.176.

28 Rales co-founded the manufacturing and technology company, Danaher Corporation, with his brother, Steven Rales. According to Forbes' 2018 Richest Americans Top 400 list his estimated net wealth is $3.7 billion and is ranked number 207.

29 Gwathmey Siegel & Associated Architects.

30 Vogel, Carol, 'Like Half the National Gallery in Your Backyard', *The New York Times*, 18 April 2013.

31 Shnayerson, Michael, 'Inside the Private Museums of Billionaire Art Collectors', *Town & Country*, 16 January 2017. Ford Bell, president of the American Association of Museums. Valdez, Angela. 'A Very Private Collection'. *Washington City Paper*, 6 June 2008.

32 Valdez, 2008, n.p.

33 Valdez, 2008, n.p.

34 Vogel, 2013, n.p.

35 Christian Boros, Magill, R. Jay Jr., 'From Nazi Bunker to Artistic Haven', *Spiegel Online*, 24 April 2008.

36 Dr Christoph Becker, interview with the author.

37 Stoschek comes from a wealthy industrialist family – her great grandfather Max Brose founded the automotive supplier company Brose GmbH & Co. KG in 1908. She is currently a shareholder and sits on the board of the board of Art Association of the Rhineland and Westphalia and Kunsthalle Düsseldorf, KW Institute of Contemporary Art in Berlin and MoMA PS1 in New York.

38 A self-made entrepreneur, Boros emigrated to Germany as a young child – a refugee from then-Communist Poland. He grew up in the provincial city of Wuppertal, where he lived until recently, and founded his own communications and publishing company – The Agency Boros.

39 In 2007, Stoschek employed five museum and administrative professionals to manage the Collection, stage and curate exhibitions, liaise with artists, publish exhibition catalogues and promote the Collection. Currently, they have a team of five people in Düsseldorf and 30 (including exhibition guards) in Berlin. Monika Kerkmann, interview with the author.

40 Monika Kerkmann, interview with the author.

41 Monika Kerkmann, interview with the author.

42 'I Want to See How You See – Julia Stoschek Collection', Deichtorhallen, Hamburg, 16 April–25 July 2010; 'High Performance. Time-Based Media Art Since 1996, The Julia Stoschek Collection Guests at ZKM', 16 March–22 June 2014; 'Turn On', Tel Aviv Museum of Art, 31 March–29 August 2015.

43 The Boros Foundation's recently appointed director Juliet Kothe, is an accomplished cultural scientist and curator (formerly the director at *me*, Collectors Room, Berlin).

44 Christian Boros, Hegenbart, Sven Mündner and Sarah, 'Christian Boros – Interview by Sarah Hegenbart and Sven Mündner', Sammlung Boros, 2012, translated author Henrike Dessaules.

45 The building occupied by Boros' firm – Agency Boros, Berlin – also draws on the strong sculptural concrete aspects of the Bunker and its aestheticised presentation manner. The Agency Boros – communications agency and publishing firm – was founded in 1990 and represents several key public and private cultural institutions, government agencies and business corporations. Bradley, Kimberley, 'A Day in the Life: Christian Boros', *Art Review* November, no. 63 (2012), p.140.

46 'Boros Collection' website.

47 Magill, 2008, n.p.

48 Christian Boros, Mündner, Sven and Hegenbart, Sarah, 'Christian Boros – Interview by Sarah Hegenbart and Sven Mündner', Sammlung Boros, 2012, translated author Henrike Dessaules.

49 Christian Boros, Hohmann, Silke. 'A Talk with Christian and Karen Boros', Sammlung Boros, 2013.

50 Based on the work by Clemens von Wedemeyer *Das Bildermuseum Brennt [The Museum Burns Pictures]* 2004–2005.

51 Falkenberg Collection (2007), Neue Museums and the Lange Foundation (2004) and Charles Saatchi and the YBAs (1993). Stoschek, Julia, 'Collector Julia Stoschek in Conversation with Art Cologne Director Daniel Hug', Art Cologne.

52 Exhibition titled *I Want To See How You See – Julia Stoschek*, 16 April–25 July 2010.

53 Exhibition titled *100 Years (Version #1, Düsseldorf), Julia Stoschek* Collection Düsseldorf, 10 October 2009–29 July 2010. Julia Stoschek Collection website. Notes from author's visit 21 December 2011.

54 Exhibition titled *Rhine on the Dnipro: Julia Stoschek Collection/Andreas Gursky, Pinchuk Art Centre, Kiev*, 28 September 2008–December 2008. Julia Stoschek Collection website.

55 Monika Kerkmann, interview with the author.

56 Monika Kerkmann, interview with the author.

5 The emergence of the stand-alone museum

Museum Folkwang, Hagen (1902–1921) and Essen, Germany (1922)

Collecting at the turn of the twentieth century was largely a personal affair that became a public concern when the collector was no longer active. Lady Wallace's bequest to the nation saw the Wallace Collection emerge as a public institution in 1900. Similarly, Isabella Stewart Gardner's posthumous act of benefaction allowed her Venetian palazzo in Boston and collection of Old Master paintings to transition into the public sphere by 1903. Karl Ernst Osthaus' (1874–1921) Museum Folkwang Hagen (1902–1921) was established from a very different philanthropic model: it was the first museum in Europe that was dedicated to the collecting and exhibiting of modern art and intended to be publicly accessible from the beginning.[1] For a number of years, it also functioned as both a home for the collector and his family and a museum for his collection. Osthaus' focus on design, contemporary art and culture and the active promotion of them to a broader audience signals a shift in cultural patronage. He placed greater emphasis on collecting and championing the new in art, rather than collecting Old Master paintings and eighteenth- and nineteenth-century decorative art objects and furniture. The Museum Folkwang was

> intended not just to educate the people or even as a place of light entertainment. It was also intended to celebrate the unity of art and life, in other words, it was to heighten and intensify life by aestheticising it.[2]

Osthaus' progressive ideas, championship, emphasis on the aesthetic presentation and juxtaposition of modern art alongside non-Western objects, tribal art and sculpture was unprecedented.

A similar stance was later adopted by American collector Duncan Phillips (1886–1966) who would in 1921 offer unrestricted access to his town house in Washington, DC, when it was formally opened to the public as the Phillips Memorial Art Gallery.[3] Phillips conducted talks and guided tours of the collection as he sought to establish a more personal and intimate experience for the viewing and contemplation of art – where one was free to learn and appreciate the fine examples of contemporary art practice. Although Phillips was keenly interested in modern art, he wanted to present the art

Figure 5.1 Portrait of Karl Ernst Osthaus, 1907. Photo: Jacob Hilsdorf. © Osthaus
    Museum, Hagen.

of his time alongside earlier works. Not unlike Osthaus, he felt that the
juxtaposition of old and new would allow for different interpretations and
an alternative way of seeing both, whilst serving to encourage and promote
contemporary artists.

To appreciate the transition from house to museum over time, it is useful to examine the pioneering role Karl Ernst Osthaus and Museum Folkwang played in determining the shift in collecting the avant garde, the role of the collector as patron and the desire to make private holdings publicly accessible by way of a purpose-built museum that is constructed within the collector's own lifetime. It is not surprising that the founding of the Museum Folkwang triggered an interest in modern art and influenced other European art collectors such as Helene Kröller-Müller (1869–1939) and Knud W. Jensen (1916–2000) who went on to foster the development of modern and contemporary art within their own private museums.

Kröller-Müller was greatly influenced by Osthaus' modern art collection and bold public spiritedness. She amassed one of the largest private collections of van Gogh's works and in 1938 established the Kröller-Müller Museum in a remote setting within the Hoge Veluwe national park in Otterlo, the Netherlands. The museum was designed by Henry van de Velde, who also designed the interior of the Museum Folkwang and Osthaus' private villa Hohenhagen in 1908.[4] Jensen's Louisiana Museum of Modern Art, Humlebæk, Denmark, was founded upon the collecting of modern Danish art in 1958, however, this focus soon shifted to international modern art. Both collectors placed the visual arts alongside architecture and the natured world allowing audiences to engage with art in a non-conventional manner. This was innovative at a time when many public museums were being constructed formally in major urban cities. Integrating art, architecture and culture within a regional, urban or rural location is a concept that many contemporary collectors have sought to emulate: The Museum of Old and New Art (MONA) discussed in Chapter 2, Glenstone Museum in Chapter 4 and Museum Frieder Burda in Chapter 7 are three such examples.[5]

The chapter is a critical examination of the emergence of the stand-alone museum and the various issues and difficulties that can emerge. By investigating Osthaus' personal trajectory, I will set out the limitations associated with founding one's own private museum including the difficulties that dramatically altered the collector's fortune and the fate of his holdings and private museum. I will discuss how this serves as a cautionary reminder for many contemporary collectors who are intent on securing the destiny of their private museums within their own lifetimes (to be discussed in Chapters 6 and 7). The Museum Folkwang, Essen, in 1922, set a precedent in the way private benefactors and the public museum sector have and continue to coexist within the German cultural landscape. The Museum Folkwang in Essen continues in its 96th year as a private-public art museum. The relocation to Essen in 1922 that ensued from Osthaus' passing, will be discussed at length in the later part of this chapter.

As Osthaus' personal financial situation was greatly impacted by Germany's defeat in the First World War, the period of economic and political uncertainty that followed prevented him from providing for the museum.

Figure 5.2 Exterior view seen from the park, Kröller-Müller Museum, Otterlo, 2014. Photo: Georgina Walker.

Figure 5.3 Exterior view of the Old Villa seen from the park, 2010. Photo: Kim Hansen. © Image courtesy Louisiana Museum of Modern Art.

Figure 5.4 Exterior view of the North Wing. The Glass Hallway and Sculpture Park, 2013. Photo: Kim Hansen. © Image courtesy Louisiana Museum of Modern Art.

Figure 5.5 Exterior view of the North Wing Gallery. The two-storey gallery with sculptures by Alberto Giacometti, 2012. Photo: Kim Hansen. © Image courtesy Louisiana Museum of Modern Art.

Upon his death in 1921, his heirs sold the collection and the museum's naming rights to a private art consortium in Essen – the *Folkwang-Museumsverein e.V* – that was formed to purchase the collection in 1922. It was intended that the Osthaus collection would merge into the *Essener Kunstmuseum's* holdings (founded 1906). Osthaus' heirs negotiated a contract with the city of Essen permitting the *Essener Kunstmuseum* to be renamed the Museum Folkwang. It was agreed that a private consortium of art collectors would bring the collection to Essen and the city would provide the means to care for the works and maintain the museum. The agreement with the city of Essen is a very brief and simple binding contract that continues to be the basis by which the museum operates to date. The collection remains privately owned within the publicly operated museum. Much of Osthaus' collection remains intact and today resides in the Museum Folkwang Essen.[6] To examine this more clearly, I will start with the Museum Folkwang's early phase in the city of Hagen (between 1902 and 1921), and with an insight into Osthaus the collector and benefactor.

Osthaus the collector, the patron and the educator

Osthaus was born into an educated wealthy banking and industrialist family. In 1896, he inherited three million Deutsch Mark upon the death of his grandparents.[7] Six years later (with the help of his inheritance), Osthaus founded the Museum Folkwang, on the outskirts of the town of Hagen. Despite its focus on the modern, the Museum Folkwang occupied a Neo-Renaissance building that was designed by established Berlin architect Karl Gérard. It was well into the construction phase before Osthaus began to question the relevance of Gérard's historical style, given the shift towards modern architecture and design. Gérard was allowed to complete the building's exterior, but another architect was commissioned to design the interior of the museum – Belgian architect-designer Henry van de Velde.

The influential German art critic and writer Julius Meier-Graefe, noted that the art nouveau architecture and design journal *Dekorative Kunst,* was the catalyst for Osthaus' change of heart and ultimate decision. Historical architectural design was redundant in modern society and instead championed van de Velde's new approach to architecture and the decorative arts.[8] Although the museum was originally conceived as a natural science museum, van de Velde convinced Osthaus to replace it with an art museum; Osthaus set about compiling his art collection once the museum was completed. This lead him to review not only his plans for the museum, but also his own aesthetic sensibility and social imperative.[9]

Osthaus soon dedicated his time to promoting a more enlightened society by emphasising the value of modern architecture, design and contemporary art and culture within his hometown.[10] The Museum Folkwang's galleries

Figure 5.6 Exterior view after draft by Carl Gérard, c.1902. Museum Folkwang,
    Hagen. © Osthaus Museum, Hagen.

displayed modern art alongside historical works, applied art and scientific
objects. They were arranged outside of their chronological, art historical or
national boundaries and juxtaposed in a way that would encourage a more
visceral and powerful engagement between the artwork and the visitor. Over
time archaeological, mediaeval, textile works, tapestries, ethnographic and
applied art objects found their way into Osthaus' disparate holdings that
can still be viewed in the lower galleries at the Museum Folkwang Essen.

   Thus, it is not surprising to know that Alfred Barr – founding director of
the Museum of Modern Art, New York, was greatly influenced by Osthaus'
juxtapositions of modern art and tribal sculpture. French museum director and curator Jean-Hubert Martin, adopted a similar curatorial stance;
although Martin's inspiration stems more from the French writer, poet,
collector and founder of Surrealism André Breton (1896–1966), it differs
little from Osthaus' approach in practice.[11] I would also suggest that the
curatorial practice of Dominique de Menil and her mentors expanded on
Osthaus' presentation methods to complement their own visual aesthetics
and appreciation of modern and non-Western art, albeit many decades later.
A similar influence can also be seen at Thomas Olbricht's *me* Collectors
Room in Berlin (2010) where his traditional *Wunderkammer* collection is
exhibited alongside contemporary art and design objects.

Figure 5.7 Photograph of south side of master bedroom. Photo: Marc Riboud. © The Menil Archives.

Figure 5.8 Installation photograph of *Art Has Many Facets: The Artistic Fascination with the Cube*, Jones Hall Fine Art Gallery, University of Saint Thomas, Houston, 23 March–12 May 1963. Photo: Maurice Miller. © The Menil Archives.

Osthaus acquired works from artists who had not yet established a reputation for themselves. His art collection included the works of several unknown artists from the collector's time that included Vincent van Gogh, Henri Matisse, Georges Braque and various French Post-Impressionist and German Expressionist artists. Many German collectors did not favour French art as they considered it to be morally dangerous and poorly executed. Such a position stems from the political conflicts that date back to the Napoleonic Wars and the tense historical relationship between the two nations. The Museum Folkwang hosted the first exhibition of van Gogh's work in Germany (1905). Edvard Munch's, Emil Nolde's and Ferdinand Hodler's works were exhibited the following year, and by 1907, the Brücke artists were displayed at the museum. In 1909, Wassily Kandinsky's solo show was staged at the Museum Folkwang; in 1911 Franz Marc followed and 1912 saw the first Blauer Reiter exhibition at the museum. Hence, his support for local and European contemporary artists, who were relatively unknown at the time, paved the way for other collectors to follow in his footsteps. Osthaus' patronage sought to pursue a broader cultural mission with the creation of artist and artisan studios, the commissioning of specific art projects, architectural, interior and graphic design ventures, thereby providing ongoing financial support for living artists; Ernst Ludwig Kirchner was one such artist that benefitted from Osthaus' patronage.[12] He went on to exhibit their work in his museum and in turn evaluated contemporary art practice and culture more broadly in his own art journal.

Osthaus belonged to a progressive intellectual circle of art collectors, patrons, museum directors, writers, critics, publishers and architects who advocated for the promotion of the contemporary artistic avant-garde, applied arts and design alongside modern architecture. They promoted an art form that extended beyond high art that was known as the German *Kunstgewerbe*. The *Kunstgewerbe* was closely aligned to the applied arts and design. This evoked a sense of peacefulness and control in an aesthetic sense and was consistent with a moral and political order that was seen to be lacking. It was not merely defined by one's personal taste but seen as an effective tool that could potentially form the basis of a balanced society at a time of social unrest.[13] As Mark Jarzombek has noted, the *Kunstgewerbe* argued that the future of modern Germany lay in the hands of the educated upper middle class who had a commitment to both capitalism and 'social responsibility through control of its own aesthetics'. One catch cry was: 'Power lay in the economy of everyday things'.[14]

This was a reaction to Germany's rapid period of industrialisation says Jarzombek, and what was seen as a subsequent split between art and society by the supporters of the *Kunstgewerbe*. They prescribed to the philosophy that an enlightened society could be integrated within a modern industrialised one.[15] This was a way that *Kunstgewerbe* sympathisers could be seen to address the anti-industrialist sentiment amongst the masses and the predicament of industrialisation it had created. Osthaus sought to transform his home town into a place of culture, not just of industry. He took it upon himself to introduce contemporary culture and aesthetics to a public audience in Hagen in the hope that the working-class masses would also come to his art museum.[16] In Osthaus' own words, the museum 'should have the goal of winning our artistically desolate industrial district near the Ruhr over to modern artistic work'.[17]

Van de Velde's inviting interiors served Osthaus' objective well, providing an enticing and inclusive cultural space that complimented the display of his exotic and disparate collection. The pale museum walls and art nouveau design features helped to further aestheticise Osthaus' personal arrangements. This can also be seen in the placement of large freestanding sculptures and individual objects within the many timber cabinets and vitrines that were elegantly arranged at various heights to create a sense of intrigue and a closer engagement with them. Osthaus' decorative approach was seen as a way to educate the citizens of Hagen on the benefits of modern art and design, albeit in a less didactive manner than public institutions. For instance, the museum's entrance hall and its ornate art nouveau embellishment served to offset George Minne's iconic circular sculpture 'Fountain with Kneeling Boys' (1905–1906) well. Framed by a series of interconnecting curved arches, alcoves, stained glass doors and an ornamental cupola the entrance hall serves as an introductory welcome to the museum while reinforcing the importance of modern art and design. The museum's archival images provide a rare glimpse into the numerous displays – none more captivating than Matisse's 'Still Life with Asphodels' (1907) alongside Paul Gauguin's 1902 painting entitled 'Barbarian Tales' that are carefully placed on either side of Minne's Fountain (refer to Figure 5.9).

The adjoining Picture Gallery and its domestic proportions allowed for a more intimate engagement with the paintings and sculptures. Elaborately adorned by a patterned moulding around the cornice the heavy marble dado served to frame and ground the room and the works displayed within it. Decorative curved cabinets are tucked into the octagonal shaped gallery allowing small figurines, busts, vases and urns to be displayed amongst the many pictures. A curious touch is the small Persian rug that is placed directly in front of Auguste Rodin's life-size bronze sculpture 'The Age of Bronze' (1880) that is mounted atop a marble pedestal (refer to Figure 5.13). This can also be seen in an earlier newspaper article where a Persian rug is seen on the floor ahead of Minne's sculpture in the entrance hall. This personal and unpretentious touch is not a coincidence when seen in the context of the Museum Folkwang as Osthaus and his family lived above the museum until 1908, before moving into villa Hohenhagen on the outskirts of the city near the lush national park (*Gartenstadt Hohengagen*). The new villa was also designed by van de Velde and adopted similar design and display aspects that can be seen in the museum. The elaborate windows, contrasted veined marble dado and columns, the informal placement of paintings and sculptures alongside elegant furniture cannot be ignored.

Villa Hohenhagen and the Museum Folkwang share a similar approach to the presentation of art and cultural objects: works of art, antiquities (classical, Egyptian, Oriental), graphic art, cultural and decorative art objects, African masks and sculptures are all seamlessly integrated. Through his travels to the East, Osthaus was introduced to Islamic art and culture; his visits to Spain, Hungary, Romania, Turkey, Greece, Asia Minor, Syria, Russia, Egypt and Italy also influenced his appreciation of non-Western cultures, their artworks and objects that can be appreciated in the company of

Figure 5.9 View of the entrance hall with George Minne's fountain and works by Gauguin and Matisse, circa 1907. Osthaus Museum, Hagen. © Osthaus Museum Hagen.

Figure 5.10 Interior view of the Rotunda with George Minne's fountain. Museum Folkwang Essen, circa 1930s. Photo: Renger-Patzsch, Albert, 1897–1966. ©Museum Folkwang Essen/ARTOTHEK.

European art and design. Osthaus' modern tendencies signalled a departure from the collecting style of his German, European and American contemporaries who built their holdings around established traditions of German art and European Old Masters. Within his dense arrangements of Western and non-Western fine and graphic art, he managed to reposition the art of the new and the viewing of it by inverting the perceived hierarchy of the fine arts and the European Old Masters.

A hybrid of private and public: Museum Folkwang, Essen (1922)

The broader economic and political developments ensured Karl Ernst Osthaus was unable to financially secure the future of his collection and museum beyond his own lifetime. Upon his death his heirs sold the naming rights to the museum and collection to a private art consortium in nearby Essen who in turn reinstated the collection within the *Essener Kunstmuseum* renamed Museum Folkwang (1922). His estate that included the Villa Hohenhof was later sold to the city of Hagen. The vacated Henry van de Velde designed museum was in due course taken over by the city of Hagen. In 2009, it was renamed the Emil Schumacher and Karl Ernst Osthaus

Figure 5.11 Interior view of the collection in the Old Building Folkwang with view of the *Fountain* by George Minne and works by Edvard Munch and Ferdinand Hodler at the Museum Folkwang, Essen, 2017. Photo: Giorgio Pastore. © Museum Folkwang.

Museum. As much of the museum's original art nouveau interior features were destroyed during World War II, the building has been remodelled to include the major construction of the new glass cubic structure erected alongside the original museum.[18]

Today, the Osthaus Museum in Hagen sits in the adjacent corner of the court yard with its restored galleries hosting a diverse collection of early-twentieth-century art through to contemporary works, albeit in a disjointed manner. At the time of my visit, works of art were displayed alongside objects of kitsch. They appeared randomly placed with some crudely displayed in alcoves or tucked into odd spots whilst many spaces were left unoccupied. This made it difficult to not only establish a consistent curatorial narrative or relationship between the works and the individual spaces but to envisage Osthaus' own displays within them. The original picture gallery and adjoining intimate rooms with their display of German Expressionist paintings and Sigrid Sigurdsson's installation 'Architecture of Memory – The Museum at the Museum' (1988/2009) were the exceptions.[19]

Although these galleries once stood at the vanguard of contemporary art, design and culture, today they appear somewhat neglected with the focus on the Emil Schumacher building. It was through visiting Osthaus' family home Villa Hohenhof (1908) and viewing works from his collection at the

Figure 5.12 View of the entrance hall, Hagen. Osthaus Museum, Hagen. 2014.
Photo: Georgina Walker.

Museum Folkwang Essen, that I was able to understand how the museum may once have been during the collector's lifetime. The impact of his visit to Granada, Spain and the exotic East at the turn of the twentieth century was immediately apparent: architectural aspects were incorporated within the design of the house and museum and juxtaposed with van de Velde's elegant art nouveau design features. This would have served as an ideal back

Figure 5.13 View of the main picture gallery, Hagen. Osthaus Museum, Hagen. ©
Osthaus Museum, Hagen.

Figure 5.14 Exterior view of Hohenhof, Henry van de Velde, Hagen-Eppenhause,
Stirnband 10. © Osthaus Museum, Hagen.

Figure 5.15 Interior view of the Large Gallery. Museum Folkwang Essen. Photo: Renger-Patzsch, Albert, 1897–1966. ©Museum Folkwang Essen/ ARTOTHEK.

Figure 5.16 Interior view of the Basement Gallery. Museum Folkwang Essen. Photo: Renger-Patzsch, Albert, 1897–1966. © Museum Folkwang Essen/ ARTOTHEK.

Figure 5.17 Interior view of the collection in the old building of the Museum Folkwang with view of the Minne fountain by George Minne and works by Edvard Munch and Ferdinand Hodler, 2017. Photo: Giorgio Pastore. © Museum Folkwang, Essen.

drop for Osthaus' eclectic collection of late-nineteenth and early-twentieth-century Western and non-Western art and cultural objects.

A hybrid of private, corporate and public

The Essen based *Folkwang-Museumsverein* was founded by a group of art connoisseurs and collectors that consisted of largely Jewish bankers who wanted to prevent Osthaus' heirs from dispersing the collection. They acquired most of his holdings. In return the new private owners of the Osthaus collection negotiated a contract with the city of Essen (located 57 kilometres from Hagen) renaming the Municipal Art Museum in Essen (that was established in 1906), Museum Folkwang. Prominently displayed at the museum in Hagen, George Minne's marble sculpture 'Fountain with Kneeling Youths' (c.1900), was also relocated to Essen (refer to Figure 5.17). The recreation of the original green marble floor pays tribute to its original location and installation, however, today's more conventional white cube setting somehow falls a little short of the magic created through Osthaus' thoughtful adjacencies. Similarly, the copy of Minne's Fountain at the Osthaus Museum in Hagen casts a melancholic tone in light of its stark placement within a space that is, today, largely devoid of art (refer to Figure 5.12).

It was agreed that the collective of private individuals would supply the collection of art and the city would provide the means to fund and maintain the museum.[20] Thus, half the collection at the Museum Folkwang Essen continues to be privately owned.[21] This includes the Osthaus collection and other artworks that came into the collection after this time. The administration, governing board of the museum, known as the *Kuratorial,* includes heirs of the Osthaus family and museum professionals from the Museum Folkwang. The position of chairman changes annually with the mayor of Essen assuming the role every odd year. Such a relationship between private and public requires a balance that needs to be constantly negotiated.

Without wealthy individuals and families in the local area the Museum Folkwang looks to the corporate sector to provide philanthropic support, more specifically, banking and energy corporations and the Krupp Foundation that are based in Essen. The Thyssen-Krupp industrial corporation has existed in Essen since 1811 and is synonymous with the city. It was the Krupp Foundation who in 2006 – at the behest of Professor Berthold Beitz, Chairman of the Alfried Krupp von Bohlen and Halbach-Foundation's Board of Trustees – who announced their intent to fully fund the museum's redevelopment. The new addition was designed by David Chipperfield Architects. The museum reopened to the public in January 2010.[22] The city of Essen did not contribute to the construction budget of 55 million Euros which was met by a single benefactor – the Krupp Foundation. The Foundation exercised total control over the building, its design and how it should look with little or no consultation with the city of Essen or the museum professionals employed to manage it. As former director of Museum Folkwang Essen Dr Tobia Bezzola notes:

> It is an example of a building constructed by the private sector – by a company – and given to the people. The Krupp Stiftung [Foundation] however they did not provide additional money for the running costs or operations of the museum; the city has to carry that ongoing responsibility.[23]

The Krupp Foundation provided the city and the museum with a new building and facilities to display and store their outstanding collection of art, it also raised many challenges for the museum and the city itself, as the larger museum requires additional funding and that is not easily addressed. The Foundation has since continued to support the museum by way of bequests and donations, however, this is only possible when the corporation itself makes a profit. Due to the deteriorating economic situation their contributions have stalled with the Foundation's capital –albeit large – have at times been in decline. Furthermore, the city's fiscal situation is under pressure with the whole region in a prolonged state of economic crisis. The City of Essen continues to pay for the museum's running costs and staff salaries, even though the city's budgets are in constant decline. Hence, the museum needs to look more broadly to philanthropic and corporate support

Figure 5.18 Entrance areas of the Museum Folkwang, 2017. Photo: Giorgio Pastore.
© Museum Folkwang, Essen.

for the additional funds needed to live up to the high standards that have been set by the new building.[24] I will examine prevailing financial concerns within the German public sector in the following chapter.

Conclusion

Although Karl Ernst Osthaus aimed to make art and culture more broadly accessible to members of the working class, we cannot disregard his attempts to also make modernity, modern art and alternative cultures more appealing to the conservative members of the upper middle class who did not often share his enthusiasm. The fostering and collecting of modern art at the time was far from fashionable, thus Osthaus was often seen to challenge conservative points of view even within his own social circle. The museum and Osthaus' cultural initiative was a catalyst for social discourse and enlightenment that can be seen as a justification for the social and economic imbalances caused by the wealthy upper middle class of which Osthaus was part of. Similar parallels can be drawn with John and Dominique de Menil's approach to the patronage and promotion of modern art and architecture in their adopted city of Houston and sensibility towards collecting and exhibiting Western art alongside non-Western art and objects. In Chapter 8 I will expand on this, along with the Menil Collection's financial concerns that arose within Dominique de Menil's own lifetime and the challenges the museum faced upon her death, thereby, sounding a cautionary tone over the sustainability of private museums beyond their charismatic creators' life.

I would argue that Osthaus' decision to allow his heirs to determine the destiny of his greatest passion – his private museum and art collection – inevitably jeopardised their future.[25] This has prompted a number of German collectors to ensure their own collections and museums do not suffer the same fate (refer to Chapter 7). This chapter has also shown that private-public relationships are not unheard of in Germany; the Museum Folkwang Essen, in 1922, demonstrated how private benefactors and the public museums have and continue to coexist within the German cultural landscape. The following chapters will examine how the German private and public museum sectors have evolved from the 1990s to the present day so as to understand why an unparalleled number of private museums have been established in Germany over the last two decades.

Notes

1 The name 'Folkwang' was taken from the German poem 'Edda Folkvangar' (in German, Palace of the Goddess Freya, that is, People's Hall). Sorensen, Lee (ed.), *Osthaus, Karl Ernst* in *The Dictionary of Art Historians*, California, Creative Commons, n.d.

2 The Museum Folkwang, *Museum Folkwang – Learning by Seeing*, Munich, Berlin, London & New York, Prestel Verlag, 2005, p.20.

3 Founded as a tribute to his recently deceased father and brother who passed away in 1917 and 1918 respectively. The renaming of the Phillips Collection corresponded with the opening of the new wing to the house in November 1960.

4 By 1933, the Kröller-Müller collection consisted of 4,000 drawings, 275 sculptures and several hundreds of fine paintings. Kröller-Müller Museum Staff, 2nd ed. Haarlem, The Netherlands, Joh. Enschedé en Zonen Grafische Inrichting, 1977, p.11.

5 Langen Foundation and Museum Insel Hombroich, Neuss, the Marguerite & Aimé Maeght Foundation, France, the Fondation Beyeler, Riehen, Sammlung Goetz, Munich, Tarra Warra Museum of Art, Victoria, Inhotim Centre for Contemporary Art, Brazil, Anita Zabludowicz Collection, Finland, Glenstone, Potomac, Burrell Collection, Glasgow, Storm King Art Centre, New Windson, Gibbs Farm, Makarau and MONA, Hobart.

6 More than 1,000 works from the Museum Folkwang, including works from the Osthaus collection were deemed to be Degenerate Art and seized by the Third Reich in 1937. Many were repurchased in the 1960s and 1970s, however, a greater number remain in private and public holdings as the museum lacks the funds to buy them back. Dr Tobia Bezzola, interview with the author.

7 Equivalent to 30 million Euros in 2012.

8 Wehle, Sean, 'Matisse's Ceramic Triptych: Nymph and Satyr in Germany', *The Oak Door* no. 4, (2013), p.1.

9 Wehle, 2013, p.2.

10 Schulte, Birgit, 'Karl Ernst Osthaus, Folkwang and the "Hagener Impuls" – Transcending the Walls of the Museum', *Journal of the History of Collections* 21, no. 2 (2009), pp. 213–214.

11 The eclectic collection of art, ethnographic objects and sculpture, scientific specimens and photographs from André Breton's apartment and studio is replicated are permanently displayed at the Centre Georges Pompidou, Paris.

12 Osthaus was Kirchner's patron until Osthaus' death in 1921. The Museum Folkwang, 2005, pp.22–23.

13 Jarzombek, Mark. 'The Discourses of a Bourgeois Utopia: 1904–1908, and the Founding of the Werkbund', in *Imagining Modern German Culture*: 1889–1910, Françoise Forster-Hahn (ed.), pp.127–145. National Gallery of Art, Washington, 1996, p.127.

14 Jarzombek, 1996, pp.127–128.

15 Based on Friedrich Schiller's notion of 'the aesthetic education of man'. Jarzombek, 1996, p.127.

16 Albert Barnes conducted educational seminars for workers in his factory in Philadelphia. This stems from his time in Germany – more specifically in Berlin or Heidelberg – where efforts were made to educate ordinary workers. Attempts were also undertaken to champion the value of aesthetics to members of the working class in England. Rudenstine, Neil L., *The House of Barnes: The Man, the Collection, the Controversy*, Philadelphia, American Philosophical Society, 2012, pp.10–11; Wehle, 2013, p.3.

17 Karl Ernst Osthaus. In German: 'Ich bin mit der Gründung eines Museums beschäftigt, das den Zweck haben soll, unsern kunstverlassenen Industriebezirk an der Ruhr für das moderne Kunstschaffen zu gewinnen.' Also Wehle, 2013, p.2.

18 Designed by Lindemann Architects, Mannheim, the new addition houses the Emil Schumacher collection.

19 Sigurdsson's captivating archival installation of photographs, documents, newspapers, objects, books, letters et cetera trace individual narratives during the Nazi Regime drawing on aspects of memory and trauma.

20 Dr Tobia Bezzola, interview with the author. Director of Museo d'arte della Svizzera Italiana in Lugano, Switzerland, as of 2018.

21 Dr Tobia Bezzola, interview with the author.

22 Museum Folkwang, 'The History of the Museum', Museum Folkwang website.

23 Dr Tobia Bezzola, interview with the author.

24 Dr Tobia Bezzola, interview with the author.

25 Many works remain on permanent display at the Museum Folkwang Essen, however, a greater number were seized by the Third Reich during World War II; many works still remain in private hands as the museum is unable to reacquire them.

Part III

The (re)emergence of the single patron collection museum

6 The German model of the private-public art museum

An unprecedented number of private art museums that have been founded over the last two decades are situated in Germany (42). Although Germany has a lower percentage ratio (eight per cent of collectors worldwide), it has a disproportionally large number of private museums.[1] So why are so many wealthy German collectors looking to the private collector's museum and what has prompted this shift? Furthermore, what are the ramifications on the public museum sector and how fiscally sustainable is the private museum model over time?

To adequately address these questions, we need to consider them alongside the developments that took place during the reunification of the Federal Republic of Germany (3 October 1990). The reappointment of Berlin as the official capital allowed the government to display Germany's cultural credentials and maturity within a European and global context and thus reassert the museum as an exemplar of civilisation within major cities. The repositioning of many museums, during the reunification process, highlighted significant gaps within public collections and their holdings of modern and contemporary art. This was reflected in the poor representation of twentieth-century European and German avant-garde and American postwar art within many German museums. It was through a number of significant private bequests that museums were encouraged to develop their collections of contemporary art. With this in mind, this chapter will set out the challenges that face many public art museums, the often-complex agreements they have entered into with private benefactors in their attempt to rebuild public collections of modern and contemporary art and to secure permanent access to important works of art.

This is an aspect that will help to frame the examination of Museums Brandhorst and Frieder Burda in the following chapter and to better understand the development of the private museum in Germany. While Museums Brandhorst and Frieder Burda might appear to indicate a new model between private and public museums, as I have shown in Chapter 5, the Museum Folkwang Essen, in 1922, set a precedent in the way private benefactors and the public museum sector have and continue to coexist within the German cultural landscape.

It is important to note that tax benefits associated with making private museums and collections available to the German public, despite the not-for-profit status, are modest and not the major factor in such cultural actions. To suggest that motivation is driven largely by individual tax inducements in this instance would be inaccurate. Even so, the tax incentives associated with creating a private foundation which makes artworks accessible to the public are generally better than donating artworks to public museums.[2] Official transfers, gifts, part sales or long-term loan agreements between private benefactors and the public sector must be sanctioned by the German Ministry of Culture; it is only through the endorsement of such contracts that benefactors are eligible to receive significant tax incentives. On the whole, most philanthropic acts are not generally motivated by tax benefits and gains; the motivations are far more complex and personal.

The repositioning of German art museums

Between the 1970s and 1990s a significant number of European public art museums refurbished or extended their museum buildings, or built new ones to address a growing interest in the museum.[3] This reinvestment in art and culture by governments toward the end of the twentieth century can be linked to cultural tourism, the positioning of main capital cities as cultural centres and to the perceived financial benefits associated with museums.[4] This period coincided with the changing political events and economic developments in Germany that prompted the redevelopment of the nation's cultural landscape. Many German public museums underwent dramatic refurbishment, expansion, rebadging and mergers during the nation's reunification process that started in 1990.[5]

The repositioning of Berlin as an important centre for art and culture soon prompted intense competition between German cities and public museums that were equally keen to strengthen their holdings and prestige.[6] This would see a dramatic reconstruction of key German museums including the Neue Pinakothek, Munich (1974–1981),[7] Neue Staatsgalerie, Stuttgart (1977–1982) and Museum für Kunsthandwerk, Frankfurt (1979–1985).[8] As scholars Frederick Baker and Gottfried Korff note, 'Museums have become the new way of representing local patriotism: when Stuttgart built itself a new Staatsgalerie, Munich did not want to be left behind and nor did the new provincial capital, Düsseldorf'.[9] They argue that Cologne soon followed suit as it sought to reposition itself as the significant cultural city it once was with its important museums and history of culture.[10]

This prompted public institutions to look to the private sector to assist them and to allow them access to the works they want to show. Coincidentally, a growing number of wealthy German industrialist collectors who began to develop important holdings of modern and contemporary art, looked to the public museum as a suitable home for their collections. Several large private donations prompted the desire to collect the new again as there were few works of contemporary art to compliment the Old Masters in many public museums. Important private bequests to the Pinakothek der Moderne in Munich include the 1964 gift from the Sofie and Emanuel Fohn Collection that was previously regarded as 'degenerate' art by the Nazi regime; the Günther Franke Foundation's donation of Max Beckman's work in 1974; and the Martha and Markus Kruss bequest followed in 1977 comprising of German Expressionist art.[11]

For much of the mid to late twentieth century, the public sector was seen as a suitable destination for private collections of art says Adrian Ellis.[12] The public endorsement of private collectors and their holdings was paramount with such arrangements as was the appropriate care and presentation of their holdings.[13] Ellis suggests 'The courting of collectors has always been a more significant source of acquisitions for public museums than buying or commissioning'.[14] Even though several German collectors made their private holdings available to key public museums, this proved problematic in the years following the reunification of Germany. This is because numerous long-term loan arrangements have over time, been withdrawn from the public sector. Thus, public museums found themselves in a difficult predicament negotiating new contracts and withdrawals of large private holdings that were previously made available to them. The rapid increase in museums, private wealth, the speculative art market and the predominance of the private museum presented collectors with alternatives beyond the public museum.

Although the reunification of Germany stimulated the remodelling and expansion of the public museum sector it became difficult for the already fiscally challenged cities to support the institutions they are charged with. Dr Tobia Bezzola, the former director of Museum Folkwang Essen points out that

> the private museum is a result of the changed economy. The weakened position of the public art museum is a direct consequence of the impoverished cities. Cities are in a disastrous financial state [in Germany] – they are in debt, they are poor, they are struggling to pay the money needed for infrastructure.[15]

For this reason, many collectors feel that they are better qualified to create their own museums. As Bezzola suggests:

> Private collectors tend to view their collection as a work of art. They feel that they are creating something that is unique. By founding a museum or a foundation it is seen as a natural step to provide for the future – to establish some form of guarantee that this will remain intact.[16]

It could also be argued that that private museums help to maintain large collections of art in one piece, during the collector's lifetime, compared with other models, however, they struggle to endure beyond the original founder's lifetime without substantial endowments. Collector and founder of the Falckenberg Collection in Hamburg, Dr Harald Falckenberg concurs: 'Usually it is not for a long time. Private museums usually have a limited lifetime, different from public museums'.[17]

When examining contemporary German private museum, we need to also consider how the public sector perceives the private museum in its most recent manifestation. Many public institutions offer what Dr Bezzola, refers to as a 'full service museum'.[18] He says public institutions often find themselves:

> faced with a competition that calls itself a museum. Often, they do little more than preserve the collection – sometimes without conservators doing any conservation. You will find many of these private museums provide a restricted service and have a limited understanding of what it means to be a museum, that is, the true concept of a museum.[19]

The public museum sector's criticism of the private collector's museum, their role and cultural contribution, the calibre of individual holdings and the museological expertise that is required in the management of museums is clearly evident. The tension between public and private is further heightened as collectors look to the public sector to secure the future of their museums as they recognise the precarious predicament of providing for their private museums, beyond their own lifetime. Director Kunsthaus Zürich Dr Christoph Becker, puts it this way: 'It is good for public institutions to see private ones grow, but private museums should remain private. They should not be funded by the state or the city; if it is over, it is over'.[20] This can often impinge on limited public funds that may be redirected away from public institutions so as to financially support private initiatives. Museum Brandhorst's partnership with the Pinakothek der Moderne in Munich, is one such example that will be discussed in the next chapter.

While the growing popularity of German private collector museums can be attributed to the difficult economic climate that is negatively impacting public museums and the cities charged with their care, many German cities are finding themselves in a difficult financial predicament, despite the nation's powerful international economic role during the Global Financial and continuing European Crises. This is because a smaller group of art museums are operated by the Federal Government in Bonn and Berlin – a greater number of German public museums are managed and funded by individual states, cities and local governments. Worst still, city and local governments in difficult financial situations might even consider bringing works to the market and liquidating assets to offset debt. Dr Bezzola points out that 'there have been several cases in recent years where German cities have sold off works from their public art collections'.[21] While this might appear alarmist, there are a number of examples where this has occurred. Berkshire Museum in Massachusetts is a very recent example. In 2013, the City of Detroit looked to sell off parts of the Detroit Institute of Arts' holdings to offset $18 billion of municipal debts. To secure the museum and its collection, the citizens of three counties that surround the city voted in favour of a modest increase in real estate taxes, over the next ten years, so as to secure the Detroit Institute of Arts and its collection and to provide them with $23 million to cover two-thirds of their annual operating budget.

In 2007, Essen politicians looked to the Museum Folkwang's internationally renowned collection to bolster their budget strategies. At the time, the museum's holdings were valued at around $250 million Euros. It appears that the city of Essen perceived the collection as an asset that could be liquidated to address shortfalls on the city's balance sheets. As fate should have it, and as noted in Chapter 5, 50 per cent of the museum's holdings continue to be owned by the private consortium in Essen – the *Folkwang-Museumsverein e.V.* and could not be sold by the city. This leaves them with a smaller number of works that could potentially be sold, should the museum's association agree to such a deed in the future.

This is not an isolated incident as there appears to be somewhat of a trend in deaccessioning works of art in the North Rhine-Westphalia region as museums, governments and corporations attempt to address declining fiscal fortunes by selling significant artworks from their holdings or those that are permanently displayed in key institutions. In 2006, the city of Krefeld's Kaiser Wilhelm Museum (located near Cologne) sought to sell one of Claude Monet's series of London Parliament paintings to address urgent repairs that included a leaking roof. Not surprisingly, such a decision met with immense controversy and debate when considering the consequences of selling cultural heritage to address the museum's much needed repairs.

In 2014, Jackson Pollock's 1951 'Number 5 (Elegant Lady)' was auctioned by Christie's New York for $11,365,000. The work was owned by the Essen-based energy company E. ON, for the last 34 years, and was on long-term loan to the Museum Kunstpalast, Düsseldorf for ten years. Similarly, in 2014, the German state-owned casino WestSpiel (owned by the state bank of North Rhine-Westphalia) sold two Andy Warhols ('Triple Elvis' (1963) and 'Four Marlons' (1966)), netting a combined $151.50 million. The Westphalian State Museum for Art and Cultural History's holdings were placed at risk during this time as a number of works from WestSpiel's 400-strong holdings were on permanent display at the museum. Museum directors and their publics fear that once such collections are sold to private collectors, it is most unlikely that they will return to the public sector. In light of such concerns, in 2016, the German state of North Rhine Westphalia acquired 297 works from WestSpiel's art collection for $30 million Euros.

Despite these difficulties collectors Frieder Burda, Udo Brandhorst, Harald Falkenberg and Ingvild Goetz have entered into individual long-term partnerships with the public museums sector, even though they have established their own private collection museums. Aged in their 70s and 80s respectively, they have elected to return to the public sector in order to secure the future of their individual holdings and to ensure their personal legacies endure indefinitely. In doing so, I question how secure their holdings might be within the already challenging public museum sector in light of the issues discussed thus far. On 9 March 2018, it was announced that 1,200 works from Erika Hoffmann's collection (founder of the Hoffmann Collection, Berlin) will transition to Dresden's State Art Collection over the next five years. Although the exact agreement between the collector and Dresden's State Art Collection is not publicly stated, it can be seen as a way to protect Hoffmann's holdings within the public museum sector as the collector nears her later years.

Considering the difficult financial predicament that public museums are currently faced with, this prompts us to ask why is this taking place, and on what terms? Although the reasons for this are numerous and personal, we can draw some general conclusions: 1) benefactors in the later stages of their lives are considering a more 'secure' future for their museums and collections; 2) generous tax benefits are available through an agreement struck with the German Ministry of Culture; 3) private museums require large endowment funds to finance them indefinitely. Fixed funds may last two or even three generations, or as long as it takes for the money to run out; 4) the original founders' heirs may not share their passion or wish to continue paying for the running of the museum indefinitely. What is more, they may not be in a financial position to do so; 5) the avoidance of estate tax for the collectors' heirs; and 6) the larger visitor numbers attending public institutions also allows private museums to be publicly visible and well-attended. The latter point, however, will be contested in relation to the Museum Bramdhorst in the following chapter.

Private-public partnerships since 1990

Private and public partnerships are complex and can often be fraught with uncertainty. This is because many private collectors want to maintain control over their respective holdings even when placed within public institutions. They often negotiate strict clauses to ensure their collections are permanently exhibited while allowing themselves a considerable degree of flexibility and curatorial involvement. This can often include the removal of artworks that are placed on long-term loan or the opportunity to increase the number of works of art on display as collectors generally like to show as much of their collections as possible. Such a dilemma can be seen with the opening of Berlin's Hamburger Bahnhoff in 1996 that included the permanent display of the Erich Marx Collection. The twentieth-century art collection that was assembled by the entrepreneur and art collector Dr Erich Marx, remains on display to date; however, the relationship between the museum and the collector has not been without its problems. In April 2007, Marx threatened to remove his collection from the Hamburger Bahnhoff after the sudden departure of his former dealer and curator Heiner Bastian, who was appointed to look after the collection. The agreement was renegotiated despite Marx's attempts to sell off part of the collection. Some 40 works were again placed on long-term loan with the museum incorporating the works within their holdings rather than displaying them as one.[22]

By 2004, the museum also agreed to the long-term loan of 1,500 works from the Friedrich Christian Flick Collection. The controversial collector's holdings were previously rejected by several museums before being accepted by Berlin. The Flick family's involvement with the Third Reich underpinned those decisions.[23] In 2008, Flick gifted 166 works to the museum from the collection. It was the single largest gift the museum has received to date.[24] In 2011, Harald Falckenberg partnered with Hamburg's Deichtorhallen, despite being pursued by the Hamburger Bahnhoff in Berlin.[25]

In 2005, the entrepreneurial German tax lawyer and art collector Dieter Bock, decided to withdraw his 500-strong collection from the Museum of Modern Art in Frankfurt. The works were on permanent display for 15 years. Bock's sudden withdrawal sparked concerns for the museum's holdings and future. His decision to sell some of the works proved advantageous for the collector as did the association with the Museum as the market value of the collection benefitted greatly from such an arrangement.[26] Similarly, the international avant-garde collection, collated by gallerists Paul Maenz, was withdrawn from permanent display at the Neues Museum Weimar in 2004, after only five years. The museum was opened to the public in late 1999, after extensive renovations. Works that were gifted or sold to the museum remain on display.[27] Several publications and catalogues of the Maenz collection were produced during this time by the museum, thereby strengthening its profile and credentials.

In 2005, Hans Grothe, the Duisburg based construction magnate and collector, agreed to a long-term loan agreement with the Kunstmuseum in Bonn. His collection of postwar German art was to be on permanent display until 2025. Grothe retracted his pledge and instead sold 400 works from his significant collection to billionaire collectors Sylvia and Ulrich Ströher, who also took over Grothe's private museum – Museum Küppersmühle in Duisburg. The museum was designed by architects Herzog & Meuron and opened to the public in 1999.[28] In September 2014, Grothe announced his decision to place a total of 38 works by Anselm Kiefer on long-term loan at the Kunsthalle Mannheim. This was actioned in June 2018 when the museum's redevelopment was completed. The agreement is in place for ten years with the option of renewing it for a further decade.[29]

Influential private collectors have a tendency to use their wealth and notable art collections to exert authority over the museums they appear to support: advancing their own cultural ambitions or seeking to benefit financially from the association with key institutions can often quash their sense of public spiritedness. In Chapter 9 I will outline how American collector and philanthropist Eli Broad has sought to exert influence over the Los Angeles County Museum of Art and the Museum of Contemporary Art in Los Angeles when seeking to support them. This approach signals a significant departure from the traditional role of the private collector as patron, bene-factor and passive supporter of public institutions. The new financial and patronage model that has emerged over the last two decades can at times appear a little elastic and difficult for institutions to manage. However, in the real world, if museums want the support of private collectors, they have to either adapt to the new system or establish a way that appears to balance the interests of the museum, its stakeholders and those of the individual collectors.

Conclusion

The reunification of Germany stimulated the remodelling and expansion of many public art museums, yet it is proving difficult for cities to uphold as many are heavily in debt and struggling to finance the public institutions they are charged with. A number of public museums are finding it difficult to stage the shows and programs they want to host, with little or no money allocated for acquisitions. These restrictions are not easily or quickly over-come; thus, museums are relying on private individuals and their foundations for financial support and long-term loans to offset their limited acquisi-tion budgets. Furthermore, the emergence of a growing number of private museums and shifts within the overall cultural landscape over the last two decades has prompted further challenges for public museums that are not so easily avoided as private-public agreements are often signed between gov-ernment departments and individual collectors.

Notwithstanding the current fiscal dilemmas faced by many German public institutions, we are seeing private museums looking to merge with them, albeit in various ways. While the perception that the private museum is seen to provide a secure future for personal collections is widespread, this cannot be guaranteed as the funds required to finance the management and ongoing operating costs associated with such an endeavour are immense. Although the endowment funds accompanying private public negotiations appear generous, they are usually insufficient to sustain personal collection museums indefinitely. That is why collectors are electing to find suitable partners within the public museum sector to ensure their legacies endure beyond their own lifetimes.

The following chapter will continue the discussion about the com-plex long-term agreements between the German Ministry of Culture and collectors Udo Brandhorst, Frieder Burda, Ingvild Goetz and Harald Falkenberg who sought more permanent solutions to ensure their private museums and collections remain intact, indefinitely. More specifically it will examine Museums Frieder Burda and Brandhorst: Museum Frieder Burda's transition into the public sector is clearly defined as is the private ownership of it, the Museum Brandhorst, on the other hand, remains a hybrid between private and public. Such arrangements might even appear to counter the current perception that the creation of the private museum is often seen to be a unique and natural step to provide for the future – one that establishes some form of guarantee that the collection will remain intact indefinitely. It also appears to contradict the premise that many private museums are founded because of the weakness of the public sector and the limitations of the public museum itself. So why are collectors looking to merge their private museums with the public sector?

Notes

1 Bossier, Max, Noe, Christoph, Resch, Magnus and Steiner, Lasse, *Art Collector Report*, edited by Larry's List, Hong Kong, Modern Arts Publishing, 2014, pp.28, 51.

2 Dr Tobia Bezzola, interview with the author. Director of Museo d'arte della Svizzera Italiana in Lugano, Switzerland, as of 2018.

3 Korff, Gottfried and Baker, Frederick, 'National, Heimat and Active Museums: An Outline of the Development of German Museums into the 1990s', In *Museums and Europe 1992*, edited by Susan Pearce, pp.116–133, New Jersey, Athlone Press, 1992, p.117.

4 Lorente, J. Pedro, *Cathedrals of Urban Modernity: The First Museums of Contemporary Art, 1800–1930*, Burlington, Vermont, Ashgate Publishing, 1998, pp.16–17.
   Ritchie, Ian, 'An Architect's View of Recent Developments in European Museums', In *Towards the Museum of the Future: New European Perspectives*, edited by Roger Miles and Lauro Zavala, pp.7–30, New York, Routledge, 1994, p.16.

5 Hickley, Catherine, 'Berlin Does $174 Million U-Turn on Modern Art Museum', *Bloomberg*, 21 August 2013.

6 This spurred the city of Munich to construct a museum of modern art – Pinakothek der Moderne (2002). The development of the new museum was at the behest of private donors. They presented the State of Bavaria with ten per cent of the funds required to build the $120 million museum.

7 It was the first museum dedicated to the display of contemporary art. The original 1853 building was lost during the war and replaced with the current building on the former site. Pinakothek, Neue, 'Neue Pinakothek – the Collection – History', Bayerische Staatsgemäldesammlungen, Munich.

8 Sheehan, James J, *Museums in the German Art World: From the End of the Old Regime to the Rise of Modernism*, Oxford and London, Oxford University Press, 2000, pp.187–188.

9 Korff and Baker, 1992, p.122.

10 Korff and Baker, 1992, p.122.

11 Schulz, Bernhard, 'Pinakothek Der Moderne', Staatliche Museen zu Berlin; Staatliche Kunstsammlungen Dresden; Bayerische Staatsgemäldesammlungen München. Pinakothek der Moderne, 'Pinakothek Der Moderne – the Four Museums – Tour', Bayerische Staatsgemäldesammlungen München.

12 Ellis, Adrian, 'The Problem with Privately Funded Museums', *The Art Newspaper*, February 2008, p.24.

13 Ellis, 2008, p.24.

14 Ellis, 2008, p.24.

15 Dr Tobia Bezzola, interview with the author.

16 Dr Tobia Bezzola, interview with the author.

17 Dr Harald Falckenberg, correspondence with the author.

18 Dr Tobia Bezzola, interview with the author.

19 Dr Tobia Bezzola, interview with the author.

20 Dr Christoph Becker, interview with the author.

21 Dr Tobia Bezzola, interview with the author.

22 Allen, Jennifer, 'Marx Collection to Neue Nationalgalerie', *Artforum International Magazine* no. 16 July 2007 (2012), n.p.

23 Wendland, Johannes, 'Farmed out to the Public: The Sammlung Falckenberg', *Metropolis M* 1, no. Feb./Mar. (2012).

24 Nationalgalerie Staatliche Museen u Berlin, 'Hamburger Bahnhoff: Museum Für Gegenwart – Berlin / About the Collection'.

25 Operated as Deichtorhallen Hamburg – Sammlung Falckenberg since January 2011. Falckenberg elected to partner up with the Deichtorhallen as he did not wish to place his collection alongside those by Friedrich Christian Flick and Erich Marx in Berlin. Wendland, 2012, n.p.

26 Gillard, Michael, 'Dieter Bock Obituary', *The Guardian*, 10 June 2010.

27 Neues Museum Weimar, 'Neues Museum Weimar / History', Neues Museum Weimar.

28 Ahead of this decision Hans Grothe looked to construct his own museum in Bonn –The Herzog & Meuron 'Kunstkiste' (Art Box). As the architectural plans met with local hostility Grothe abandoned the project and renovated the former cereal mill – The Museum Küppersmühle in his home town of Duisburg. Michalska, Julia, 'Largest Private Collection of Anselm Kiefer Lent to Kunsthalle Mannheim', *The Art Newspaper*, 7 August 2014.

29 Hansson, Hendrik, 'Kunsthalle Mannheim Acquires Anselm Kiefer Collection', *Artnet Worldwide Corporation*, 18 September 2014.

7 The private-public collection museum

Museum Brandhorst, Munich (2009) and Museum Frieder Burda, Baden-Baden (2004) Germany

> Private museums, at their best, provide alternative viewpoints to state sanctioned museums; but at their worst they are sterile mausolea.
>
> Mark Fraser[1]

This passage points up the broader issues facing a number of contemporary private museums. Although the private collector's museum has gained momentum over recent times it faces a twofold challenge: how fiscally sustainable is the private collector's museum beyond the original founder's lifetime and how can they differentiate themselves from other private and public museums? In the late 1970s, Dominique de Menil cautioned against the construction of monumental private museums and argued that they are financially unsustainable: 'What I feel is that in a few years no one will have any money for the monumental museums. That I am pessimistic about how things will be'.[2] Time has proven that de Menil was indeed correct as we cannot take for granted that museums will endure indefinitely – even pre-eminent examples such as the Menil Collection has been challenged, both within and beyond the collector's own lifetime.

What is often missing in many of today's private museums is Dominique de Menil's original way of thinking. In seeking to differentiate the Menil Collection from other museums, de Menil not only questioned established museum and curatorial practices but sought to redefine them through her unique way of seeing while making a stance against repetitive installations within starkly lit galleries. While the Museum Brandhorst looked to the Menil Collection's Cy Twombly Gallery for inspiration they struggled to capture the ambient aspects of the naturally lit galleries and the intimate human scale that helps to frame Twombly's evocative paintings. It is not sufficient to merely emulate the design elements of a particular museum or space; I would argue that an individual collecting and curatorial approach is also required to set private museums apart from other private and public institutions.

This chapter will consider the two points in more detail and question the prevailing perception that the creation of the private collector's museum is

Figure 7.1 Exterior view of the Museum Brandhorst. © bpk | Bayerische
Staatsgemäldesammlungen.

seen as a natural step to provide for the future and to establish some form
of guarantee that the museum will be permanent.[3] Particular case study
examples will show that more recently, collectors Udo Brandhorst, Ingvild
Goetz, Frieder Burda, Harald Falckenberg and Erika Hoffmann secured
complex long-term agreements with key public art museums with perpetuity
in mind. Perhaps, Karl Ernst Osthaus' personal trajectory and decision to
allow his heirs to determine the fate of his collection and museum serves
as a critical reminder for many contemporary German collectors who are
intent on securing the future of their museums and holdings within their
own lifetimes. Museums Brandhorst and Frieder Burda will lead this examination into the changing and complex nature of private-public museums
and their relationship with the public museum sector. The unconventional
transfer of ownership, partial sale and long-term loan agreement between
Udo Brandhorst and the State of Bavaria Museum is seen to challenge the
public museum's ability to operate effectively as their role and financial
security is being challenged. This will be juxtaposed with Frieder Burda's
distinct approach to the creation of the private collector's museum and its
trajectory into the public sphere.

Museum Brandhorst, Munich, Germany (2009)

Terms of the agreement

Udo Brandhorst's (born 1939) lengthy discussions with the State of Bavaria and Bavarian State Painting Collections (*Bayerische Staatsgemäldesammlungen*) started in 1999 upon the death of his wife Anette Brandhorst.[4] The dialogue between the various government departments and Udo Brandhorst resulted in the partial sale and long-term loan agreement of some 700 works from the Brandhorst Collection of twentieth- and twenty-first-century paintings, sculptures, media works and installations. The partial sale may have allowed Brandhorst to contribute 120 million Euros towards the museum's endowment fund. The agreement was secured on the proviso that a museum would be built (within a designated period) to house and display Brandhorst's personal collection. The museum was opened to the public in 2009 at a cost of 60 million Euros and was fully funded by the State of Bavaria. The interest earned from the Brandhorst Foundation endowment fund (around two million Euros annually), is allocated to new acquisitions for the Brandhorst Collection. To place this into a broader context, the Brandhorst's annual acquisition budget of two million Euros exceeds that of all state-operated museums in Bavaria, which have to make do with 200,000 Euros per annum for new acquisitions.

So, it is not difficult to understand that the construction of the Museum Brandhorst has generated much public debate. The funds allocated to the building of the new museum and the acquisition of much of Brandhorst's collection has meant that a significant amount of money has been redirected away from existing public museums in Munich. For this reason, it is considered a great expense and drain on limited public funds. Museums such as the Pinakothek der Moderne are required to work within rigid operating and often declining budgets with little in the way of acquisition funds available to them to grow their collection. The quality and suitability of Brandhorst's holdings was judged by a jury and external art expert appointed by the government department; the Pinakothek's professional and curatorial staff had little or no say in the matter. Because of this process many agreements between the Ministry and private benefactors have a tendency to meet with public hostility and controversy as there is little in the way of public debate and consultation with the partnering museum.

As custodians of important public institutions, the Bavarian State Painting Collections can be seen to be compromised when museum professionals are not consulted ahead of such negotiations. Too often governments undervalue the expertise and connoisseurship of museum directors and curators and are reluctant to seek their critical input. The reasons for this are not known, but one can assume that the Ministry places greater emphasis on the opinions of influential collectors and external advisers who might be seen to be more objective than their own staff who have a greater insight into the museum's holdings. In doing so, they risk compromising the calibre of the collection and its overall character.

As I have noted, long-term commitments with private collectors can come at a cost to the public museum sector and thus require rigorous consultation and debate. Redirecting already limited funds away from the Pinakothek der Moderne is a direct symptom of not only the construction of the new museum, but also the acquisition of a large number of works from Brandhorst's private collection. This in turn reduces the museum's existing funding while also shifting their focus away from their own collections to that of the Brandhorst's and the new museum.

A less visible outcome was the rejection of a significant and smaller private bequest as it coincided with the establishment of the Museum Brandhorst. The proposed gift by Christof and Ursula Engelhom was originally declined due to poor timing. As long-standing patrons of the Pinakothek from 1967 to 2003, they promoted contemporary art and supported the museum's *Galerie-Verein München e.V.* (known today as PIN: Friends of the Pinakothek der Moderne e.V.). In 1967, Christof Engelhom played a key role in the Pinakothek der Moderne's development and assisted them with the purchase of a number of works including the Francis Bacon triptych 'Crucifixion' and with the acquisition of Joseph Beuys' works (in 1983) for the Bavarian state painting collections. After the death of Christof Engelhom in 2010, his private collection was transferred to the Swiss Art Mentor Foundation Lucerne. It was not until Ursula Engelhom's death in 2016, that 58 works from the Engelhoms' private collection were once again offered to the museum (by the Foundation), and on this occasion, were accepted in the same year. If it was not for the Foundation's persistence such works of art would have been redirected to other public institutions.

The consistency and quality of Brandhorst's holdings has also been scrutinised by museum practitioners. This is because the nature of personal collections varies greatly as individual collectors buy according to their own taste, budget and often on the advice of curators, artists and art market professionals. Hence, the quality of the works can reflect their choices and advice received. This is not a matter of concern providing these collections remain private; however, upon entering institutional collections it becomes a topic of interest for the museum and its public. One might question why the State of Bavaria agreed to fund a separate museum to display Brandhorst's holdings as not all private collections warrant their own museum. While some have argued that the Brandhorst collection is not of a high quality and is not deserving of a private museum, others believe that the decision to take over much of the Brandhorst collection will in the long-run be a very fruitful collaboration – it probably is even now. The collection is seen to be complimentary to those of the Pinakothek der Moderne with important works by Andy Warhol and Cy Twombly filling in significant collection gaps for the Pinakothek.[5]

The collector's museum

The Museum Brandhorst is situated within Munich's cultural precinct alongside the Pinakothek der Moderne, Alte Pinakothek and the Neue Pinakothek. It is constructed over 12,100-square-metres. The architectural competition for the Museum Brandhorst started in 2002 and involved four architectural firms of which Sauerbruch Hutton won the jury's approval and the deciding vote of Udo Brandhorst. This was their first museum project. The foundations were laid in October 2005, and by end 2008, the shell construction was completed. The long rectangular plot of land available alongside the Pinakothek der Moderne dictated the new museum's cubic design.

The exterior shell is made up of 36,000 vertical rods glazed in 23 different colours that are placed over the top of a metal structure. The coloured rods are carefully graduated with the entrance and lower section of the museum wrapped in darker colours with medium tones placed in the middle and light ones on the top front section. The kaleidoscope of colours from a distance present a more even surface, however close up one is able to see the three-dimensional qualities with the layers of materials and surfaces clearly visible. The coloured rods are representative of the Munich cityscape and cover the entire building except for the horizontal windows that wrap around the building's shell. The colours merge within the museum's immediate location and buildings creating a harmonious and pleasant structure.

The museum entrance is set apart from the rest of the building with its raised head firmly orientating the structure on the perimeter of Türkenstrasse and Theresienstrasse; this is at the opposite end of the internal courtyard that is occupied by the Pinakothek der Moderne. This begs the question, if you decide to partner up with an institution, why do you decide to turn your back to it? The positioning of the entrance – facing away from both the Pinakothek der Moderne and the Alte Pinakothek – was at the behest of the collector. This could be seen as a disrespectful gesture by many at the Pinakothek der Moderne, Alte and Neue Pinakothek as Brandhorst sought to distinguish himself from his public counterparts. Even so, the vista from the visitors' room, at the rear of the Museum Brandhorst, provides an impressive view of the Pinakothek der Moderne, Alte Pinakothek and Eduardo Chillida's monumental sculpture 'Buscando la Luz (1924–2002), thereby firmly placing the new building within Munich's established museum precinct.

Despite its location amongst Munich's distinguished museums, the Museum Brandhorst has experienced a decline in visitor numbers. This may be a symptom of the unchanged display of the collection; until quite recently, the museum has focused on exhibiting works of art from the collection with much of the gallery space dedicated to the permanent display of it. If the museum is to remain relevant to contemporary audiences, a greater emphasis should be placed on interpreting or juxtaposing works from the collection and presenting new narratives and relationships between the many works

Figure 7.2 Exterior view of the Pinakothek der Moderne and Alte Pinakothek, Munich, 2017. Photo: Georgina Walker. Eduardo Chilled Juantegui 'Buscando la Luz'. © Eduardo Chillida Juantegui/VEGAP. Copyright Agency.

within and outside the collection. Even though the Brandhorst has revised their temporary exhibition program, it can at times be a difficult to determine the point of departure between permanent and temporary exhibits when looking at the museum's web site. This is because a number of the exhibitions (between 2011 and early 2015) were quite similar and appear as mere modifications of previous shows. It is for this reason that many of the exhibitions have a tendency to appear homogenous in the way they are curated. The recent shift in the Museum Brandhorst's exhibition program and curatorial approach might be seen as a response to the museum's lower than expected attendances. As former director of Museum Folkwang Dr Tobia Bezzola observes:

> It is one thing to have the money to spend on these museums – it is another thing to attract an audience. It is usually by doing the big exhibitions that attracts large audiences. What you have on display at many private museums of contemporary art is nice, but often founders have to learn that it is not something that will attract a huge audience or members of the public.[6]

It would appear that a number of recent temporary exhibitions at the Museum Brandhorst have drawn on the Pinakothek der Moderne's curatorial expertise to reposition their exhibition program in response to the declining visitor numbers. The exhibition entitled 'Creating Realities. Encounters between art and cinema' (16 April–31 May 2015) saw the collaboration between the Pinakothek der Moderne, Museum Brandhorst, Goetz Collection and Kino der Kunst. Similarly, the recent survey exhibition of American artist Seth Price (21 October 2015–8 April 2018) saw the collaboration between the Museum Brandhorst and the Stedelijk Museum Amsterdam, thereby, deviating greatly from their earlier exhibition format. Seth Price's works dominated much of the space with 150 works presented throughout numerous galleries and levels. On my initial visit in December 2013, the smaller lower level galleries displayed works by Andy Warhol whilst the permanent collection was displayed across the first and second levels. Upon my return in December 2017, a similar exhibition of Andy Warhol's works remained on show with only a slight change to the exhibition format and narrative. The third level is dedicated exclusively to the permanent display of Cy Twombly's paintings and sculpture. The Museum Brandhorst owns the largest single collection of Twombly's work outside the Menil Collection. It is the focal point of Brandhorst's holdings and consists of 170 works – paintings, sculptures and works on paper.[7] The large polygonal gallery at the rear of the building, aptly named the Lepanto Gallery, is dedicated to the display of the 12 panel 'Lepanto Cycle' (2005). I would suggest that this is one of the museum's highlights.

Upon viewing the Cy Twombly galleries for the first time, it became immediately apparent that the Museum Brandhorst looked to the Cy Twombly Gallery (1995) at the Menil Collection when considering the presentation of Twombly's paintings and sculptures. At first glance, it became difficult to distinguish between the two displays as even the pale timber floor boards and design of the spaces looked similar. After closer scrutiny, however, one can clearly see that the large-scale spaces at the Museum Brandhorst and the stark lighting vary greatly from the more intimate naturally lit rooms at the Cy Twombly Gallery in Houston. More recently, the top-level Roses Gallery has been dramatically reconfigured and includes a number of asymmetrical partition walls. The partition walls are designed to break up the large gallery and to create a more intimate and less foreboding engagement with the many smaller works on paper (largely Twombly's photographs and sketches), while also making the space more welcoming. I am not sure that it does this effectively as the numerous partition walls disrupt the natural flow of the space and disturb the visual adjacencies between the many artworks. That being so, it does allow visitors to appreciate a number of Twombly's smaller works on paper that are seldom exhibited in most museums. Thus, the Brandhorst has the capacity to introduce audiences to various aspects of the artist's oeuvre that may not always be possible in larger institutions due to ongoing limited exhibition spaces or acquisition budgets.

Figure 7.3 Installation of the 'Lepanto Gallery' (Cy Twombly), Museum Brandhorst, Munich. © bpk | Bayerische Staatsgemäldesammlungen.

Figure 7.4 Installation of the 'Rose Gallery' (Cy Twombly), Museum Brandhorst, Munich. © bpk | Bayerische Staatsgemäldesammlungen.

Figure 7.5 Installation of the 'Rose Gallery' (Cy Twombly), Museum Brandhorst, Munich. © bpk | Bayerische Staatsgemäldesammlungen.

A complex relationship between private and public

The agreement with the Ministry of Culture affords Udo Brandhorst generous tax benefits and prestigious naming rights for the new museum that is named in his honour – even though the Museum Brandhorst remains publicly funded and operated. The State of Bavaria agrees to pay for the staffing (two to three curators) and running costs of the museum and the Brandhorst Foundation pays the director's salary. The Pinakothek der Moderne, the Alte and Neue Pinakothek operate with around 12 curators collectively and are overseen by a single director. The disparity between the Bavarian State Painting Collections and Museum Brandhorst is immediately apparent as influential private collectors lobby and court ministers in pursuit of private agendas.

Udo Brandhorst and his contemporaries are redefining the notion of philanthropy by merging private museums and collections with the public sector and establishing exclusive arrangements with them. This is because private collectors look to the public museum sector with perpetuity in mind as they recognise that private collections and museums have a limited lifespan.[8] Formal guidelines and protocol are yet to be established as museum professionals and private benefactors are finding individual ways to work together. Such agreements are not conventional bequests or gifts and to present them to the public as philanthropic and civic deeds can therefore be misleading; nonetheless, the personal nature of these agreements makes them difficult to define.

To better understand how contemporary collectors are challenging philanthropic models we need to consider how they differ from past collectors.

In doing so, it is important to acknowledge that bequests are seldom unconditional. They are generally accompanied by a number of stipulations
that include permanent, exclusive and specific displays, the creation of
new structures and even a dedicated team of curators and conservators to
care for the collection. At the time of his death in 1969, American banker
Robert Lehman, bequeathed 2,600 works to the Metropolitan Museum in
New York. The basis of the bequest included the creation of a new addition (the Robert Lehman Wing), dedicated to the permanent display of his
collection. The new wing opened in 1975. It was furnished in a manner that
replicated Lehman's own private domestic interiors: furniture, drapes, wall
coverings and decorative art objects present a homely presentation of his
life as an important collector and connoisseur. The bequest was not accompanied by an endowment and Lehman's personal collection continues to be
displayed in much the same way 43 years later.

So, how does Lehman's arrangement with the Metropolitan differ from
that of Brandhorst's agreement with the Pinakothek? The Lehman wing
has been replaced with a stand-alone museum with both structures funded
and operated by the respective public institutions. Whilst the galleries at the
Museum Brandhorst adhere to a minimalist white cube method of presentation that is indicative of our time, the Lehman wing is presented in a way that
was representative of museum displays during the 1970s. There are, however, three significant points of distinction: Brandhorst's active philanthropic
deed replaces Lehman's posthumous one, thereby allowing him to exercise
authority over what is a quasi-private-public museum. While Lehman gifted
his collection to the Metropolitan, Brandhorst's arrangement includes an
endowment of 120 million Euros and a complex mix of gifts, long-term loan
and partial sale agreements. With this in mind, is the Museum Brandhorst a
private or public institution? I would argue it is a hybrid of private-public: it
is publicly owned, but privately operated on public funds as Brandhorst and
his director manage the Museum Brandhorst and exercise control over it
and the collection, not the State of Bavaria or the Pinakothek der Moderne.

Similarly, in January 2014, Ingvild Goetz 'donated' 375 works of art
along with the building that houses and displays the Goetz Collection in
Oberföhring, Munich, to the State of Bavaria. The 'donation' allows her to
exercise total control over the museum and its holdings, curate exhibitions,
arrange loan agreements with other institutions even though the government is charged with the running and operating of the museum and its staff.
Through this agreement 5,000 works have also been made available to the
Pinakothek der Moderne, the Haus der Kunst and the Neues Museum in
Nuremberg over the next ten years. When the works are not on show they
are kept in storage. The sale of the works to the German Ministry of Culture
has ensured that Goetz's heirs are remunerated accordingly. This is reminiscent of the £20,000 fee paid to Sir Hans Sloane's heirs upon his bequest
in 1753 that helped to establish the British Museum. The 2017 exhibition
at the commercial gallery of Hauser & Wirth in New York might also

suggest Ingvild Goetz's intention to sell works from her notable Arte Povera collection.

The agreement with the Ministry of Culture allows for the bulk of the collection to remain the property of the collector and her family. To define such arrangements as a 'donation' is arguable as this is not a straightforward donation or gift as the collector has the authority to preside over her collection and private museum, indefinitely. The Bavarian Minister President Horst Seehofer declares it as so: 'This is a unique opportunity for the state of Bavaria to secure the future of one of the most internationally recognised collections of contemporary art. It will lastingly strengthen Bavaria as a centre for art and culture'.[9] So, why are governments willing to agree to such arrangements? Perhaps it has more to do with regional competition and fear that collectors will embark on an agreement with neighbouring cities if they are refused? If this is so, it is reminiscent of the intense competition (discussed in Chapter 6), between German cities and public museums that were equally keen to strengthen their holdings and prestige during the 1970s and 1990s.

Although the agreement between Harald Falckenberg and the Deichtorhallen in Hamburg appears to be more clearly articulated it is equally individualistic. The contractual arrangement allows access to the Falckenberg Collection and Phoenix-Hallen until 2023. The Deichtorhallen is able to stage additional exhibitions in this suburban located space with complete access to Falckenberg's collection.[10] While the Collection provides the Deichtorhallen with an additional exhibition space, access to the collection permits lending arrangements with other institutions. As part of this agreement the city of Hamburg contributes 500,000 Euros per annum along with 70,000 Euros towards the appointment of a curator and assistant that is employed by the Falckenberg Collection.[11] All additional charges are paid for by Falckenberg.[12]

In agreeing to idiosyncratic partnerships, governments can often relinquish public institutions' autonomy and restrict their access to additional public funds as they are being redirected towards securing private initiatives and collections. Allowing private collectors to exercise authority over their museum and holdings, despite renouncing responsibility of them, raises concerns over the credibility of such arrangements. Private benefactors and museum professionals are thus required to tailor a respectful relationship and collaboration that can be productive and mutually advantageous, without losing sight of their respective responsibility to the public they seek with whom to engage with.

Although the Museum Brandhorst is a complex mix of private and public, the old Türkenstrasse Barrack that is situated between the Museum Brandhorst and the Pinakothek der Moderne can be seen as a symbolic gesture of their partnership and cooperation. Built in 1826, the gatehouse for the Royal Bavarian Infantry Lifeguards Regiment, was restored during 2008 and 2010. It was opened to the public in 2010 to accommodate the

Figure 7.6 Exterior view of the Türkentor, Türkenstrasse and Museum Brandhorst, Munich, 2017. Photo: Georgina Walker.

permanent display of Walter De Maria's 'Large Red Sphere' (2002). The De Maria installation was an idea that originated from the Pinakothek der Moderne's curatorial teams. The renovation of the building was funded by the Stiftung [Foundation] Pinakothek der Moderne.[13] The acquisition of the sphere. (which is not the entire work and includes the room), was acquired by the Foundation Brandhorst. The redevelopment project can be seen as a cooperation and collaboration on different levels and one that will continue to develop over time.

I would argue that the Pinakothek der Moderne and its curatorial staff are not able to exert much influence over the Museum Brandhorst's collection and display, within Brandhorst's lifetime; they are restrained by his presence and the control he exerts over both the collection and the museum, despite being publicly funded and operated. Even so, the key force behind the Museum Brandhorst comes from the Pinakothek as an established and respected cultural institution; the Museum Brandhorst's standing is heightened through its association with a world-renowned group of state-owned art museums. Why else would private collectors seek to partner up with public institutions? Despite current financial challenges facing many public museums, I would suggest the prestige and the association with government-owned museums can be most attractive to individual benefactors such as Udo Brandhorst and his contemporaries, hence its appeal. Even though it is not known if the private museum model will continue to be as important as it is today, many private benefactors continue to focus on the present in their quest to establish a lasting public legacy for themselves. In doing so, some are challenging public museums' ability to operate effectively as their role and financial security is being challenged. It might be the case that the name Brandhorst will continue to live on as a legacy to the collector, but at what price?

Museum Frieder Burda, Baden-Baden, Germany (2004)

A private foundation museum

Frieder Burda's philanthropic deed is more clearly stated than that of Udo Brandhorst's agreement with the Pinakothek der Moderne. The deal struck between Burda and the State of Baden-Württemberg is concise and unconditional: upon the original founder's passing the museum and his collection of 1,000 works of German Expressionism, American Abstract Expressionism, Postwar West German and contemporary art will be bequeathed to the State. Until that time, the Museum Frieder Burda remains privately funded with the collector and the Foundation Frieder Burda (established in 1998) exercising total control and ownership of the museum and its holdings.[14] The State

Figure 7.7 Frieder Burda. © Museum Frieder Burda, Baden-Baden.

does on occasion contribute funds towards joint programs and exhibitions staged between the Museum Frieder Burda and Staatliche Kunsthalle.

Frieder Burda constructed his new museum alongside the State-owned Staatliche Kunsthalle Baden-Baden. It opened to the public in February 2004. The two institutions are connected by a glass bridge which is seen as a symbolic gesture of their cooperation. The Kunsthalle, by nature, is not a collecting institution and thus the partnership with a collecting museum is seen to be a complimentary arrangement. The cost to construct the museum is estimated to be around 20 million Euros – a third of the amount needed to build the Museum Brandhorst. The collector financed the cost of the entire building whilst the Foundation Frieder Burda continues to meet the operating and running costs associated with the collection museum.

Born into a wealthy German family whose fortune was made in printing and publishing, Frieder Burda (born 1936) grew up surrounded by the works of German Expressionist artists and those of his father's generation. He began collecting in the 1970s and has developed an important collection of modern and contemporary art by renowned German and American artists along with late works by Pablo Picasso.[15] Included are works by Max Beckman, Ernst Ludwig Kirchner, August Macke, Willem de Kooning, Jackson Pollock, Mark Rothko, Clifford Still, Gerhard Richter, Georg Baselitz, Sigmar Polke and John Chamberlain. More recently, the collection's focus has been on works by contemporary German artists.[16] Burda has also sat on the Centre Georges Pompidou's acquisition commission. This connection has allowed the two institutions to coordinate reciprocal exhibitions from their respective permanent collections including those by young German and French artists; works from Burda's holdings have been exhibited in Paris and those from the Pompidou in Baden-Baden.[17]

Within the first five years the Museum Frieder Burda attracted over one million visitors.[18] The museum hosts four main exhibitions a year and is not restricted to the display of works within the collector's holdings. The exhibition program is varied with the focus on thematic or solo survey shows of artists represented in the collection, loans from other private and public holdings and collaborations with contemporary artists and curators. The 'James Turrell' exhibition (9 June–28 October 2018) was designed and planned in collaboration with the artist. More recently, the curatorial team decided to show highlights from particular sections of the collection to compliment temporary exhibitions on a more regular basis. Works from the collection are also integrated within the individual shows. This also prevents the museum from running into the remit of the Kunsthalle whilst attracting interested audiences to the museum throughout much of the year.

Highlights from the Burda Collection are exhibited at different times of the year and on occasion span across to the Kunsthalle with the curatorial teams presenting two distinct perspectives of it: the inaugural show and the celebratory exhibition – 'Forty Years of the Collection – Ten Years of the Museum' (12 July–26 October 2014) – are two such examples.[19] The partnership with the Staatliche Kunsthalle allows for joint programs and exhibitions to be staged across the two venues throughout the year while also pursuing their individual curatorial mandates. For example, the show 'In Focus: German Expressionism' (1 March–29 June 2014) was on display alongside the retrospective exhibition of French contemporary artist JR: 'The Exhibition JR the Museum Frieder Burda and in Public Space in Baden-Baden' (1 March–29 June 2014). This also incorporated many of JR's large outdoor projects entitled 'UNFRAMED BADEN-BADEN'. The artist's focus was on the presentation of the historical relationship between Germany and France and placing it within a new and current context. Local citizens were invited to submit old private photographs that were projected on the exterior of many of the city's neo-Baroque buildings during the course of the exhibition.

The museum does not shun its responsibility to tackle sensitive historical issues and topics nor does it turn its back on contemporary social and political concerns. On my first visit to the Staatliche Kunsthalle Baden-Baden: the exhibition 'Power of the Powerless' (16 November 2013–9 February 2014) the theme of 'escape and expulsion' featuring works from dOCUMENTA (13) captured my attention and curiosity.[20] The Kunsthalle galleries were tailored around the specific exhibits. Silke Wagner's 'Buergersteig (Pavement)' (2001–2002) was one such work that prompted visitors or those merely strolling by to stop and question why the Volkswagen van, resembling that of Lufthansa's, marked boldly with the words 'Deportation Class' was parked in front of the Kunsthalle's entrance? At the time, the work drew attention to the growing number of refugees deported from Germany (around 35,000 per annum were leaving Frankfurt on Lufthansa flights in the early 2000s).[21] Not only is this is a stark awakening amongst the tranquil surroundings of Lichtentaler Allee, but also an issue that still continues to prompt international political debate in Germany and throughout much of Europe.

A clear demarcation of private and public

By the late 1990s, Frieder Burda began to consider a permanent home for his expansive art collection. He initially intended to build his museum in Mougins – a town in the south of France where he has a residence. Burda decided to build it in his hometown of Baden-Baden on the historical Lichtentaler Allee – the charming park lined with old copper beeches. Located at the northern tip of the Black Forest in south-west Germany, Baden-Baden is an affluent and picturesque thermal spa town. The town's proximity to France and Switzerland makes it a popular destination for French and Swiss visitors, with the Museum Frieder Burda a popular tourist and cultural attraction.

Figure 7.8 Exterior view of the Museum Frieder Burda, Baden-Baden. © Museum Frieder Burda, Baden-Baden.

Considering and often rejecting many architectural plans submitted for his new museum, Frieder Burda eventually settled on those by New York architect Richard Meier. The new museum was constructed next to the century-old Neoclassical Kunsthalle designed by Hermann Billing (1867–1946) in 1909. Meier's building is compatible with Billing's Kunsthalle and does little to disturb the serene and historic character of the seventeenth-century avenue it now occupies. Approaching Lichtentaler Allee from the centre of town visitors are immediately captivated by the harmonious placement of Meier's three-level structure in his signature colour white; the museum stands at the same height as Billing's roof line allowing the Kunsthalle's portico to peak above it. The Museum Frieder Burda's building mirrors aspects of the Kunsthalle's design and elegant sandstone proportions: Meier replaces Billing's symmetrical Ionic plasterwork with the vertical asymmetrical placement of the white painted metal plates and glazing. What is more, Meier's off-centre entrance is not unlike Billing's; entry into the Frieder Burda is on the ground level the Kunsthalle's is elevated to the first floor. It is at the mezzanine level that the two buildings come together by way of the glass interconnecting bridge and the joint café.

Figure 7.9 Exterior view of the Museum Frieder Burda, Baden-Baden facing Lichtentaler Allee. © Museum Frieder Burda, Baden-Baden.

Meier does not seek to dominate Billing's architectural presence, nor does he disturb the immediate parklands with much of the landscape left undisturbed electing to build the museum on a hilly plot that backs onto a residential area. This can also be seen in the way that Meier constructs the Arp Museum Bahnhof Rolandseck (2007) in Remagen (outside of Bonn), to compliment the Bahnhof Rolandseck. The contemporary structure is carefully embedded within the mountains of the Siebengebirge, and the overall romantic and picturesque Rhine landscape. The historic Neo-Classical Bahnhof was designed by the prominent Prussian architect Karl Friedrich Schinkel (1781–1841) and completed in 1856; Schinkel's other distinguished projects include the Altes Museum in Berlin (built between 1823 and 1830) and St. Nicholas' Church, Potsdam (built in the years 1830–1837). Today the church sits opposite the new Museum Barberini that serves as a replica of the Roman original. It was privately funded by billionaire collector and software magnate Hasso Plattner and his foundation and opened to the public in 2017.

Meier's wide angled white ramp is an important architectural, artistic and practical feature of the Museum Frieder Burda's interior; it serves to

Figure 7.10 Exterior view of the Museum Frieder Burda, Baden-Baden and Staatliche
Kunsthalle Baden-Baden. © Museum Frieder Burda, Baden-Baden.

orient visitors within the immediate landscape and scenic Lichtentaler Allee
while leading them into the numerous galleries on the lower, mezzanine and
top levels. The floor to ceiling glazed panels merge the interior and exterior
spaces seamlessly as does the uninterrupted visual aesthetic from one point
of the museum to the next. The south wall louvres control the daylight into
the large galleries, with sunscreens placed over most of the remaining large
glazed panels throughout the museum. Galleries are situated on either side
of the ramp with the large spaces placed toward the back of the museum.
The central gallery floor on the first level is suspended above the ground
floor; the hovering tabletop design creates a lightness of space and perspective as it stops well short of the glazed panelled south wall. This is also
enhanced by the thoughtful placement of the individual partition walls that
are freestanding and not fixed to the ceiling. They are of human proportions
and allow for an uninterrupted view of the interior and exterior spaces and
the presentation of works of art, irrespective of their scale.

The large central exhibition spaces are juxtaposed with smaller intimate
areas that contain the viewing experience. Even though large works are
shown to great effect in the Museum Frieder Burda, smaller works are not
compromised as they are often hung low and asymmetrically, often in small
clusters to create individual points of interest. This was clearly apparent on

Figure 7.11 Exterior view of the Staatliche Kunsthalle Baden-Baden, 2014.
Photo: Georgina Walker.

my recent visit to the exhibition 'Die Brücke 1905–1914' (17 November
2018–24 March 2019). Individual artist's works were hung within a thematic
narrative while temporary partition walls were erected to address conservation concerns associated with works on paper and their sensitivity to light.
Even so, this did not detract from the gallery's overall display aesthetic. What
is more, the daylight and economical selection of works promotes a contemplative exhibition environment despite the large central galleries. At the time
of my first visit to the Frieder Burda they hosted the survey exhibition of
the Swiss hyperrealist artist Franz Gertsch entitled 'Franz Gertsch: Nature's
Secret' (26 October 2013–16 February 2014). A total of 30 large paintings
and woodcuts were displayed throughout the museum. The canvases and
works on paper were lowly hung allowing the viewer to immerse themselves
within the individual works. Most of the works in the exhibition came from
the Museum Franz Gertsch in Burgdorf, outside of Bern in Switzerland. The
museum has thus looked for individual ways to curate their exhibitions within
the diverse and naturally lit galleries that are thoughtfully constructed around
the art collection and the museum's surroundings.

The Museum Frieder Burda does not adopt an insular approach to their
exhibition programs as it seeks to broaden its appeal and promote more
regular visits to the museum and Baden-Baden. It can also be said that the

Frieder Burda and Staatliche Kunsthalle Baden-Baden are well matched: one pursues a distinct collecting approach while the other is a non-collecting institution. The Kunsthalle's innovative and intellectual curatorial approach is also a good fit for to the Burda's exhibition programs. We can conclude that the two institutions adhere to a clearly articulated mandate: the Museum Frieder Burda is at the behest of its original founder and his foundation and the Kunsthalle to its public. This is clearly articulated by the Staatliche Kunsthalle Baden-Baden:

> The neighboring Museum Frieder Burda is beholden to the extensive collection of its patron Frieder Burda. The Kunsthalle, on the other hand, is not bound to the personal preferences of its direction or curatorial staff ... Its close proximity to a private museum offers an excellent starting point for taking up new discussions concerning the public function and responsibilities of a national art gallery at the beginning of the twenty-first century.[22]

Conclusion

We can surmise that Udo Brandhorst, Frieder Burda, Harald Falckenberg, Ingvild Goetz and Erika Hoffmann recognise that the funds required to finance the ongoing management and operating costs associated with

Figure 7.12 Interior view of the Museum Frieder Burda, Baden-Baden. © Museum Frieder Burda, Baden-Baden.

Figure 7.13 Interior view of the Museum Frieder Burda, Baden-Baden. © Museum
　　　　　Frieder Burda, Baden-Baden.

private collection museums is immense. With this in mind, they are equally
concerned about the eventual dispersal of their respective holdings over
time and seek to avoid it at all cost. Although the endowment funds accompanying some of the agreements appear generous, they are usually insufficient to sustain personal collection museums indefinitely. That is why
collectors are electing to find suitable partners within the public museum
sector to ensure their legacy lives on beyond their own lifetimes. Even so, the
formation of individual partnerships with the public sector indulges private
benefactors by allowing them to exert total control over their museums, art
collections and the curatorial display of them. Whilst the Museum Frieder
Burda's transition into the public sector is clearly defined as is the private
ownership of it, the Museum Brandhorst, on the other hand, remains a complex mix of private and public.

The Museum Frieder Burda demonstrates a desire to embrace a more
individual approach to their exhibitions formats – one that compliments the
neighbouring Staatliche Kunsthalle's innovative stance while recognising that

Figure 7.14 Installation view of the exhibition *America! America!* at the Museum
Frieder Burda, Baden-Baden, 9 December 2017–21 May 2018. Photo:
Volker Naumann. © Museum Frieder Burda, Baden-Baden.

they also need to attract visitors to the museum with frequently changing
and diverse exhibition programs. This not only supports the museum's financial situation but also serves as a major cultural attraction for the city of
Baden-Baden. Creating a distinct character and curatorial approach is thus
essential for private museums – why else must they exist if they do not distinguish themselves within the competitive and busy global cultural landscape.
Despite the number of private museums that have been founded in Germany
since the late 1990s, maintaining private collection museums and holdings
intact, in perpetuity, continues to be the biggest challenge facing many contemporary art collectors and benefactors. Hence, they are looking for individual ways to plan for a longer future, and as cost effectively as possible.

Notes

1 Mark Fraser, interview and correspondence with the author.
2 Dominique de Menil's Notes Handwritten by K. Davidson Dated 15 October,
  1976, Menil Archives, The Menil Collection, Houston.
3 Dr Tobia Bezzola, interview with the author.
4 Anette Brandhorst was the great-granddaughter and heiress of the founder of the
  Henkel manufacturing company that produced chemicals, detergents, adhesives
  and personal care products.

5 The Pinakothek der Moderne has one of the finest collections of modernist and contemporary artists in Germany: Georg Baselitz, Joseph Beuys, Andy Warhol, Rosemarie Trockel, Arnulf Rainer, Blinky Palermo, Anselm Keifer, Dan Flavin, Gerhard Richter are strongly represented within their holdings.

6 Dr Tobia Bezzola, interview with the author.

7 Museum Brandhorst, 'Cy Twombly', Museum Brandhorst website.

8 Dr Harald Falckenberg, correspondence with the author.

9 Sammlung Goetz, 'Donation: Goetz Collection, a State-Owned Collection in Bavaria', Sammlung Goetz website.

10 Wendland, Johannes, 'Farmed out to the Public: The Sammlung Falckenberg', *Metropolis M*, 1, no. February/March (2012), n.p.

11 Dr Harald Falckenberg, correspondence with the author.

12 Wendland, 2012, n.p.

13 The Foundation was founded in 1994 and provided the State of Bavaria with 13 million Euros towards the construction of the Pinakothek der Moderne's new building.

14 Museum Frieder Burda website, 'The Frieder Burda Collection Opens New Museum in Baden-Baden. Press Release 22 October 2004'.

15 Frieder, Burda Foundation, *Museum Frieder Burda: Architect Richard Meier*, edited by Frieder Burda Foundation, Ostfildern, Germany, Hatje Cantz Verlag, 2011, p.6.

16 Museum Frieder Burda website, 'The Frieder Burda Collection'.

17 Museum Frieder Burda website, 'Press Release. Centre Pompidou in Paris and Museum Frieder Burda in Baden-Baden Enter Cooperation Agreement'.

18 Museum Frieder Burda website, 'Five Years after Its Inauguration: Museum Frieder Burda in Baden-Baden Welcomes Millionth Visitor'.

19 This was also the case with the Georg Baselitz – 'Baselitz. A Retrospective' (21 November 2009–14 March 2010).

20 Staatliche Kunsthalle, Baden-Baden, 'Power of the Powerless 16 November 2013–09 February 2014'.

21 Regine, 'Brussels Biennial: Lufthansa Deportation Class', 17 December 2008.

22 Staatliche Kunsthalle Baden-Baden, 'Dear Friends of the Staatliche Kunsthalle Baden-Baden'.

8 In defiance of the monumental museum

Menil Collection, Houston, USA (1987)

> The criteria for a successful plan are inventiveness and beauty. I believe this museum can offer a unique approach to the exhibition of art.
>
> Dominique de Menil, 1980[1]

The use of 'philanthropy' and 'public access' in the context of the collecting, patronage and philanthropic practices of John and Dominique de Menil implies an active and unique sense of civic duty. The uniqueness stems not only from their generosity but from Dominique de Menil's unwavering ethical position that avoided the overt display of benefaction and any signs of money or ego orientated gestures. This approach departs from traditional and contemporary expressions of benefaction that are often publicly celebrated as significant cultural milestones. This chapter will chart how the de Menils went to great lengths and personal expense to make their disparate collections of art freely accessible to all Houstonians. They also set out to support the curatorial practices of key museum professionals, act as cultural ambassadors for the promotion of modern art and architecture within the city of Houston and financially support art and culture along with other wealthy Houstonians with the single purpose of placing their adopted city of Houston on the cultural map. When Dominique de Menil set out to create the Menil Collection she garnered support from her peers who financially contributed to the construction of the museum and also made generous donations of money to assist the museum in its greatest hour of need. The ability to muster the support of third party individuals and their foundations when creating a private museum is unique to the Menil Collection.

This chapter outlines that the founding of the Menil Collection in 1987 reinstated the single patron collection museum in the United States and much of Europe. The development of the American model of the private collector's museum is marked by two distinguishing markers: one, the large freestanding museum has usurped the house museum; and two, the private museum is no longer established as a posthumous philanthropic gesture. Although the Menil Collection signalled a move away from the opulent design aesthetic and personalised house museum display favoured by earlier

American benefactors, I will assert that the de Menil house served to define the museum's distinct appearance, character and design aesthetic.[2] The individual character of the house that was designed by Philip Johnson, in 1951, in the postwar International Style, set the de Menils apart from their contemporaries in Houston's affluent suburb of River Oaks. Its stark, minimalist rectangular brick box-like appearance challenged architectural design conventions as did the 'un-museum-like' appearance of the Menil Collection, as ultimately built in an institutional format by Renzo Piano.

I will touch on how Dominique de Menil used the collection and display of art and objects within their private domestic interiors and the use of particular architectural, design and curatorial styles as an expression of her subjectivity that was later transferred to the Menil Collection, an aspect of her life not critically discussed to date. De Menil's interiors and the way that objects and works of art are displayed can also be seen in a series of images taken of the numerous exhibitions they supported. The de Menil home reveals similarly decorated interiors, albeit over thirty years after they first appeared as museum displays. While the Menil Collection's understated architectural design was a format that many American and international private collectors sought to emulate,[3] the curatorial and philosophical beliefs that underpinned the museum's unique character was not easily adaptable. This is because the museum was a personal reflection of its founders, their unique circle of mentors and particular relationship with the art of their time – the collecting and display of it – and the manner and reasons in making it publicly accessible. The exuberant nature of the twenty-first-century private museum model has deviated greatly from the understated nature of the Menil Collection. The grandiose scale of many of these initiatives is making it difficult for the public to distinguish between private and public institutions. This is evidenced by the examination of The Broad in Chapter 9.

John and Dominique de Menil

John (1904–1973) and Dominique de Menil (1908–1997) moved to the United States in 1941 and were granted American citizenship in 1962. Dominique de Menil and their three young children fled the family's apartment in Paris, before the German army occupied the city. She made her way through Europe while John de Menil was working with the Resistance in Rumania destroying Schlumberger oil drilling equipment to ensure it did not fall into the hands of the Third Reich.[4] The company was one of the world's biggest drilling technological corporations and was developed and patented by Dominique de Menil's father Conrad Schlumberger and uncle Marcel Schlumberger. The family was reunited in New York making their way to Houston where the Schlumberger corporation had set up an office in 1935.[5]

On their many travels to New York, the de Menils befriended and associated with other émigré intellectuals that also found themselves in

Figure 8.1 Photograph showing table of African sculptures on north side of living room, in front of courtyard. Photo: Marc Riboud. © The Menil Archives.

Figure 8.2 Menil Collection, Arts of the Pacific Islands Gallery, Houston. View of the internal tropical courtyards. © Menil Collection.

America during the war years and with whom they shared an appreciation of the development of a 'Catholic avant-garde' where religion and contemporary culture could coexist. The devastating war years challenged individual concerns with modern life and triggered a shift towards a more relevant faith that would offer greater consideration of contemporary world events. They looked to modern art as it addressed the many concerns held by contemporary society at the time.[6] This is evidenced by the de Menils' endeavours to transform the conservative and racially segregated Houston into an open and cosmopolitan city through the promotion of modern art and architecture.[7]

In order to understand the de Menils' distinct vision it is important to recognise that they often differed from many of their wealthy and more conventional Houstonian contemporaries. This can be seen in their overt gesture in both the positioning and design of their home that faced the service road rather than the picturesque view of River Oaks. Philip Johnson's understated design signalled the de Menils' disapproval of ostentatious structures favoured by other wealthy Houstonians. Similarly, the offer of Barnett Newman's 'Broken Obelisk' (1963–1967), as a partial gift to the City of Houston in 1969, was rejected because it was dedicated to Dr Martin Luther King. Upon the city's refusal the de Menils bought the work for themselves and installed it at the Rothko Chapel.

Figure 8.3 Exterior view of the de Menil private residence in River Oaks, Houston. © Menil Collection.

The de Menils' belief that they could make an important contribution to Houston's long-term cultural and civic development was determined soon after their arrival and thus their public commitment was established long before the construction of the museum itself.[8] Their actions included the funding and commissioning of not only the Menil Collection (1987), but also the ecumenical Rothko Chapel (dedicated in 1971), Cy Twombly Gallery (1995), Byzantine Fresco Chapel (1997–2012) and Dan Flavin Installation in the former grocery store at Richmond Hall (1998). Other less publicly visible achievements include the championing of international conferences, research and various publications, the commissioning of scholars to compile comprehensive *raisonnés* of René Magritte's and Max Ernst's art as well as funding the purchase of several works for public museums.[9] They established a comprehensive teaching collection that was made available to students and scholars at the neighbouring St. Thomas and Rice Universities, founded the Art Department and the Media Centre at the University of St. Thomas and the Institute for the Arts and Rice Media Centre at Rice University.[10] The de Menils organised various scholarly and curatorial programmes and sponsored several professorial positions at both universities, at the Contemporary Arts Association (CAA) in Houston (Jermayne MacAgy's directorship from 1955 to 1964) and the Museum of Fine Arts, Houston (MFAH) (James Johnson Sweeney's directorship from 1961 to 1967). Due to the scope of the de Menils' accomplishments this chapter will focus exclusively on the formation of the Menil Collection.

De Menils the experimentalists, the collectors and their exhibitions

Patronage of the arts, throughout much of the US has traditionally been the domain of the wealthy, both as a civic obligation and form of prestige – Houston was no exception. A little over 100 years old, Houston in the 1940s had a population of 385,000. The city's fortunes at the time were made in agriculture and industry. The war, the growing demand on petroleum and air conditioning coincided with the development of the petroleum and oil industry in Houston. At the helm of Schlumberger's international operations, John de Menil played a pivotal role amongst the city's industrial leaders. As Houston allowed the de Menils to see through their many unconventional endeavours and collaborations, they applied themselves, their time and financial resources in the hope that exposing local audiences to modern art and architecture, and to an alternative point of view, might help to overcome discontent with modernism and notions of the new.[11]

Founding director of the Menil Collection Walter Hopps, notes that the war years in America differed greatly from the situation in Europe; artists, architects, composers, intellectuals and art dealers banished from Europe ultimately inspired and influenced America's cultural development by exposing them to the cutting edge of European art and culture, that they may not have otherwise known. Thus art and life in America continued uninterrupted during the war years, and as Hopps suggests, it even flourished.[12] The de Menils felt that art was for all to appreciate and for this reason wanted to share their art collection with the public: they believed that art brings people together and connects 'individuals to a collective human past and provides a deeply personal experience with the sublime in the present day'.[13] Recognising that artistic and spiritual connections existed between contemporary art practice, prehistoric, 'primitive' and indigenous cultures, the de Menils compiled, lived and surrounded themselves with their disparate holdings that included Byzantine, Antiquities, modern and contemporary American and European art works through to objects from Africa, the Pacific Islands and the Pacific Northwest.[14]

Although the Menil Collection was a culmination of its founders' life work as cultural ambassadors and art patrons, the contribution of key intellectuals, artists, art dealers, architects, museum directors and curators they associated with and were influenced by, cannot be ignored. Their sphere of influence was broad – guiding the de Menils' collecting philosophy, steering them towards specific artists that they inevitably collected and supported, and exposing them to contemporary art practice and the presentation of it. This informed a distinct visual aesthetic that is often referred to as a different way of 'seeing' and arranging works of art from different cultures and periods. This particular perspective was informed by the French writer, poet, collector and founder of Surrealism André Breton (1896–1966). Breton and his followers exercised an unorthodox curiosity with surreal images, sculptures, fetish, ethnographic, scientific and everyday objects. The de Menils' mentors – Father Marie-Alain Courturier, Alexandre Iolas and Jermayne MacAgy – were greatly influenced by the philosophical and artistic practices of the Surrealists. MacAgy's exhibitions repositioned the viewing of modern art through the unconventional presentation of it alongside non-Western art and non-art objects. As I shall outline, MacAgy's pioneering practice helped to define Dominique de Menil's distinct curatorial approach.

In their quest to bring high culture to Houston, the de Menils continued to push the city's potential by challenging the status quo. Their friendship with the French émigré Dominican priest Father Marie-Alain Courturier (1897–1954) exerted tremendous influence over the de Menils' collecting and patronage style and served as their mentor. He advocated that the Catholic Church should commission only the finest artists, regardless of their faith. He believed genius was far more important than faith alone: that is, a work by a lesser artist who was Catholic was not preferable as it merely promoted mediocrity. Father Courturier's appreciation and respect for outstanding artistic talent and quality was shared by the de Menils.[15] As Walter Hopps put it, 'His ideas and convictions were catalytic for the de Menils'; introducing them to various New York gallerists and educating them of the virtues of modern art, they went on to purchase their first works by Paul Cézanne, Georges Braque, Fernand Léger, Joan Miró and Henri Matisse.[16]

The New York gallery owner and collector Alexandre Iolas (1907–1987), also influenced the de Menil's cultural development, distinct patronage style and engagement with art.[17] Iolas advised and persuaded the de Menils to collect modern art and steered them towards the Surrealists – whom they showed little interest in initially. The de Menils' went on to purchase works by René Magritte, Victor Brauner, Giorgio de Chirico, Marcel Duchamp, Max Ernst, Joan Miró, Yves Tanguy, Man Ray and others.[18] Hopps points out that Iolas believed 'art embodied the magical and enigmatic' and with this in mind he went about promoting the works by the Surrealists and other emerging contemporary artists to the de Menils during the 1940s.[19] They trusted his judgement and learnt a great deal from him. As Dominique de Menil recalls:

> At first, I resisted Surrealism; it was such a strange world. I felt outside of it. But Iolas kept showing us great works. He was so convincing; he was himself so convinced of the importance of what he was showing. I remember my skepticism in front of our de Chirico, 'Hector and Andromache'. I was not taken in; I bought it on his word, on faith . . .[20]

Despite de Menil's initial reluctance to embrace Surrealism the Menil Collection's structure is built around it. They collected many of the artists's works in depth – Ernst, Magritte and Brauner – along with various

Surrealists manifestos published by Breton and others. Thus, it has been argued that the de Menils sympathised with the anxiety expressed by the Surrealist artists: challenging the dichotomy between the old and the new, the tangible and the mystical and the everyday and the spiritual.[21]

The third person who was to influence the de Menils' involvement with art and their presentation of it was the curator and museum director Jermayne MacAgy (1914–1964). MacAgy was Museum Curator and Acting Director of the California Palace of the Legion of Honor, San Francisco, for 14 years (1941–1955). Her unorthodox exhibition installations and designs ultimately formed the basis of Dominique de Menil's aesthetic sensibility and that of the Menil Collection. I will examine McAgy's curatorial practice and influence over de Menil in the following section of this chapter. I will outline how MacAgy subverted established museological and art historical hierarchies by positioning non-art objects, that she perceived to be of high quality and creativity, within a museum context.

Through her unorthodox and dramatic arrangement of disparate objects MacAgy challenged public perception of what was understood to be high and low art. She dared to overturn longstanding nineteenth-century European modes of presentation that continued to dominate museological practice as she perceived them to be staid and 'backward'.[22] MacAgy articulated her installation philosophy thus:

> Each kind of collection of objects . . . has been tenderly manoeuvred . . .
> To create an aura, an atmosphere, belonging personally to the objects,
> rather than merely building an edifice against which the objects look
> well, in the purpose of the museum's installation plans.[23]

Her philosophical perspectives were consistent with those of Father Couturier and Iolas who expressed a similar desire to leverage art's exceptional qualities through considered and ambient arrangements. As Hopps points out:

> She [MacAgy] had an innate sense of visual theatre, and with resourceful
> alchemy mounted exhibitions of exceptional appeal and invention.
> She pioneered thematic exhibitions, mingling periods, cultures and
> genres. Her brilliant installations combined enchantment and erudition,
> drawing from the de Menils' diverse collections.[24]

Jermayne MacAgy – a new way of seeing

Jermayne MacAgy's exhibitions were thematic and placed little or no emphasis on didacticism or art historical narratives. She created distinct juxtapositions of works and objects 'provoking a visceral response that would exceed, and perhaps subvert, intellectual readings'.[25] As de Menil asserts: 'Jermayne MacAgy was a master at seduction. She could cast a spell on practically anything. If she decided an object should be raised to the dignity of an art object, an art object it became'.[26] It was as guest curator at the opening of the Cullinan Hall at the Museum Fine Arts Houston, that MacAgy drew much attention. The new wing was designed by architect Mies van der Rohe and funded by the benefactor Nina Cullinan.[27] MacAgy's exhibition 'Totems Not Taboo' (26 February–29 March 1959), not only challenged the notion of high art and appropriate museum exhibits, but also attracted the interest of the Museum of Modern Art in New York.[28] The largely tribal art exhibition attracted around 35,570 visitors.[29]

MacAgy arranged over 200 exhibits that were presented on numerous white pedestals with objects and carved statues precariously placed upon them. They were arranged along the temporary staircases and platform that she constructed on either side of the exhibits. Once on the platform viewers were intimately positioned at eye level with the many statues that were placed on tall pedestals, thereby creating a carefully orchestrated relationship that was both confronting and engaging. Descending the stairs, one could see that the objects were placed in all manner of ways: some were displayed directly on the white gravel along with the densely arranged

Figure 8.4 Menil Collection, Arts of Africa Gallery, Houston. View of the internal tropical courtyards. © Menil Collection.

tropical plants, others on the green polished Venetian terrazzo floor or on a row of high pedestals along the perimeter of Mies van der Rohe's floor to ceiling windows. MacAgy's use of potted tropical plants soon became her trademark and would later become Dominique de Menil's. The exotic internal courtyard positioned within the African, Pacific Islands and Pacific Northwest art galleries at the Menil Collection draws on this concept amongst others.

Although MacAgy was intent on creating an ambient environment around the many exhibits and works of art, she did so without compromising their integrity. In the foreword of *The Menil Collection: A selection from the Palaeolithic to the Modern Era* (1987) de Menil reinforces MacAgy's emphasis on visual aesthetics: '. . . the natural longing for enchantment is discouraged in our culture. And what is art if it does not enchant? Art is incantation . . . It is the fusion of the tangible and intangible . . .'[30] Art historian Pamela Smart, argues that not unlike MacAgy, de Menil sought to educate the public of the beauty of art by creating an environment 'in which visitors would engage with artworks, not as mere admirers, nor as passive consumers of high culture, but as interlocutors actively participating with the artwork' in what de Menil referred to as 'a process of "mutual interrogation"'[31] I would also add that MacAgy's implementation of an interior design approach to exhibition making, was a powerful and evocative medium in creating an all-consuming engagement with works of art and one that de Menil adopted.

Figure 8.5 Installation photograph of 'Other Voices: An exhibition of Artefacts of Religious and Supernatural Beliefs of Other Cultures', 25 October–16 December 1962, University of Saint Thomas, Houston. Photo: Maurice Miller. © The Menil Archives.

Considering a museum

> A museum should be a place where we lose our head.
>
> Father Marie-Alain Couturier

> Alas, we rarely lose our head in a museum. Great museums are overloaded with masterpieces, each fighting for attention, and we are bombarded with information that distracts from contemplation and remains foreign to the magic of great painting. The truth is also that we are not prepared to lose our head. We have been trained not to, trained by emphasis on analysis, on virtuosity, on 'accomplishments'.
>
> Dominique de Menil[32]

As early as the 1970s the de Menils looked to find a suitable solution to permanently store and display their vast art collection of paintings, sculptures, antiquities, Byzantine and Medieval art, prints, non-Western art, photographs and rare books that were scattered across various sites.[33] The de Menils considered creating a 'gallery with open storage' in 1972 and started to discuss their ideas with renowned architect Louis Kahn (1901–1974).[34] John de Menil's premature death to cancer in 1973 disrupted their plans. Although Dominique de Menil hoped to see through the project her ideas had changed as she feared the initial concept was too formal, advising Kahn accordingly: 'this project needs to be conceived of as a park, quite compact, with no monumentality . . .'.[35] Kahn's own untimely death, only months after John de Menil's, put a stop to the project with de Menil taking up the challenge nearly a decade later.[36] She was determined to find a way to maintain their collection intact.

The Menil Foundation was formed in 1954, as a not-for-profit charitable organisation to oversee the de Menils' large holdings and the Menil Collection. A board of directors was appointed to preside over the Foundation's assets and projects. The Schlumberger corporation provided for the Foundation – with de Menil serving as president. Its charter, as expressed by Dominique de Menil in 1976, was to support new creative and bold ventures that sat outside conventional projects. Quality, discernment and independence of mind where key.[37] As the Menil Foundation's holdings functioned essentially as a teaching collection – since 1960 until the opening of the museum – de Menil believed the collection ought to remain in Houston for the promotion of research and the appreciation of art.[38]

The Menil Collection was not intended to be a conventional museum, but rather a storage facility with a small gallery. Storing the de Menils' private collection and that of the Menil Foundation's under one roof, underpinned this concept. It was conceived within two distinct spheres: public and private. The public spaces were illustrated in former Menil Foundation Curator, Kathryn Davidson's own hand-drawn diagrams as a scaled-down version of what would later become the museum. In the original plan the six small galleries – now seven larger spaces – were assigned to the display of African, Prints, Film and Audio and miscellaneous works of art. The galleries fanned out from the main entry lobby and the central larger gallery for modern art. The central interior courtyard linked the public spaces with the 'private' sections which included five large individual areas for storage, administration, offices and filing areas, curatorial and exhibition workshops, conservation and photographic laboratories, print room, rare book and library.[39] The concept of establishing distinct private and public spaces developed into two complimentary areas – display and storage. De Menil articulated the housing and display of the collection thus:

> Works of art will be shown in small, intimate surroundings. Simple, frequently changing, imaginative displays of works in the collection should continually intrigue and entice the public to come see and come back again. This will provide a complimentary alternative to the traditional museums' large areas of permanent display.

Many museums store works of art not on exhibit in a manner which makes them completely inaccessible: in basements, in crates, in areas with no provisions for supervision or viewing. All works in the proposed museum would be stored in a manner making them accessible, even when not formally 'on exhibit'.[40]

Davidson's diagrams articulated de Menil's vision for the proposed museum's layout and aesthetic philosophy and can be seen in several aspects of the Renzo Piano designed building. The notion of the interior court evolved into two distinct spaces incorporated within the large African, Pacific Islands and Pacific Northwest galleries – one along the perimeter of the building and one positioned between the two galleries. Likewise, the small intimate spaces evolved within the seven large galleries permanently partitioned into smaller spaces to create the intimate viewing environment of a house museum collection. This is not unlike the many modest scale rooms within the Menil house that surprisingly unfold beyond the large public spaces. As expressed by de Menil: 'One gets with art in intimate contact not big spaces . . . few objects . . . treasures . . . small rooms'.[41]

In preparation of the museum de Menil chartered a private jet to undertake an exploration trip from 28 June to 3 July 1976. Accompanied by Phillipa de Menil, Houstonian architect Howard Barnstone, Menil adviser Harris Rosenstein and Mary Jane Victor, they examined great number of small-to-medium size museum designs: Pittsburgh (Carnegie Institute); Cleveland, Toledo, Detroit (Tannerhill Collection); Milwaukee, Des Moines Art Centre, Minneapolis (Walker Art Centre); Kansas City (Museum of Fine Arts and Williams Rockhill Nelson Gallery); Denver (Denver Art Museum); Seattle (Burke Museum, University of Washington); San Francisco (Museum of Modern Art; de Young Museum and Asian Museum); Berkeley University Art Museum; Oakland Museum and Los Angeles (LACMA and J.P. Getty

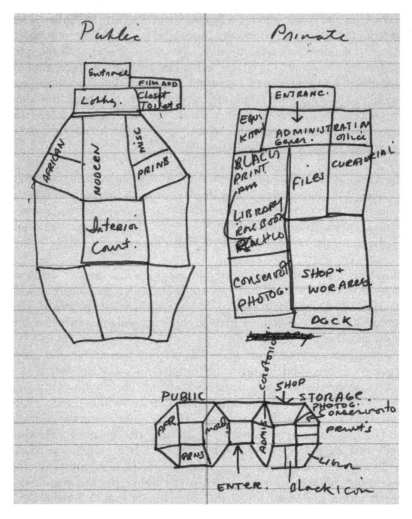

Figure 8.6 Excerpt from the notes of Kathryn Davidson. © The Menil Archives.

Museum).[42] Each institution was evaluated in much detail as was the overall visitor experience, thereby, forming the basis of de Menil's own research and the type of museum she sought to create. Louis Kahn's Kimbell Art Museum in Fort Worth, Texas (1972) was closely considered. Kahn's complementary relationship between the museum's internal and external spaces and masterly use of natural light was of much interest to de Menil. A 1977 draft document served to publicly express de Menil's decision to upgrade the storage gallery into a permanent museum that allowed equal focus on storage and workshop spaces. Many of the records from her trip provide an accurate insight into de Menil's preference for understated architectural

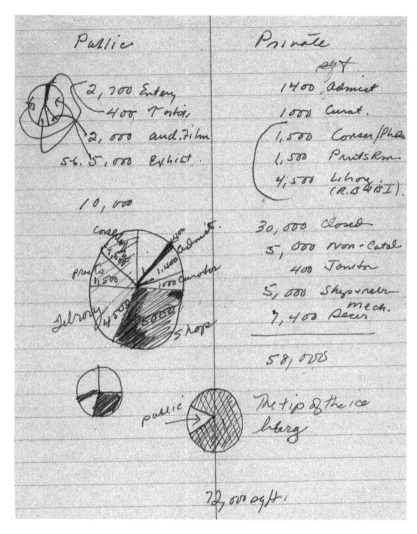

Figure 8.7 Excerpt from the notes of Kathryn Davidson. © The Menil Archives.

designs rather than the boldness adopted by many American museums and their uniform approach to display and design.

De Menil wanted to create a space for scholarly pursuits and a relaxing environment for the contemplation and appreciation of art – a space of 'enchantment' rather than one that was predictable and 'boring'. She was deeply concerned with museum fatigue and sought to avoid it in her own museum – exhaustive displays and repetitive installations did little to stir the imagination of viewers and were thus perceived to be dull. Seeking to recreate the museum as a space that would counter such perceptions of

Figure 8.8 Photograph of Dominque de Menil, seated in New York home. Photographer: Marc Riboud. © The Menil Archives.

boredom and detachment, required an aesthetic that the Menil Collection would address and make it its trademark.[43] The de Menil house informed such intentions to recreate the intimacy between the viewer and works of art that de Menil experienced in her own home. The understated simplicity of the museum's interior design, and the considered visual aesthetic and distinct mode of presentation is unmistakably linked to de Menil's desire to avert any hint of museum fatigue. This is clearly expressed in de Menil's own words:

> The building should be of an intimate human scale rather than monumental. The visitor's experience should be personal and intriguing. One must be drawn space to space with a feeling of anticipation and excitement. A balanced interplay between exterior and interior spaces must exist, with natural light used as a source of illumination . . . The criteria for a successful plan are inventiveness and beauty. I believe this museum can offer a unique approach to the exhibition of art.[44]

The Menil Collection: 'big inside and small outside'

By 1980, Dominique de Menil met with the emerging Genoa-based architect Renzo Piano. She presented herself as a well-informed client with very clear ideas regarding the display of art and the storage of the collection, and how best to incorporate it in the overall design of the museum.[45] De Menil's instructions to Piano at their inaugural meeting in Paris, were clearly articulated: she wanted a building that was 'big inside and small outside', that is, one devoid of all distractions.[46] She did not want a museum that was monumental in its architectural exterior. In her own words: '. . . I dreamed of preserving some of the intimacy I had enjoyed with the works of art'.[47] This was a quality she wanted to capture and share with the broader public. To allow them to feel like the painting or sculpture they are standing before is theirs, if only momentarily. De Menil insisted on a museum interior that was intimate, serene, aesthetically inspiring and enchanting. The similarity between the public spaces of the house and those seen at the Menil Collection suggests that de Menil may have created a museum version of her ideal house museum – one that captured the subjective aspect of a home without the fussy domestic interiors.

Although it was not intended to be grandiose, the 400-foot-long horizontal museum that comprises of two levels and a basement, is imposing, albeit in an understated manner. Sheathed in grey Cypress planks the museum's skeletal structure was made of solid metal with heavily insulated walls and fireproof materials. The museum's external panelling was painted the same grey colour as the many (forty in total) neighbouring 1920s bungalow-style weatherboard dwellings that were preserved by the de Menils and continue to be owned by the Menil Foundation. The grey timber bungalows with their white trimmed porticos mirrored the museum's grey walls and white steel borders.[48] The original guidelines required the building to be in harmony with the tranquil surroundings of its leafy suburban location of Montrose. While she adhered to the residential stipulations, de Menil vehemently opposed any form of ostentatious architectural design and refused to succumb to it.

De Menil did however want the interior to be awe-inspiring and 'big' in terms of 'spatiality, of light, of luminosity, of transparency' says Piano.[49] The internal largeness was a matter of practicality and necessary to accommodate the Menil Collection's immense holdings. 'What goes on in the museum itself is essentially a ritual – the ritual of art and its contemplation – and preparation for exhibitions' says Piano.[50] Thus, the aspect of creating perfect lighting conditions was of paramount concern. Without it de Menil would be unable to create the peaceful contemplative museum space that was important for her: she sought to devise an environment 'of suspension, for a museum is a place of suspension. You go in, and you have to be able to lose your head' says Piano recalling his patron's own words.[51]

Piano's white I-steel beams that surround and support the 300 thin, curving ferrocement (flexible material of steel and cement) louvres form part of the highly engineered roof that provides much of the light within the museum. The series of curved ferrocement louvres are also visible within the individual galleries and the long corridor that spans the entire length of the museum. They offer a sculptural and individual quality to the otherwise

Figure 8.9 Exterior view of the de Menil Collection, Houston. © Menil Collection.

Figure 8.10 Exterior view of the neighbouring 1920s bungalow-style weatherboard dwellings opposite the Menil Collection, Houston. © Menil Collection.

minimalist white cube space. Achieving optimal natural lighting conditions within the Menil Collection was a critical factor for de Menil.[52] Houston's changeable weather and hot climate made it difficult to manage the lighting throughout the museum and to maintain a stable climate-controlled environment with only overhead lighting. That is why many of the galleries rely on a combination of natural and artificial light.

More often than not, the galleries at the Menil Collection can be experienced without any artificial lighting. The constant changes in the weather, time of the day and year influence not only the amount of light within the museum galleries, but also the way that works are viewed and experienced. The fluctuations in the daylight and the scale of each gallery allows visitors to engage with the works of art in a unique and experiential manner. The character of individual galleries is constantly transformed with such dramatic shifts in daylight. The ambient spaces help to lure visitors into the labyrinth of smaller galleries that provide an element of surprise as they make their way through them.

This unpredictability ensures constant stimulation as the museum tries hard to avoid visual fatigue. It is not through spectacle or theatrics that this is achieved, but through a distinct approach and aesthetic. One is encouraged to make sense of the works autonomously and within the context they are presented. What is more, artificial lighting alone would create a clinical environment that would counter de Menil's subjective exhibition aesthetic. Her determination and passion to build the museum 'her way' – is ultimately the reason it was such a successful project says Piano. As a result, the museum formed its own personality, one that reflected its creator.[53] The compatibility between architect and patron combined with a masterly architectural approach has since set the benchmark in museum lighting and design. The Fondation Beyeler (1997) was one of the first museums to emulate the Menil Collection's design aesthetic. The subtle manner in which Piano embedded the building within Berowerpark in Riehen pays homage to de Menil's desire to situate the museum within a tranquil parkland. Likewise, the layout and dimensions of individual galleries, the merging of internal and external spaces within the museum and Piano's masterly use of natural light are elements that are reminiscent of the Menil Collection.

The de Menil home within the museum

The Menil Collection comprises three discreet levels: Menil archives, storage spaces and receiving docks are situated in the basement; exhibition galleries on the ground level; with curatorial offices and the 'Treasure House' situated on level one. The long spine or 'promenade' runs through the museum on both the ground and first levels. Visitors are led into the seven distinct public galleries: Modern and Contemporary Art, African, Pacific Islands and Pacific Northwest, Byzantine and Antiquities, Surrealism and three temporary exhibition galleries. The Collection's holdings are stored in the

Figure 8.11 View of Renzo Piano's curving ferrocement louvres at the Menil Collection, Houston. © Menil Collection.

basement or on open display within the custom-built rooms and walls in the 'Treasure House'. The Treasure rooms are situated around the perimeter of the building with easy access to natural light should it be required. The visible storage areas (eight in total) have been designed to make works from the collection accessible to scholars, curators and researchers.

The entrance into the Menil Collection is self-effacing and discreet. So much so that the front entrance on Sul Ross Street and the rear staff entrance on Branard Street are identical. They are exactly parallel to one another with only an internal partition wall to separate the two once inside. The lack of distinction between the front and rear entrances demonstrates de Menil's democratic zeal just as the de Menil house faces the service road rather than the picturesque view of River Oaks. The dark stained pine floor boards that have been installed throughout the museum are a result of de Menil's aversion to harsh, cold floor surfaces. It is also a domestic reference and link to the de Menils' private residence where porous black Mexican floor tiles are laid throughout much of the house. De Menil favoured the impermanence of the almost black stained timber because she felt it would serve as a permanent mark of human contact over time:

> It's as if the ghosts of everyone who has been in were still here. It's as if you could sense them, sense their presence. A museum is a bit like a home. It's much prettier when it bears the marks of time.[54]

Such references to the personal are not coincidental. Just as every visitor has left their mark on the museum's floor boards, so too has the founder and creator; not through sentimental or obvious road maps but by way of discreet markers. The internal tropical courtyards running off the African and Pacific Islands and Pacific Northwest galleries, take their lead from the de Menil house.[55] Philip Johnson devised the courtyard so as to allow the interior spaces to merge with the exterior of the house and its surrounding garden. The tropical internal garden serves as an informal backdrop to the eclectic private collection of ethnographic objects and modern art. The disparate objects are casually presented in artistic arrangements amongst furniture, books and personal ornaments. Everything is set out in a considered and economical manner. The streaming of natural light through the internal garden helps to define the ambient space that is key to both house and museum.

De Menil was not alone in devising a direct relationship between the museum's exterior and interior spaces. Philip Johnson's eight-domed circular pavilion at Dumbarton Oaks Research Library and Collection in Washington, DC, was most definitely a source of inspiration. Mildred and Robert Woods Bliss' Pre-Columbian Collection was installed in the new naturally lit pavilion in 1963. Perspex pedestals and displays are arranged in a way that does little to disturb the viewer's vista. The individual pavilions provide an intimate viewing space allowing visitors to move around individual

Figure 8.12 Interior view of the Menil Collection, Houston. © Menil Collection.

Figure 8.13 View of the internal tropical courtyards. Arts of the Pacific Islands Gallery, Menil Collection, Houston. © Menil Collection.

works while maintaining a close connection with the immediate treescape. Johnson's design sought to incorporate the curved glass structure with its immediate landscape – to merge the displays with their surroundings in much the same way as de Menil had hoped to do.

Although Piano was charged with the architectural design of the Menil Collection, many of the museum's key features can be linked to de Menil's research and determination to see through her own ideas. Even though she drew inspiration from existing museum designs and sought the advice of those she respected and trusted, the museum also turns to the de Menil home in River Oaks. Human-scale architectural features and the manner in which spaces simply unfold as one navigates through larger galleries is reminiscent of the way that Johnson incorporated the many rooms within what appears to be a modest minimalist designed home. In addition, the streaming of natural light through the internal tropical garden helps to create the ambient space that is key to both house and museum. Once inside the museum the collection, exhibition and gallery layouts and interior-design aesthetic pay tribute to the de Menils' mentors who opened their eyes to a different way of seeing, experiencing and sharing their collections of art. Even so, it is de Menil's personal aesthetic and aura that is indelibly inscribed into the museum's psyche. Thus, the Menil Collection's 'difficult-to-articulate' quality is the result of de Menil's single-minded quest to create a museum – a place of enchantment – where it is possible for us 'to lose our heads'.[56]

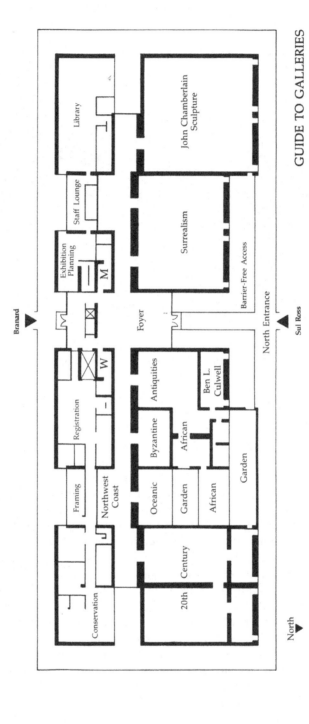

Figure 8.14 Menil Collection, Gallery guide for the opening of the Menil Collection, Houston. © The Menil Archives.

Funding the collector's museum

In examining Dominique de Menil's steps in the creation of the Menil Collection it is necessary to consider the years ahead of the museum's founding and those following her death to appreciate much of what was at stake when the museum began to experience financial and administrative difficulties. I will touch on two factors: the somewhat unconventional manner in which the Menil Collection was founded and to the concerns many private museums face at the death of their creator. Whilst the museum experienced a financial crisis upon its opening in 1987, this was not fully corrected until 1992 – for reasons I shall outline. Moreover, the years between 1999 and 2004 exposed the Menil Collection to a strategic and institutional challenge from its board members and newly appointed director Ned Rifkin. This period of change placed the museum's individuality and the de Menils' legacy most at risk.

To consider the museum's financial trajectory we need to step back momentarily. In 1977, it was proposed that a museum would be built in Houston on the land owned by the Menil Foundation Inc. The land was purchased in the late 1950s. By testamentary arrangement much of the de Menils' private collection was transferred to the Menil Foundation. Although placing a monetary value on the art collection was difficult, in 1977, it was estimated at over $30 million. It was announced that the Foundation would establish an initial endowment of $1.5 million.[57] According to the Menil Collection's 2017 Annual Report (published on 6 August 2018), the museum's investment portfolio consists of $264 million with annual operating expenses placed at $18.5 million. The transfer of $240 million from de Menil's estate to the Foundation at the time of Dominique de Menil's death in 1997, bolstered the value of the endowment; currently it provides the museum with an annual income of around $12.22 million.[58]

The Menil Collection was built largely through the support of the Menil Foundation. However, we cannot ignore the significant contributions from a number of founding benefactors who played a key role in its creation. The Brown Foundation, Inc. (donated $5 million), the Cullen and Hobby Foundations, Houston Endowment Inc. and numerous private contributors,[59] including Mrs Theodore N. Law who played a key role in the funding of the Menil Collection.[60] Despite the museum's unique character it did not deter other individuals from enlisting their financial support, from the beginning and during the museum's difficult years. This continues to date with many temporary exhibitions, public programmes, new acquisitions, capital expenditure and expansion projects continue to be funded through the generosity of private Houstonian foundations and individuals. By June 2017, the *CAMPAIGN for the Menil* raised $117,464,624 (exceeding the goal of $115 million) to fund the new Menil Drawing Institute (opened in 2018) and other key museum initiatives and upgrades of adjoining infrastructure and parklands, while also bolstering their endowment fund. Even though the museum is named in the de Menils' honour, many Houstonians were keen to contribute towards the construction of the museum. This is because the de Menils generously contributed to the funding of a number of new art, cultural, academic and architectural initiatives that were founded in Houston since their arrival.

Founding donor names appear in the stone base of Michael Heizer's 1991 'Charmstone' sculpture outside the museum's entrance. Once inside the Menil Collection the absence of naming rights and bold signage alluding to its benefactors, including the de Menils, is evident. Credits acknowledging bequests and exhibition support are applied economically and discreetly on wall and individual label texts. It is only on the exterior of the museum's glass entrance that 'The Menil Collection' is discreetly inscribed. There are no banners or large signage on the museum's exterior or surrounding area. Whilst the museum continues to expand their support base, it does so in a manner that is understated and uncommercial. De Menil maintained a rigid ethical position that avoided the overt display of benefaction and any signs of money or ego orientated gestures; it is a long held Menil tradition to uphold the museum's moral integrity by not succumbing to personal whims.[61] Even so, the philanthropic support from many individuals and their private foundations cannot go unnoticed, as it is unusual for founders of private collection museums to attract the financial support of their peers within their own lifetime and beyond.

Institutionalising 'the Menil way'

The Menil Collection's concerns with rising operating costs and endowment issues arose from the moment it was decided that the museum was to be built. De Menil undertook a $20 million fund-raising campaign to bolster the museum's endowment fund and offset operating costs. The problem was exacerbated by the dramatic decline in oil prices during the 1980s, disrupting Houston's economic fortunes. As the Menil Collection and Foundation were endowed by Schlumberger's stock, their declining value proved problematic for the museum.[62] The oil crisis hampered efforts to raise the desired funds, hence the Menil Foundation elected to cover the $2.9 million operating costs associated with the museum along with the $1 million acquisition fund.

Two years after the opening of the Menil Collection it began to experience financial difficulties forcing the museum to embark on a $35 million endowment campaign. De Menil contributed $17.5 million towards the endowment, the Brown Foundation a further $5 million, with other foundations and private individuals helping the museum reach its target by 1992. The museum's operating costs, however, increased dramatically during this time: the $3.4 million budget was no longer achievable with annual spending rising to $7.9 million by 1994. The Menil Collection needed to not only extend its financial base, but also restructure if the operating costs were to be reduced to $5.5 million annually. This resulted in the loss of staff and a dampening of moral.[63]

Following de Menil's death, the Menil Foundation managed to avert several attempts by previous board members and directors keen to secure the museum's financial position by institutionalising it and ensuring it conformed to established museum standards and protocol. The implementation of distinct bureaucratic and budgetary departments that are common place at most conventional museums were seen to be contrary to the Menil's original structure. This clashed with the hands-on approach by the de Menil, Walter Hopps and Paul Winkler management team, who ran the museum, its curatorial programmes, exhibition schedule and installations. Their informality was not in keeping with conventional museum practice, hence its appeal. The resignation of Paul Winkler, as director in 1999, saw the Menil Collection enter a critical point.[64] His departure was prompted by the forced resignation of the Foundation's chief financial officer for the last 30 years – Miles Glaser. Winkler's resignation was thus seen as the end of the continuity to de Menil.

The appointment of Ned Rifkin as director in February 2000, cast the museum in further crisis. His entrepreneurial style alienated many long standing Menil employees and prompted their departure as his style was seen to be foreign to the museum and at odds with its character and culture. One could argue that the museum's quirky private character was in tension with the public managerial model of the institutional museum. The restructuring of the museum during Rifkin's directorship saw several new external appointments in his quest to bring the Menil Collection in line with other conventional museums: to increase audience numbers, the endowment and formalise its function. The increased number of temporary exhibitions, at the expense of the permanent collection, and their installation, demonstrated little understanding or affinity with de Menil's curatorial practice. Pamela Smart argues that they no longer resembled Menil Collection exhibitions; the chief curator had no affinity with 'the Menil way' or in preserving the character of the museum through its exhibitions. As she points out, under such conditions, it becomes increasingly difficult to determine exactly what defined 'the Menil way' because it was such an abstract and difficult concept to articulate and implement.[65] I would also add that de Menil's visual display aesthetic was complex and innate; it was not a science that could be explained, but rather felt and seen through a particular lens. Perhaps Jermayne MacAgy's unique exhibition practice informed the Menil's distinct way of seeing and displaying objects?

Rifkin's dramatic changes were unsuccessful and thus resigned his post in the second year of his five year contract. Two interim directors – before and after Rifkin – did little to stabilise the museum. As we have seen, to institutionalise a museum that was created as a reaction to the conventional museum model would contravene its original mandate. The appointment of

Figure 8.15   Photograph of Dominique de Menil, seated in entrance hall of the Menil
Collection, 1987. Photo: Adelaide de Menil. © The Menil Archives.

Dr Josef Helfenstein as director in January 2004, has seen a more consulta-
tive, scholarly and curatorial focus than that under Rifkin.[66] Smart describes
him as a scholar rather than a 'museum person' who is intent on promoting
institution change and audience reach at the expense of establishing an
environment that is conducive to more meaningful engagement between
audiences and the collection itself.[67] She notes that Helfenstein recognised,
'that the distinctive project of the Menil Collection (if it is to be maintained)
will always be in tension with the standards and accountabilities of any
business model, and with the conventional model of the museum'.[68] Thus if
much progress is to be made, despite such tensions, Smart argues that they
must ultimately be tackled around the question of 'what Dominique would
have done'.[69] Helfenstein's direction at the Menil Collection remained stable
and true to its original founder's vision, curatorial and public foresight while
developing audience engagement and ongoing support. During his 12-year
tenure, Helfenstein doubled the attendance numbers, increased the value of
the museum's endowment by nearly 50 per cent and oversaw the acquisition
of around 1,000 new works of art.

Even though de Menil exercised vigorous control over the museum,
within her own lifetime, she did not apply strict conditions to the final deed
of gift as the museum was never intended to be a personal memorial for her
and John de Menil. The communication between John de Menil and their
daughter Philippa, in 1970, eloquently expressed such intentions:

I'm glad you leave flexibility – it's not a tomb but a reincarnation. I would dislike being on the board of something which acts like an undertaker carrying out minutely the last wishes of you and mother. He replied: You're right . . . not sclerosis but continuity.[70]

In their book entitled *Art and Activism: Projects of John and Dominique de Menil*, Josef Helfenstein and Laureen Schipsi suggest that Dominique de Menil's belief in the ability of others to see through their unique vision and commitment to the connection between art and activism meant that they did not impose strict guidelines to their benefaction; 'rather they viewed their collections, projects and foundations as living and organic, elastic enough to adapt to changing circumstances'.[71]

The Menil Collection's original character remains intact despite the formalisation of the museum's administrative structure and previous unsuccessful attempts to institutionalise and commercialise the museum at the passing of its charismatic founder. As Peter Marzio, the longtime former director of Museum Fine Arts Houston (1982–2010) noted:

Anytime you go through the death of a founder, it's not easy. Without Mrs de Menil's presence, and her vision and her energy and compassion that she always conveyed, it would just be another place. Now the institution has to stand on its own, without that kind of magician.[72]

Conclusion

Dominique de Menil had the foresight to create the Menil Collection in a way that engaged local support and interest. For decades the de Menils, along with many of their contemporaries, generously invested their time and funds with the hope of transforming the city of Houston and cultivating Houstonians' appreciation for modern art and architecture. In return, key individuals and private foundations reciprocated by financially supporting the creation of the Menil Collection. The de Menils' ultimate aim was to share their passion and make quality art available to all that were interested through education and open access. They sought to erode the social and racial barriers that existed by making their art collections publicly accessible as a teaching library and through the many captivating exhibitions they sponsored and curated. Dominique de Menil's collaborative approach has served the museum well in the years following her death with private foundations and individuals continuing to financially support the Menil Collection, its development and innovative projects.

We have seen that private museums benefit from a distinct character and curatorial approach, why else must they exist if they do not set themselves apart from public institutions and the existing cultural landscape? Dominique de Menil not only questioned established museum practices she sought to redefine them through the Menil Collection's unique museum style. She wanted to make a stand against the dominance of the monumental museum and the repetitive installations within starkly lit galleries.[73] One only wonders how de Menil would view Eli Broad's enormous museum and galleries where there is little room for intimacy and seduction.[74]

Notes

1 Dominique de Menil, Letter of Invitation, Draft Dated 26 February 1980, Architectural Competition, Menil Archives, The Menil Collection, Houston.
2 The Menil house is not open to the public. It serves as a research tool for curators, researchers and scholars.
3 Sammlung Goetz, Munich (1993); Beyeler Foundation, Basel (1997); Rosengart Museum, Lucerne (2002); Tarra Warra Museum of Art, Victoria (2003); Langen Foundation, Neuss (2004); and BCAM @ LACMA, Los Angeles (2008). Earlier European examples may have influenced the de Menils' own museum – Museum Folkwang, Essen (1922); Kröller-Müller Museum, Otterlo (1938); Louisiana Museum of Modern Art, Denmark (1958) and the Marguerite & Aimé Maeght Foundation outside Nice (1964).
4 Browning, Dominique, 'What I Admire I Must Possess', *Texas Monthly*, April 1983, n.p.
5 John de Menil was in charge of Schlumberger's South America, Middle East and East Asia operations joining the company in 1936 upon the death of Conrad Schlumberger. Browning, 1983, n.p.
6 Smart, Pamela G., *Sacred Modern: Faith, Activism, and Aesthetics in the Menil Collection*, Austin, University of Texas Press, 2010, pp.22–25.
7 The house made a strong political and social gesture in both the positioning and design; it signalled their disapproval of ostentatious structures favoured by other wealthy Houstonians.
8 Their holdings were publicly accessible as a teaching collection to students at both St. Thomas and Rice Universities from the 1950s to 1972.
9 Works by Picasso, Calder, Miró, Léger, Mondrian, Braque and an entire Tinguely exhibition were purchased for the Museum of Fine Arts Houston (MFAH). John de Menil was a board member at MFAH during the late 1950s and early 1960s. Smart, 2010, pp.56–57.
10 Constructed buildings to accommodate their initiatives and offered scholarships – privately and through their foundation. Helfenstein, Josef and Schipsi, Laureen (ed.), *Art and Activism: Projects of John and Dominique De Menil*, Houston, Menil Foundation, 2010, p.12.
11 Smart, 2010, p.22.
12 Hopps, Walter, Comments by Walter Hopps, Building Project and Opening, Menil Archives, The Menil Collection, Houston.
13 Helfenstein and Schipsi (ed.), 2010, p.12.
14 Nelson A. Rockefeller began collecting 'Primitive' art as early as 1930, helping to found the Museum of Primitive Art in New York in 1956.
15 Smart, 2010, pp.33–34.
16 Hopps, 1987, pp.2, 11.
17 Father Courturier maintained that modern art and architecture played an integral role in the repositioning of faith and spirituality within contemporary life.

He believed the Catholic Church was failing contemporary society's spiritual requirements as it was not addressing their concerns. Smart, 2010, pp.26–27.

18 Over time they purchased 100 works by Ernst, 54 by Magritte and Brauner; acquiring a total of 300 works. Smart, 2010, pp.75–77.

19 Hopps, 1987, p.11.

20 Dominique de Menil, The Menil Collection: Comments by Walter Hopps, Press Release, June 1987, p.2, Menil Archives, The Menil Collection, Houston.

21 James Clifford paraphrased. Smart, 2010, p.76.

22 Goldsmith, Meredith, 'Pleasures and Problems in Jermayne Macagy's Eclectic Exhibitions', *The Task of the Curator Conference, University of California*, Santa Cruz, 2010, pp.2–3.

23 MacAgy, Jermayne, 'On Installation', California Palace of the Legion of Honor, *Bulletin* 11 nos. 1–2 (May–June 1953) as quoted in Jermayne MacAgy, 'A Life Illustrated by an Exhibition', University of St. Thomas (1953), p.21.

24 Hopps, Walter, The Menil Collection: Comments by Walter Hopps, Press Release, June 1987, p.3, Menil Archives, The Menil Collection, Houston.

25 Dominique de Menil. Smart, 2010, p.63.

26 Dominique de Menil. Smart, 2010, p.51.

27 When MacAgy's contract at the CAA was not renewed in 1959, the de Menils continued to sponsor her exhibition projects. They underwrote her salary when they created a position for her as the chair of art history at the University of St. Thomas. Smart, 2010, pp.59–61.

28 The exhibition draws on the 1946 exhibition of Oceanic art, *Arts of the South Seas*, at MoMA. Museum of Modern Art, 'The Museum of Modern Art "Arts of the South Seas Opens at Museum of Modern Art", Press Release', New York, The Museum of Modern Art, 1946, pp.1–3; Smart, 2010, pp.52–53.

29 In 1954, the exhibition *Primitive Sculpture from the Collection of Nelson A. Rockefeller* was held at Century Association, New York; *Ancient Arts of the Andes*, held at MoMA; other exhibitions followed at the Museum of Primitive Arts from 1958–1969. The museum's collection and library were transferred to the Metropolitan Museum of Art by Rockefeller in 1969. The Metropolitan Museum of Art, 'The Nelson A, Rockefeller Vision', in *Pursuit of the Best in the Arts of Africa, Oceania, and the Americas*, 8 October, 2013–5 October, 2014, Press Release, New York, The Metropolitan Museum of Art, 2014, pp.1–6; Goldsmith, Meredith, 'Pleasures and Problems in Jermayne Macagy's Eclectic Exhibitions', in *The Task of the Curator Conference, University of California*, Santa Cruz, 2010, p.8.

30 Dominique de Menil, The Menil Collection: Comments by Walter Hopps, Press Release, June 1987, p.8, Menil Archives, The Menil Collection, Houston.

31 Smart, 2010, p.63.

32 Father Marie-Alain Couturier and Dominique de Menil, Dominique de Menil: Comments on the Menil Collection and Museum, Press Release, June 1987, p.2, Menil Archives, The Menil Collection, Houston.

33 The collection stands around 17,000 objects and continues to grow.

34 The de Menils pledged $2 million towards a Louis Kahn designed Gallery at Rice University. When the plans for Rice University's Sewall Gallery fell through they shifted their focus to establishing their own storage gallery. The University decided not to proceed with the project as it would have meant handing over greater autonomy to the de Menils, thus contravening their organisational structure. Smart, 2010, pp.107–108.

35 Dominique de Menil, Smart, 2010, p.110.
36 Louis Kahn died 17 March 1974, only nine months after John de Menil (1 June 1973). Louis Kahn left behind only preliminary sketches, however Dominique de Menil did not pursue the project. The City of Houston offered de Menil land so that she could build a museum – their offer was declined. Browning, 1983, n.p.
37 Dominique de Menil. Smart, 2010, pp.87–88.
38 Dominique de Menil, Curatorial Museum storage records: Dominique de Menil's notes, 1975–1977, Menil Archives, The Menil Collection, Houston.
39 Kathryn Davidson's handwritten diagrams of the storage space dated 15 October 1976. Articles for Menil Foundation storage space museum, 1976–77, Menil Archives, The Menil Collection, Houston.
40 Notes by Dominique de Menil, Draft Dated 30 March 1977, with a Second Draft Proposal Compiled 4 December 1980, Menil Archives, The Menil Collection.
41 Dominique de Menil's Typed Notes Dated 14 November 1979, Curatorial Museum storage records: Museum overall purpose, Menil Archives, The Menil Collection, Houston.
42 Curatorial Museum Storage Records: Exploration Trip for Study Storage 28 June–3 July 1976. Dominique de Menil typed up notes from her itinerary, Menil Archives, The Menil Collection, Houston.
43 Smart, 2010, p.143.
44 Dominique de Menil, Letter of Invitation, Draft Dated 26 February 1980, Architectural Competition, Menil Archives, The Menil Collection, Houston. The museum is 100,000-square-foot in size.
45 Dominique de Menil, Letter of Invitation, Draft Dated 26 February 1980, Architectural Competition, Menil Archives, The Menil Collection, Houston.
46 The de Menil commission was Piano's American debut following the 1977 opening of the Pompidou Centre in Paris, France. Dominique de Menil. Piano, Renzo, 'The Menil Collection', in *The Menil Collection: Renzo Piano*, edited by Lia Piano, Milan, Fondazione Renzo Piano, 2007, n.p.
47 Dominique de Menil, Dominique de Menil Comments on the Menil Collection and Museum, Press Releases, Menil Archives, The Menil Collection, Houston.
48 The bungalows supplement the museum's income; they are rented out to not-for-profit organisations and tenants seeking middle income residential housing. The de Menils purchased them to prevent future development in the area that may irrevocably compromise their cultural plans. The Menil Bistro is being constructed alongside the bookshop. The new structure is sympathetic to the design of the 1920s bungalows in appearance and height.
49 To achieve this Piano created a series of surfaces and depth of space that gives the impression that there were additional spaces as you moved through the museum. Piano, 2007, n.p.
50 Renzo Piano. Piano, 2007, n.p.
51 Renzo Piano paraphrasing Dominique de Menil. Piano, 2007, n.p.
52 On 25 November 1980, de Menil and Piano visited the Kibbutz of Ein Harod in Israel, to view the natural lighting system, at the suggestion of Pontus Hulton. Milestone Dates for Design and Construction, Correspondence, Menil Archives, The Menil Collection, Houston. Daylight readings were also obtained from various museums – 9.30 am, 2 pm and 4 pm – to better understand the impact of the changing light within the museum galleries. Museums including the National Gallery, Washington, DC, Kimbell Art Museum, Fort Worth, San Francisco

Museum of Modern Art, Walker Art Gallery, Minneapolis, Meter Galleries and Metropolitan Museum of Art, New York, and Tate Art Gallery, London. The Building Project: Art Storage, Houston, Texas, 1982, Menil Archives, The Menil Collection, Houston.

53 Piano, 2007, n.p.

54 Dominique de Menil. Piano, 2007, n.p.

55 The de Menils lived in Venezuela for three years and adopted the concept from the home they lived in while there. In conversation with Susan Sutton, former Assistant Curator at the Menil Collection and the author, 18 August 2014.

56 Father Couturier and Dominique de Menil. Hopps, 1987, p.8.

57 Notes by Dominique de Menil, Draft Dated 30 March 1977 with a Second Draft Proposal Compiled 4 December 1980, Curatorial Museum storage records, Menil Archives, The Menil Collection, Houston.

58 Breakup of total annual income: Fundraising 25 per cent, Endowment 64 per cent, Real Estate 9 per cent and Program Revenue 2 per cent. Menil Foundation, 2017 Annual Report: The Menil Collection, Houston, *The Menil Collection*, 2017, pp.70–71.

59 Top 7 benefactors (listed in order): Brown and Cullen Foundations, Mrs. Theodore N. Law, Hobby Foundation, Houston Endowment, Sanford E. McCormick, Balene C. McCormick. The list includes a further 49 foundations, trust funds and a large number of private individuals. The Menil Collection Dedication Booklet, The Building Project: Opening Brochures, Menil Archives, The Menil Collection, Houston.

60 Caroline Weiss Law bequeathed $135 million to the Museum of Fine Arts Houston (MFAH), the University of Texas MD Anderson Cancer Centre and the Baylor College of Medicine upon her death in 2003. She also contributed to the construction of the Rothko Chapel. Her bestowal included paintings to the MFAH valued between $60 and $85 million along with a $25 million endowment. *News, Digest Philanthropy*, 'Oil Heiress Leaves $135 Million to Houston Museum, Hospitals', 17 February 2004.

61 Smart, 2010, pp.141, 245.

62 Value of the shares declined from $87 in 1980–1981 to $38.25 by the late 1980s. Smart, 2010, pp.200–201.

63 Smart, 2010, p.201.

64 Winkler held the position of director at the Museum of International Folk Art in Sante Fe. He joined the Menil Collection in 1980 as associate director and oversaw the planning and construction of the museum. Appointed director from 1991 until his resignation. Smart, 2010, p.99.

65 Smart, 2010, pp.186–191.

66 Previously the director of the Krannert Art Museum, University of Illinois. He spent 17 years at the Kunstmuseum in Bern as chief curator of prints and drawings, and as associate director of the Paul Klee Foundation's nine-volume catalogue raisonné project. In June 2015, he took up the directorship at the Kunstmuseum, Basel.

67 Smart, 2010, p.192.

68 Smart, 2010, p.193.

69 Smart, 2010, p.193.

70 John and Philippa de Menil, 10 August 1970, Menil Archives, The Menil Collection, Houston.

71 Helfenstein and Schipsi (ed.), 2010, p.11.
72 Peter Marzio. Adams, Lorraine, 'Frame and Fortune', *Washington City Paper*, 11 October 2002, www.washingtoncitypaper.com/articles/24747/frame-and-fortune (accessed 3 September 2014).
73 Dominique de Menil's Notes Handwritten by K. Davidson, Dated 15 October 1976, Curatorial Museum storage records, Menil Archives, The Menil Collection, Houston.
74 Phrases such as 'Monumental architecture: fascist; Mussolini architecture – Statues Symbol; Grandiose. . .' were used by de Menil to describe museums she visited ahead of the Menil Collection's construction. Dominique de Menil, Curatorial Museum Storage Records: Exploration Trip for Study Storage, 28 June–3 July 1976, Menil Archives, The Menil Collection, Houston.

9 The new museum and its creator's grand plan

The Broad, Los Angeles, USA (2015)

The Menil Collection's understated architectural design was a format that many American and international collectors sought to emulate in the 1990s, however, the exuberant nature of the twenty-first-century private museum has deviated greatly from the Menil Collection and Dominique de Menil's aversion to ostentatious displays of wealth. The monumental scale of The Broad exemplifies the shift towards the contemporary monolithic museum design that has gained immense popularity in much of the US, over recent years. Situated alongside the Walt Disney Concert Hall and directly opposite the Museum of Contemporary Art (MOCA) on Grand Avenue in downtown Los Angeles, the museum spans one entire city block. At face value its institutional appearance is akin to a public museum than a private one. This chapter draws attention to the successful self-made entrepreneur Eli Broad who is attracted to the idea of creating a grand single-patron collection museum that distinguishes him on the global cultural stage. While The Broad and the redevelopment of Grand Avenue has been Eli Broad's grandest assignment to date I will assess the fiscal sustainability of the monumental museum through the examination of The Broad.

In this chapter I will also consider Broad's relationship with the Los Angeles County Museum of Art (LACMA) and MOCA and his entrepreneurial approach to philanthropy that can be likened to a corporate takeover of the cultural sector in the city of Los Angeles and therefore question if we are loosening our sense of public-spiritedness by succumbing to the dominant cultural ambitions of influential wealthy collectors? The interference of museum trustees and benefactors can challenge the curatorial authority and role of the public museum sector by injecting a corporate mindset that can dominate the museum's area of responsibility and thus raise a cautionary flag that there might be a conflict. Furthermore, influential collectors such as Eli Broad feel that if they are to commit time and funds assisting museums, then they should get something back in return. This is seen to challenge the altruistic notion of philanthropy that involves donations for which no specific material benefit is provided. Perhaps it is more closely aligned to Peter Frumkin's definition where 'the meaning of philanthropy is negotiated and defined every time donors and recipients are joined through philanthropy?'[1]

Or, could it be argued that this is not philanthropy in the truest sense, it is perhaps something else?

Overview

Eli Broad was born 6 June 1933 in the Bronx, New York, the only child to Lithuanian Jewish immigrant parents. The family moved to Detroit, Michigan, when Broad was only seven years of age; he went on to graduate with a major in accounting from the Michigan State University in 1954. The prospect of working his way to the top of a small accounting firm did little to spark Broad's imagination and desire to be financially successful. Instead, in 1957, he used his accounting skills and a $12,500 loan from his father-in-law to set up his own homebuilding company – Kaufman and Broad Home Corporation (KB Home).[2] Broad left Michigan in 1963 making his way to Los Angeles, California, where he could expand his growing business. KB Home's success – through building new and affordable suburban homes in Detroit – was reflected in its listing on the American Stock Exchange in 1961 and in 1969 on the New York Stock Exchange.[3] He went on to buy the Sun Life Insurance Company of America (that was founded in 1890) and, in 1971, he transitioned it into the retirement savings company SunAmerica. The eventual $18 billion sale of the company in 1999, to the American International Group provided fresh impetus for Broad's cultural and personal ambitions; thus, his art collection began to expand rapidly along with his various philanthropic projects.[4]

Individuals like Eli Broad played a crucial role in the cultural development of their adopted cities and their contributions cannot be ignored or trivialised. One of Broad's earliest projects was to help found MOCA in 1979. I will outline that his involvement with the museum continues to date, however, this has not always been a smooth relationship. Broad's active involvement at this formative stage of MOCA's development propelled him into the city's elite sphere, building a name and creating an important role for himself in a way that business alone could not. Broad enlisted support and funds for the building of the museum, its collection and the management of them.[5] He applied the same rigour to his fundraising and promotion of the city's cultural development as he did to his business ventures. This proved advantageous as he helped to raise $13 million towards the museum's endowment in 1979, contributing $1 million himself, exceeding the original estimate of $10 million.[6] Connie Bruck from *The New Yorker*, writes Broad was determined to distinguish himself and place MOCA on the American cultural map. He personally pursued the Centre Georges Pompidou's inaugural director Pontus Hultén for the role of director and succeeded. Broad boldly declared: 'We don't want to be a provincial museum. We want to overfly New York'.[7] His active role in the fundraising campaign was acknowledged and was therefore named 'founding Chairman' of MOCA.

My numerous attempts to interview and correspond with Eli Broad and his staff at The Broad and The Broad Art Foundation have either been ignored or politely declined as have all expressions of interest. Most of the available literature stems from journalistic interviews with Eli Broad or with his own curatorial team; his autobiographical book entitled *The Art of Being Unreasonable: Lessons in Unconventional Thinking* (2012); and journalistic articles and self-published sources. Due to the nature of such publications, the perspective is generally one-sided: they are poised in Broad's favour or against him – with little middle ground. My visits to The Broad, MOCA, BCAM at LACMA, Eli and Edythe Broad Art Centre, UCLA Department of Art (Los Angeles) and the analysis of the available literature have informed this examination of Eli Broad and his diverse philanthropic actions so as to establish a critical distance that I feel is missing from many of the current publications.

Broad the man, the collector and the philanthropist

Philanthropy is something that Broad takes very seriously. He believes his Jewish heritage plays a role in his philanthropy; American Jews, he says, have been very generous in Los Angeles and in other American cities and hopes to contribute to such a tradition.[8] His philanthropic actions over the last three decades have dominated Los Angeles with the city dubbed as a 'one-philanthropist town'.[9] Bruck writes that the absence of other significant benefactors in Los Angeles in recent times has been most advantageous to Broad. The lack of competition and interest to compete with Broad has given him an advantage over many of his peers – wielding influence over the institutions and projects he financially supports. When asked by *60 Minutes* host Morley Safer, in an interview conducted in 2011, why he likes to put his name on all the things he supports, Broad replied: 'I don't keep it a secret, that's for sure'.[10] Such a response provides an insight into Broad himself, his overt approach to cultural philanthropy and his desire to be recognised and respected within the public sphere.

The Broad Art Foundation was founded in 1984. The Eli and Edythe Broad Foundation was set up in 1999 to sit alongside the Art Foundation to fund Education, Scientific and Medical Research and Civic Initiatives. Collectively, The Broad Art Foundation and The Eli and Edythe Broad Foundation draw on assets valued at $3.02 billion.[11] The Broad Art Foundation consists of 2,000 works of postwar and contemporary art. They are publicly accessible by way of The Broad and the foundation's 'lending library'. The 'lending library' operates independently as an international borrowing resource for recognised public and university museums. According to the Foundation's web site the notion of the lending library is unprecedented '… creating a unique repository of contemporary art with the sole purpose of display and study by public institutions'.[12] It exists because of the fiscal difficulties facing many privately governed public institutions in acquiring and exhibiting contemporary art, declining government funds, increasing operating costs and the diminishing number of private bequests to museums due to the speculative art market.

The art collection has been collated with the input of two curatorial advisers – Shelley De Angelus and Joanne Heyler. De Angelus worked for Broad during the 1980s and 1990s, whilst Heyler started at The Broad Art Foundation in 1989. She curated the Broad collections and presided over the lending library from 1995 and has been appointed the founding director of The Broad. Overall, the Foundation's focus is on 200 artists spanning from 1960 to the present date. Both the Foundation and The Broad like to draw attention to the size of their holdings. This is reiterated throughout the museum's and Foundation's web sites, by the director and founder and numerous press releases. While a large private collection is seen as a distinguishing factor amongst private collectors and their museums, Bruck suggests that the Broad art collection varies greatly in quality as he pursues quantity over quality; that is, he seeks to buy works at bargain prices which often means buying lesser quality works: 'He [Broad] has artists in depth, some masterpieces. But he goes for volume and for bargains, and you rarely get great works as bargains'.[13] Broad's former curatorial adviser Shelley De Angelus, concurs adding that his tough negotiations and unwillingness to pay more for superior works of art has resulted in a collection that is at times inconsistent.[14] A similar sentiment can be seen in historian Keith L. Bryant, Jr's more general observation: 'In the Southwest entrepreneurs began to collect art in the same way that they acquired business enterprises …'.[15] While there is no way of knowing how accurate such opinions are, we can, however, form some assumptions based around Broad's actions and approaches to the way he spends and invests his money. By his own confession, Broad does not give money away, he invests it and he has a tendency to be economical with the way he spends his money – the rigid clauses attached to his donations of money, the construction of BCAM at LACMA and his refusal to endow it, cannot be ignored.

It will be shown that Broad practices an alternative style of philanthropy that is referred to as 'venture philanthropy'. Venture philanthropy is an unconventional model that is often favoured by individuals who have made their fortune through their own enterprising initiatives and seek to attach quantifiable results to their philanthropic initiatives. Broad's direct and active relationship with the institutions he supports is one key aspect of his approach. Another is the strict criteria he applies to his philanthropic projects so as to monitor the productivity of his financial contributions over time. He seeks to apply business practices to the way museums are operated, and as the *Los Angeles Times'* art critic Christopher Knight, points out 'A museum is not a company. Corporate policy doesn't function well there'.[16]

It becomes clear that Broad does not perceive philanthropy as a form of charity or about 'giving money away': 'We want our wealth to make a measurable impact' he says.[17] Before he commits to any project he considers three questions: can the project happen without the Foundation's investment? If it can, then Broad does not commit to it. Two, will this make a difference long-term – that is, 20 or 30 years from now? And three, are the right people employed to lead the project and make it happen once the money is committed?[18] This method exemplifies a business approach that seeks to establish clear cut objectives and performance indicators that can be easily quantified within a specified time frame where the commitment can be judged a failure or success in strictly commercial terms. Furthermore, the question of whether the right people are in place to see through the commitment is an interesting proposition; one that sees the donor actively involved in micro-managing his financial contributions. Thus, Knight refers to Broad as 'Eli "Strings Attached" Broad'.[19] Broad himself would counter this by saying, 'We don't give it away, we invest it. And we want a return. Remember, I started work as a CPA, so that gave me fiscal discipline in everything I did in business. I guess some of it carries over to philanthropy'.[20]

In his quest to actively manage his philanthropic funds, Broad has developed a tempestuous relationship with many cultural institutions, architects, museum directors and private benefactors over the last decade. He has fallen out with both MOCA and LACMA on a number of occasions and has returned to make amends. In Broad's words: 'I think people on the board thought I was too autocratic'.[21] Even though he has contributed around $140 million to various cultural institutions over the last three decades, he struggles to receive the respect and loyalty he seeks. Broad is perceived as controlling and powerful because of his immense personal wealth, but he is also seen as a generous benefactor, nevertheless. As Bruck put it, 'Broad inspires both admiration and fear in the LA art scene ...'.[22]

Museum of Contemporary Art (MOCA)

MOCA is an institution that Broad financially supported from the beginning and at its greatest time of need during the Global Financial Crisis in 2008. Broad and The Eli and Edythe Broad Foundation contributed $30 million: $15 million towards the museum's endowment fund on the proviso that the museum and its trustees matched this amount, and $15 million to support their exhibition programme. It was reported that the amount pledged to offset exhibition costs was to be paid in twenty instalments of $750,000 per quarter, however, records from early 2012 indicate that at least two repayments have not been made.[23] Broad's 'bail out' prevented the museum from considering a merger or selling out to LACMA who offered to take over MOCA and its collection. The museum's overspending, poor financial management and a declining investment portfolio of $36.2 million in the mid-2000s was reduced to $5 million by December 2008, before bouncing back to $14.2 million by end March 2009 through new donations. The California Attorney General's office asserts that MOCA drew heavily on its restricted assets to cover operating costs without seeking the permission of its donors.[24]

Upon accepting Broad's financial assistance, the museum agreed in December 2008 to comply with his conditions: the museum was not permitted to sell works from the collection and must continue to operate as an independent entity. It could not merge or be taken over by 'any museum located within one hundred miles of [its] Grand Avenue facility, excluding educational institutions or museums affiliated with educational institutions'.[25] The agreement also capped MOCA's annual operating budget between $13 million and $16 million; additional cash income would be needed if they were to exceed this amount and trustees would need to contribute accordingly.[26] It was not long before Broad began to exert greater influence over the museum's operational and curatorial programmes, recruiting new board members and controversial former director Jeffrey Deitch. The forced resignation of senior curator Paul Schimmel in 2010 triggered the resignation of four artists – John Baldessari, Catherine Opie, Barbara Kruger and Ed Ruscha. Deitch was accused of compromising the museum's curatorial mandate opting for more celebrity focussed and populist approach to boost visitation numbers. This resulted in the departure of senior curators and long- standing artists on the museum's board of trustees.[27]

Despite the clause that prevented Broad from interfering with the curatorial and exhibition programmes he exerted tremendous influence during Deitch's directorship. Consequently, many museum professionals and private individuals affiliated with the museum perceived Broad's influence and involvement with extreme caution; they saw this as part of a long-term plan to incorporate MOCA with his own museum.[28] As the 'biggest donor' he was seen to wield too much power. Christopher Palmeri and Katya Kazakina from *Bloomberg News*, note that his involvement was detrimental to the museum's ability to fundraise as many potential donors have retracted their pledge or are unwilling to contribute financially because they question the museum's future under Broad's influence.[29]

By 2013, MOCA found itself in a similar financial predicament needing to bolster its endowment to $100 million. Whilst LACMA's 2008 takeover offer was declined in favour of Broad's financial assistance, LACMA again extended their submission to take over MOCA, and again, it was rejected as the museum managed to secure much of the $100 million needed – setting a new target of $150 million. I would argue that the 2008 board of trustees showed limited fiscal capacity by allowing the museum's endowment to be eroded without making any financial contributions, especially as their collective net worth was estimated at $21 billion at the time. Their mismanagement jeopardised the trust that exists between donors and the museum by permitting the leadership team to access restricted funds without the approval of donors. Although they were financially equipped to assist the museum they failed to take up the option, and in so doing, Broad's large 'bail out' fund saw him dominate the board of trustees. His return to MOCA saw the board divided between the Broad and the anti-Broad camps making them divisive and unable to pursue a united agenda at the expense of the museum itself.

One issue that cannot be ignored is the constant speculation that Broad may have greater plans for MOCA, that is, a merger between The Broad and MOCA. Many have argued that this is the incentive to keep the museum on Grand Avenue and the collection intact. MOCA has a world-renowned collection of modern and contemporary art that is invaluable and inaccessible to even someone as wealthy as Broad – it would be the jewel in the Broad crown – should he succeed. Perhaps this is mere speculation, however, it is not unreasonable and when questioned on the matter Broad's response was: 'If I wanted to do that, why would I have saved MOCA?'[30] *The New York Times* reporter Roberta Smith, suggests that it is not that Broad has saved MOCA, 'as staved off its demise, and without more money either from him or other trustees, the place is more or less on life-support'.[31] I would add that such a coup would heighten his own public persona and that of his holdings; furthermore, it would top Broad's many cultural accomplishments and ensure him a sense of immortality in the city of Los Angeles and beyond.

Figure 9.1 Exterior view of BCAM (Broad Contemporary Art Museum) at the Los Angeles County Museum of Art. Photo © Museum associates / LACMA.

Los Angeles County Museum of Art (LACMA)

In 2008, BCAM at LACMA opened with an exhibition featuring 151 works from the Broad Art Foundation as well as Richard Serra's colossal 2006 sculpture 'Band', purchased with Broad's $10 million donation.[32] When Broad announced his intentions to fund the building he clearly stipulated that the new project would not be called a gallery, or simply be presented as another wing of the museum. He wanted the new entity to be a stand-alone contemporary art museum. It was anticipated that BCAM at LACMA would serve as the permanent home for part of the Broad collection. The 'gift' however never took place as Broad retracted his original pledge to donate 250 works from his private collection. Days ahead of BCAM's opening, in February 2008, Broad announced his decision to proceed with the construction of his own collection museum.[33] BCAM's opening celebrations were thrown into chaos as the general media appeared more interested in his shock announcement than LACMA's new addition.

Eli Broad's relationship with LACMA and the funding of BCAM at LACMA drew much attention within art circles and the general media, as the relationship challenged the notion of what is understood to be private and public. The terms and conditions accompanying the proposed donation of Broad's private art collection to BCAM at LACMA stipulated that the collection must be on permanent display. The museum's curatorial staff would exercise authority over the installations, but they would do so with the contribution from Broad and his then chief curator Joanne Heyler.[34] The idea of relinquishing control over the display of his private collection within a public institution was incomprehensible to Broad who wanted to have the final say on its curating. To deny himself control over the manner in which his holdings were displayed also diminished Broad's ability to manage how his collection is viewed by the public and the presentation of his public persona within a global context. LACMA's reluctance to agree to this rigid stipulation provoked Broad into withdrawing his pledge to gift 250 works to the museum. Nevertheless, the museum's strong position demonstrated their desire to maintain autonomy over their collection and exhibition programmes without having to balance private interests at the expense of public ones.

Although the $50 million 'gift' in 2003 was the single largest donation the museum had received to date, it came with a list of imperatives: BCAM would be called a 'museum' not a gallery or wing named in Broad's honour; sufficient space would be needed for his private collection; the building was to be designed by Renzo Piano; and the museum would exist as an independent entity with its own director, staff and board of trustees. The last request was declined by the then director Andrea Rich, and thus in doing so, her demise was imminent, and she resigned by November 2005. Even though Broad paid for the construction of BCAM he did not endow the museum or assist with the operating costs. He argued the extra revenue from the added membership and increased attendances to the museum's new addition should cover the operating costs.[35] Defending his decision he declared that one is not remembered for providing endowment funds, insisting that LACMA sell naming rights to the museum's galleries to raise the funds needed to operate the new addition.[36] Indeed, LACMA has needed to raise additional funds to bolster BCAM's endowment and offset curatorial and operating costs by naming rights to the individual galleries within BCAM itself.

As public institutions are reluctant to subscribe to such inflexible demands, wealthy contemporary collectors look to the private museum where they can exercise total control over the collection and their public image. Victoria Newhouse suggests that private collectors do not wish to be subject to institutional board of trustees and bureaucratic demands and thus look to alternative cultural models.[37] Furthermore, public institutions cannot permanently display the numerous and often large private collections due to curatorial and spatial restrictions, nor are they financially equipped to exhibit them in a way that individual collectors believe contemporary audiences should experience art. I would also add that today's super wealthy collections have expanded dramatically in number, size and breadth and over relatively short periods of time, making it difficult for public institutions to readily accommodate them.

In his desire to make his collection publicly accessible, Broad has toyed with numerous institutions and their suitability to display part of his art collection on a permanent basis. All options fell short of his expectations or the relationship between the collector and the various museums inevitably soured. The list of potential options included MOCA, UCLA, the Museum of Modern Art and the Guggenheim in New York and more recently BCAM at LACMA – yet they all proved unsuitable for one reason or another. LACMA, however, appears to have made more progress than other institutions as BCAM at LACMA was created specifically for Broad's holdings. Eli Broad has been seen to actively leverage his art collection in his negotiations with the various institutions even though he had no intention of gifting them to a public institution. This precarious relationship has as much to do with gaining credibility within the established art community and elite circles as it has with disingenuous philanthropic gestures. Even so, we cannot ignore the often tense and challenging relationship between public and private and the issue of who inevitably wields the upper hand.

The Broad on Grand Avenue

> The building should be of an intimate human scale rather than monumental. The visitor's experience should be personal and intriguing. One must be drawn space to space with a feeling of anticipation and excitement. A balanced interplay between exterior and interior spaces must exist, with natural light used as a source of illumination … The criteria for a successful plan are inventiveness and beauty. I believe this museum can offer a unique approach to the exhibition of art.
>
> Dominique de Menil[38]

Figure 9.2 Installation photograph, BCAM Inaugural Exhibition at the Los Angeles County Museum of Art, 8 February 2008–27 October 2008. Photo © Museum Associates / LACMA.

After much anticipation The Broad opened to the public on 20 September 2015.[39] It was designed by New York based architectural firm Diller Scofidio+Renfro (DS+R) for an estimated cost of $140 million. The museum serves as both an office and storage facility consolidating The Broad Art Foundation's headquarters – previously located in Santa Monica. The Broad on Grand Avenue in Los Angeles Foundation was formed to construct the new museum and manage the permanent display and storage of Broad's vast art collections. A board of directors, which includes Eli and Edythe Broad, preside over the museum. In Broad's own words: '… to create an institution that would exist in perpetuity, long after we were gone, so we formed a new non-profit to build and operate the museum'.[40] The setting up of The Broad as a separate entity ensured that it was governed independently of Broad's other philanthropic commitments. To do so, $150 million worth of bonds were sold – most likely Broad's – to raise the capital required to fund the construction of the building.[41] It has been agreed that the debt will be repaid within a ten-year period at an interest rate of 3.13 per cent. This effectively means that established endowment funds associated with his existing Foundations are not compromised: 'The museum received the money it needs to build. And the people of Los Angeles will get a new museum' says Broad.[42]

Securing a site for The Broad on Grand Avenue was Broad's first choice, even though he considered alternatives in Santa Monica and Beverley Hills.

Transforming Grand Avenue and downtown Los Angeles' stark surroundings was high on Broad's agenda. To obtain the land to build his museum would require careful planning and strategising as much of the land on Grand Avenue is largely owned by the county or the city, and not easily purchased. To do this he needed to prepare a plan that would allow him to secure a plot for his private museum, but also to negotiate the transformation of Grand Avenue itself. His successful fundraising for the completion of Disney Hall provided an *entrée* into such discussions with the county and the city of Los Angeles.[43] Connie Bruck argues that Broad's plans for Grand Avenue as a cultural precinct was his negotiating tool – art museums, concert hall, luxury hotels, condominiums, restaurants, retail stores and a recreation park were all part of the bigger picture. What is more, Broad began to lobby for a site on Grand Avenue suitable for his own private museum – one nearest to MOCA and adjacent to Disney Hall.[44] Despite his efforts, the $3 billion agreement struck between the various property developers, the city and the county, in early 2007, fell through at the time of the Global Financial Crisis. Determined to acquire the site, he did so in August 2009 for $7.7 million. Bruck points out that Broad negotiated a $10 million rebate upon the completion of the museum.[45]

The museum sits alongside the newly created public plaza which incorporates the redevelopment and improvements of the Grand Avenue

Figure 9.3 Exterior view of The Broad and Walt Disney Concert Hall, Los Angeles, 2016. Photo: Georgina Walker.

streetscape: olive trees, an open lawn area created in the middle of the plaza for the screening of films, performances and outdoor exhibition events, along with a new restaurant. The cost of creating the outdoor plaza and remodelling of the immediate public area and street was around $18 million. The aesthetic modifications, landscaping and the construction of The Broad alongside Disney Hall, MOCA and a new 19-story luxury residential tower has successfully repositioned Grand Avenue and downtown Los Angeles from a harsh urban environment into a cultural hub. The Grand Avenue Project appears to also be back on the drawing board with Frank Gehry's construction set to start in 2018 and to open by the end of 2022.

The Broad spans 120,000-square-feet and consists of two structural components: 'the vault and the veil'. The main concept behind the building merges archive and storage areas ('the vault') and the public exhibition spaces ('the veil'). The carved underbelly of 'the vault' frames the lobby and serves as a support for the large exhibition space known as 'the veil'. The Broad is designed for visitors to enter the museum from Grand Avenue. Once inside the museum, access to the 35,000-square-foot top floor gallery is by the 105-foot enclosed escalator or the glass cone-like elevator. A glimpse into the open storage and archive areas is only possible when using the staircase. The cave-like design of the lower ground interior is subject to minimal filtered light as only the entrance and corner points of the building allow for visual access on to Grand Avenue.

Entry into the museum's permanent collection is free of charge, hence the 'advance online reservations' are generally fully booked two months ahead. Timed tickets to the Tate Modern's travelling blockbuster exhibition 'Soul of a Nation: Art in the Age of Black Power 1963–1983' (23 March–1 September 2019) are priced at $18. The Broad was the only venue in the US to stage Jasper Johns' 'Something resembling truth' (10 February–13 May 2018) exhibition from the Royal Academy. The Broad's blockbuster exhibition programme allows them to address the issue of admission fees while ensuring the museum continues to draw large number of visitors throughout the year. Those wishing to visit The Broad, without prearranged bookings must queue for 30 to 45 minutes on weekdays and up to 90 minutes on weekends. Such delays have not dampened visitors' enthusiasm to view Broad's collection of modern and contemporary art. The surprisingly younger audiences are prepared to wait and once inside the museum are intent on navigating their way around the museum as part of a 'selfie' guided tour that can be uploaded on various social media platforms.[46] Whilst peer pressure via social media is credited with attracting younger and more diverse audiences to The Broad, one could argue that the architectural design of the museum itself, the photogenic art collection and the ongoing media hypebole has been equally effective in attracting an overwhelming response from the public at large. Advertising banners and posters are situated throughout the city of Los Angeles making it difficult to miss or ignore. The Broad team effectively manage the flow of visitors both inside and outside the museum. The use of timed tickets allows the individual galleries to feel spacious at all times, despite the large visitor numbers.

Figure 9.4 Exterior view of the public plaza and The Broad, Los Angeles, 2016.
Photo: Georgina Walker.

The economics of the private art museum

The long-term sustainability and the question of how The Broad will endure beyond Eli Broad's lifetime is of central interest here because of the brutal reality of museum economics that highlights the importance of not only

Figure 9.5 Exterior view of The Broad, Los Angeles. View of the carved underbelly of 'the vault', 2016. Photo: Georgina Walker.

founding new museums but being able to ensure their survival through the provision of a significant endowment. Despite the generosity of Broad's proposed $200 million endowment fund, the operation of private museums can be a financial drain, as we have seen through the analysis of the Menil Collection and Museum Brandhorst in the previous chapters.

Upon visiting The Broad it becomes immediately apparent that the costs associated with conservational care, storage and exhibiting the collection, operating and staffing the museum would be at a significant cost to its octogenarian founder. The speculation mounts as Broad does not intend setting up the foundation in perpetuity. If this is true, the endowment may only support an annual operating income of around $12 million. The director emeritus for the Getty, John Walsh, believes this amount is insufficient to support the museum's ability to continue to acquire new works that would be comparable to those currently in Broad's collections. To do so, Broad would need to establish a fund of a billion dollars, he says, 'if he wants to really distinguish himself, and if he wants to make something truly, lastingly great, to enable people who aren't even born yet to do great things'.[47] The Broad's $200 million endowment will endure for a limited time – perhaps a little under 20 years before it may need to be 'topped up'. So, how will The Broad generate sufficient income to supplement the shortfall or acquire new works of art and who will be prepared to support The Broad should the endowment fall short?

Most museums of this size would find it challenging to operate on a restrictive annual budget of around $12 million. The Menil Collection's operating costs for the FYE 2017 was $18.5 million with a $264 million endowment.[48] MOCA operated on over $18 million for the FYE2016, however, their costs were as high as $25 million in 2008 when their total assets were only $30 million. As of 2017, MOCA's net assets were placed at $156,567,811 with total functional expenses of $20 million.[49] Registered as a private operating foundation, The Broad Foundation's Annual Report is not expected to provide a financial breakdown of the various areas of interest, nor are the Foundation's financial details publicly disclosed. Even so, it becomes immediately apparent that it does not take long before the funds begin to run out as museums draw on the value of their assets as the income it generates can often fall short of its operating costs. Alternatively, museums may seek additional financial contributions from donors to cover expenses or to top up the endowment.

As I have outlined, the Menil Collection experienced serious financial difficulties within the first two years of its opening – and within de Menil's own lifetime – as she set out to raise $35 million towards the museum's endowment. This was unexpected as it was assumed the collection was sufficiently endowed; however, as its founder clearly stated, 'my foundation and my fortune are not bottomless'.[50] Without wishing to labour the point, The Huntington Library, Art Gallery and Botanical Gardens in San Marino faced a similar situation.[51] Opening with an endowment of $8 million, it was a third of what the institution needed to financially support itself says former director Steve Koblik.[52] The trustees and founding director Max Farrand, attempted to convince Henry Huntington at the Trustee meeting on 5 February 1927, that an endowment of $10 to $11 million was needed to run the institution. Their efforts were unsuccessful as Huntington died on 23 May 1927, with little time to make any amendments to his indenture.

In 1999, the former director of The Huntington Robert Skotheim, outlined how the institution began to incur financial difficulties within the first three decades as little surplus income was generated by the endowment to cover operating costs and new acquisitions.[53] The Huntington continued to be plagued by financial concerns for much of the time between 1958 and 1993.[54] In the 1990s, The Huntington undertook a significant fundraising campaign to rectify the situation and has since expanded its philanthropic focus. Under Koblik's directorship, The Huntington's endowment grew from $153 million to $450 million between 2001 to 2013. According to the latest report (FYE2017) their net assets sit at $669,137,810.[55] Even though The Huntington bears its original founder's name, it has been extremely successful in attracting broad philanthropic support.

It has been noted that around 75 per cent of The Huntington's philanthropic support comes from individuals – be it through fundraising, membership, donations or bequests. No one individual is seen as a dominant benefactor, but rather a collective effort and a shared passion is exercised to ensure The Huntington prospers. Naming rights have been credited to benefactors of new galleries such as the Virginia Steele Scott Galleries and Boone Gallery. As The Huntington is a multi-faceted institution – library, art gallery and extensive gardens and sculpture – it is not restricted to mythologising its original collector and founder nor is it hampered by the rigid constraints of its indenture. Huntington's original deed of gift did not seek to hamper the institution's progress.

The Broad's undisclosed long-term plan will inevitably determine the museum's future, as will the size of the final endowment. While Broad sees little value in forming collaborative partnerships or providing a substantial endowment to secure The Broad in perpetuity, I question whether the county, city or private individuals and their foundations will be willing or able to financially contribute to secure The Broad's survival, should it be needed. As Broad's future plans for the museum are not publicly articulated we are left to speculate on what he may do based on previous actions and his many media declarations. The 'gifting' of The Broad to the city or county after some twenty years may be one possible outcome to ensure Broad's legacy continues in place of a larger endowment. One is almost certain that Broad will ensure his indenture is rigid and not left to others to see through as his self-assured personality will simply not allow this.

Despite such conjecture, the construction of The Broad is Eli Broad's grandest assignment to date and has been much anticipated in Los Angeles. The media hyperbole, speculation and reception leading up to the museum's opening has been largely unprecedented in Los Angeles – attracting 177,264 visitors within the first 12 weeks.[56] The overwhelming interest in The Broad continues to date with over 800,000 people visiting Grand Avenue's new museum each year.

Conclusion

Eli Broad's bold vision of Los Angeles becoming an international cultural hub is fundamental to his personal values and motivation behind his philanthropic actions and collecting. For Broad, it is not simply about the democratisation of the arts and amassing a large collection of art, it is more personal. Broad takes his role as a cultural philanthropist and entrepreneur very seriously in a way that merges private and public and corporate and not-for-profit objectives. He adopts an active approach in all his dealings with the many public art museums he supports and applies a no-nonsense business style to museum dealings as a trustee, board member and bene-factor. As we have seen through his relationships with LACMA and MOCA, he sees little value in forming collaborative partnerships. Dominique de Menil had the foresight to create the Menil Collection in a way that engaged local support and interest. For decades the de Menils, along with many of their contemporaries, generously invested their time and funds with the hope of transforming the city of Houston and cultivating Houstonians' appreci-ation for modern art and architecture. In return, other wealthy individuals and private foundations reciprocated by financially supporting the creation of the Menil Collection. Broad, on the other hand, has sought little value in such an approach and has opted for a solitary path and even ostracised many of his contemporaries with his autocratic style.

Notwithstanding his intention to contribute to Los Angeles' cultural development, Broad's personal ambitions and the overt posturing in the public domain can often be problematic; his unexpected announcement to construct his own museum at the opening of BCAM at LACMA is a case in point. Likewise, Broad's financial plan to 'rescue' MOCA in 2008 and 2013 has been interpreted by many as an inevitable take over. In his relentless quest for unconditional power and respect Broad inadvertently commodifies art and the art museum itself. Such behaviours serve to question his integrity and genuine philanthropic intent.

Whilst de Menil sought to avoid the American model of the monumental museum and the ostentatious connotations that accompanied such a ges-ture, she nevertheless, foresaw an end to such a monumental approach, believing it to be financially unsustainable. She could be right as only time will tell if institutions such as The Broad are sustainable on a $200 million endowment.

Notes

1 Frumkin, Peter, *Strategic Giving; the Art and Science of Philanthropy*, Chicago and London, The University of Chicago Press, 2006, p.21.
2 Broad, Eli, *The Art of Being Unreasonable: Lessons in Unconventional Thinking*, edited by Swati Pandey, New Jersey, John Wiley, 2012, pp.58–59.
3 Broad, 2012, pp.20–28.
4 Broad, 2012, pp.20–28. Broad is the 78th wealthiest person in the world, according to the Forbes '400 Richest Americans 2018' with an estimated net worth of $6.7 billion. This is a drop from the 71st wealthiest person on the list with an estimated net worth of $7.3 billion in 2017. His personal art collection is valued at $2 billion with his Foundations' holdings at more than $2.4 billion.

5   Broad brokered the deal between Count Giuseppe Panza di Biumo and MOCA. Panza's American postwar art collection was acquired between 1956 and 1963 as it needed to be sold to avoid excessive taxes imposed on the collection by the Italian government. Appraised by Sothebys, it was valued between $11 million and $15 million. The collection was secured for $11 million. Broad, 2012, pp. 90–91; Broad, 2012, pp.5–6.

6   Bruck, Connie, 'The Art of the Billionaire', *The New Yorker*, no. 6 December (2010), p.53.

7   Bruck, 2010, p.53.

8   Masters, Lindsay, 'The Broad Museum: Jewish-American Billionaire Eli Broad Builds Free Museum in Los Angeles', *JewishNewsOne*, 12 October 2013.

9   Bruck, 2010, p.50.

10 Streeter, Ruth. 'Eli Broad from the 60 Minutes Interview (Transcript): Interview with Morley Safer (24 April 2011)', 2011.

11 The Broad Foundations 2015–2016 Active Report, 'Entrepreneurship for the public good in education, science and the arts', 2016.

12 500 museums have borrowed more than 8,000 works from the Foundation since its founding. The Broad Art Foundation, 'Mission: A Contemporary Art Lending Resource and the Board Collections; the Collection: Featured Artists', The Broad Art Foundation.

13 Bruck, 2010, p.56.

14 Bruck, 2010, p.56.

15 Bryant, Jr. and Keith L., 'The Art Museum as Personal Statement: The Southwest Experience', *Great Plains Quarterly*, 1989, p.101.

16 Knight, Christopher, 'Critic's Notebook: Seeing LA's MOCA as a Company – Therein Lies the Rub', *Los Angeles Times*, 8 July 2012; Kennedy, Randy, 'Museum's New Identity Causes More Fallout', *The New York Times*, 13 July 2012.

17 The Giving Pledge, 'Our Giving Pledge: Eli and Edythe Broad, 1 July 2010' (Original Pledge).

18 Broad, 2012, p.138.

19 Streeter, 2011.

20 Streeter, 2011.

21 Bruck, 2010, p.54.

22 Bruck, 2010, p.50.

23 Palmeri, Christopher and Kazakina, Katya, 'Eli Broad Misses MOCA Payment in Museum's Murky Finances', *Bloomberg*, 9 August 2012.

24 Boehm, Mike, 'LA's MOCA in Deep Financial Trouble', *Los Angeles Times*, 19 November 2008.

25 Finkel, Jori, 'LACMA Offers to Bail out MOCA', *Philanthropy News Digest*, 11 March 2013.

26 Haithman, Diane, 'MOCA Accepts Eli Broad's $30-Million Lifeline, Appoints CEO', *Los Angeles Times*, 22 December 2008.

27 Vogel, Carol and Kennedy, Randy, 'A Once-Troubled Museum Frames a Future in Los Angeles', *The New York Times*, 7 January 2014.

28 Bruck, 2010, pp.60–61.

29 Palmeri and Kazakina, 2012.

30 Smith, Roberta, 'A Los Angeles Museum on Life Support', *The New York Times*, 22 July 2012.

31 Smith, 2012, n.p.

32 Further acquisitions with the $10 million donation included Alighiero e Boetti's *Mappa* (1979) and Chris Burden's *Hell Gate* (1998) that were acquired jointly with The Museum of Contemporary Art, Los Angeles. Los, Angeles County Museum of Art, 'LACMA', Los Angeles. Los, Angeles County Museum of Art website.

33 Connie, 'The Art of the Billionaire', *The New Yorker*, 6 December 2010, p.58.

34 Freudenheim, Susan, 'Romancing the Collector: Will There Be a Storybook Ending?' *The New York Times*, 31 March 2004, p.1.

35 Freudenheim, 2004, p. 1.

36 Bruck, 2010, pp.57–58.

37 Newhouse, Victoria, *Towards a New Museum*, Expanded Edition 2006, New York, Monacelli Press, 1998, p.279.

38 Dominique de Menil, Letter of Invitation, Draft Dated 26 February 1980, Architectural Competition, Menil Archives, The Menil Collection, Houston.

39 The Broad's original opening date was 25 October 2013.

40 Broad, 2012, p.67.

41 Bonds are a type of loan that allow borrowers to fund long-term investment projects. They are sold to a financial institution or company with the investor receiving the sum in cash, as a loan that needs to be repaid within a defined term and interest rate. The bonds sold by the museum were Aa1-rated bonds. Broad, 2012, p.67.

42 Eli Broad. Broad, 2012, pp.67–68.

43 Bruck, 2010, p.60.

44 Bruck, 2010, p.60.

45 Bruck, 2010, p.60.

46 The average visitor age is 32. According to the National Endowment for the Arts' the US average age for museum attendance is 46 years of age. Museum audiences aged between 18 and 34 have declined from 2002 to 2012. Vankin, Deborah, 'What's drawing millennials to downtown L.A.'s Broad museum', *Los Angeles Times*, 20 March 2016.

47 John Walsh. Bruck, 2010, p.61. The J. Paul Getty Trust's endowment sits at $6.7 billion for the 2014 fiscal year – comprising cash and a strong investment portfolio. Moody's Investors Service, 'Rating Action: Moody's Affirms J. Paul Getty Trust, Ca's Aaa; Outlook Stable', Moody's Investors Service.

48 Menil Foundation, '2017 Annual Report: The Menil Collection, Houston', The Menil Collection, 2017, pp.70–71.

49 Charity Navigator, The Museum of Contemporary Art, Los Angeles (published 12 January 2018).

50 Glueck, 'The de Menil Family: The Medici of Modern Art', *The New York Times*, 18 May 1986.

51 Henry Huntington's estate, Library, art collection, decorative art objects, furniture and Beaux Arts private residence were transferred to a non-profit trust in 1926. This was a year before his death with the institution opening to the public in 1928. Overview; Institutional Mission Statement; The Huntington Library and Archives, The Huntington Library, Art Collection and Botanical Gardens, San Marino, Los Angeles.

52 Koblik, Steve, *Change in Context: A Case Study in Philanthropy and Institutional Transformation*. San Marino, Los Angeles, The Huntington Library, Art Gallery and Botanical Gardens, 2011, p.1.

53 Skotheim, Robert, Allen, The Pierpont Morgan Library New York City April 29, 1999 Outline for Talk by Robert Allen Skotheim, President the Huntington Library, Art Collection and Botanical Gardens, San Marino, Los Angeles, The Huntington Library, Art Collection and Botanical Gardens, 1999, p.4.
54 Skotheim, 1999, pp.5–6. Also refer to Charity Navigator, The Huntington Library, Art Collection and Botanical Gardens (published 12 January 2018).
55 The Huntington Library, Art Collection and Botanical Gardens, 'Huntington President Steven S. Koblik Announces Retirement', San Marino, Los Angeles, The Huntington Library, Art Collection and Botanical Gardens, 2014.
56 The Broad, 'The Broad to Welcome 200,000 Visitors by End of 2015', Press Release, 2016.

Conclusions
Evolving philanthropic conventions

> The Renaissance saw wealthy patrons funding churches, schools and universities. Today it is private art museums.
>
> Mark Fraser[1]

If the private collector's museum is to be more than a visible and aspirational model for wealthy collectors, then we need to ensure that its *raison d'être* is clearly articulated within the public sphere. At the beginning of this book I asked to what extent are individual collectors challenging and redefining the terms *philanthropy*, *public access* and *museum* and how fiscally sustainable is the private collector's museum beyond the original founder's lifetime? My response is that a unique vision, character and philanthropic commitment to the connection between art and engagement needs to prevail if the private museum is to endure beyond the lifetime of their often-charismatic creators. Furthermore, the private collector's museum must be supported with generous endowments so that they do not intrude upon public institutions and their area of responsibility. *The Private Collector's Museum: Public Good Versus Private Gain* has examined a series of in-depth case studies to understand the private museum through the lens of history and how they play out within a contemporary context.

Private art museums can play an important role in the overall cultural landscape, however, I have argued that they benefit from a distinct approach and curatorial style, why else must they exist? The often-homogenous approach to museum and exhibition making was precisely what Dominique de Menil was reacting against when planning the construction of the Menil Collection. To conform to such conventions would be at odds with the private museum's *raison d'être*. Hence, she undertook a lengthy and detailed analysis of 'the museum' questioning aspects of architecture and conventional museological practices and displays along the way. She wanted to create a space for scholarly pursuits and a relaxing environment for the contemplation and appreciation of art – a space of 'enchantment' rather than one that was predictable and 'boring'. She was deeply concerned with museum fatigue and sought to avoid it in her own museum – exhaustive displays and repetitive installations did little to stir the imagination of viewers and were thus perceived by her to be dull. Seeking to recreate the museum as a space that would counter such potential boredom and detachment, required an aesthetic that the Menil Collection would address and make it its trademark.[2]

Perhaps more rigorous intellectual planning is needed if private collectors and their museums are to distinguish themselves in their quest to expand the existing cultural landscape. It is not enough for wealthy collectors to embrace innovative venues, structures and juxtapositions to differentiate themselves from their public counterparts, contemporaries and predecessors in their attempt to attract local and global attention. Spectacle and wonder might be seen as one way to entice contemporary audiences to the art museum, but I question how it can continue to sustain and develop a more meaningful engagement with art on a long-term basis. Director of the Kunsthaus Zürich Dr Christoph Becker, issues a note of caution:

> Do not think of us [public museums] as being recipients but think of the general public outside who are sometimes feeling uncertain about what is going on. The variety of offers made, should not keep them from taking opportunities and that can be a problem. It is often too much of the same and we do not understand it anymore.[3]

A similar sentiment is expressed by founding director of the Museum of Old and New Art (MONA) Mark Fraser who suggests that 'Private museums, at their best, provide alternative viewpoints to state sanctioned museums; but at their worst they are sterile mausolea'.[4]

As we have seen, American collector Eli Broad has made a second career out of philanthropy; it has propelled him into elite circles and allowed him to create a name and role for himself in a way that corporate enterprise alone could not.[5] It is for this reason that many collectors – past and present – recognise that it is through their cultural, not their business initiatives, that they are able to establish a longstanding legacy to honour their individual achievements. This was the case with many twentieth-century American industrialist collectors such as Henry Clay Frick, Henry Huntington and Albert C. Barnes – as it is today for many of Broad's international contemporaries. I would suggest that the private museum model allows influential wealthy collectors to present themselves in a manner that is seen to be public-spirited. This public acknowledgement is bestowed upon them within their own lifetime and serves to validate their cultural achievements.

Even though past collectors were actively involved in the formation of their holdings and the means by which these works would, in due course, transition into the public sphere, this was determined at the later stage of their lives. Therefore, private collections and house museums, at the turn of the twentieth century, were inevitably constructed to perpetuate individual collectors and their legacies, upon their passing. Only few offered restricted access to members of the public within their own lifetime – Sir John Soane,

Sir Richard Wallace, Isabella Stewart Gardner, Albert C. Barnes and Peggy Guggenheim amongst them. Today, many private museums are conceived with the public in mind and offer general access from the outset. Private museums allow their founders to take charge and address the dilemma and shortage of exhibition space available for personal collections to be on permanent display within public museums. It can be argued that the existence of private museums may deny public institutions future access to significant donations that were once seen to ultimately benefit their holdings. It also raises questions about its long-term sustainability and how the private museum's existence may negatively impact the already challenging public museum sector.

To bequeath works of art to public museums, in the past, meant that collectors relinquished ownership of and authority over their holdings once they entered a public institution; alternatively works were bestowed posthumously. The gift usually included the permanent display of the collection, naming rights or the construction of a new museum wing to accommodate such a gesture. The Robert Lehman Collection and wing at the Metropolitan Museum of Art is an example of this type of benefaction. The act of philanthropy was clearly articulated and final. Similar characteristics can be seen in the agreement struck between the Donald Fisher Foundation and San Francisco Museum of Modern Art (SFMOMA) in 2009. Fisher reached a last-minute agreement with SFMOMA after exhausting a number of private-private and public partnership arrangements. The deal included the long-term loan of 1,100 works from the Fisher Foundation's collection and the construction of a new purpose-built wing and exclusive naming rights. Yet as I have outlined, the more traditional aspects of benefaction are being challenged by contemporary collectors, who seek to actively exercise authority over their holdings within their own lifetimes.

This is done in three ways: outright bequests are largely being replaced with long-term loan agreements that allow collectors flexibility to retract their pledge. The Fisher Foundation's loan agreement with the SFMOMA signals such a departure; furthermore, the museum was expected to pay for the $480 million wing to accommodate it. Other examples include the many long-term loan agreements between collectors and German public museums and the planned relocation of the Bührle Collection to the Kunsthaus Zürich in 2020. Secondly, private collectors seek to engage and influence the public museum sector despite creating their own museum. Broad's relationships with the Museum of Contemporary Art (MOCA) and Broad Contemporary Art Museum at Los Angeles County Museum of Art (BCAM at LACMA) has been plagued with numerous problems as he exerts influence over the museums' respective programmes and operations. And thirdly, collectors (in their later years) and more specifically those in Germany – have formed individual relationships with public museums, to ensure the future of their holdings and museums. The argument that private museums do not necessarily endure as long as public museums is supported by the ongoing financial commitment that is required to sustain them indefinitely. This has prompted individual collectors to look to the public sector to perpetuate their cultural achievements.

When I asked Dr Harald Falkenberg (founder of the Falkenberg Collection, Hamburg) why private collectors are forming permanent relationships with public institutions and whether private museums can continue to exist beyond their original founders' lifetime he responded thus: 'No, private museums usually have a limited time, different from public museums. Usually this is not a long time'.[6] With this in mind, a group of influential German collectors and public museums are entering into complex and individually negotiated agreements. They are frequently a mix of transfers, sales, long-term loan agreements and gifts. This is largely achieved on the collector's own terms and often at the expense of the partnering institution. Udo Brandhorst, Ingvild Goetz, Harald Falkenberg, and more recently, Erika Hoffmann have negotiated formal arrangements with public museums. In contrast, the agreement between Museum Frieder Burda and the Staatliche Kunsthalle, Baden-Baden, appears fair and balanced: Museum Frieder Burda will be unconditionally gifted to the State of Baden-Württemberg when the collector is no longer active. Until such time, the museum is funded and operated by Burda's private foundation. This represents a new development from earlier examples where private museums were gifted to the city, state or nation: Sir John Soane's Museum, The Wallace Collection, Isabella Stewart Gardner, The Huntington, The Frick Collection, Kröller-Müller Museum, Oskar Reinhart 'Am Stadtgarten' and 'Am Römerholz', Rosengart Museum, Amon Carter Museum, Kimbell Art Museum, Menil Collection are all such important examples.

In considering the (re)emergence of the private collector's museum in the twenty-first century, Dr Tobia Bezzola argues that 'the private museum is a consequence of the changed economy. The weakened position of the public art museum is a direct consequence of impoverished [German] cities'. That being so, it poses a number of concerns for the already challenging German public museum sector as funds are being redirected to secure private collections and museums – even constructing new ones as in the case of Museum Brandhorst. This allows collectors to continue to exert authority over their holdings and museums, within their own lifetime, despite agreeing to transfer, sell or gift them to the public sector. This not only confuses the notion of private and public, it also prevents public museums from fulfilling their curatorial, collecting and educational role as public institutions, free of individual influence. A discerning approach to institutional collecting can equally be compromised as not all private collections are constructed with the same sense of connoisseurship that public institutions are expected to exercise. The very nature of a personal collection is underpinned by the individual collector's taste and that of their advisers.

While agreements struck between private collectors and the public sector allow museums to own the works they want to show, the lack of consultation between government bodies and museum professionals questions such decisions that have long-term consequences for the institution and its public. The quality and suitability of Brandhorst's holdings was judged by a jury and external art expert appointed by the government department; the Pinakothek's professional and curatorial staff had little or no say in the matter. This process between the Ministry and private benefactors has a tendency to meet with public hostility and controversy as there is little in the way of public debate and consultation with the receiving museum. One might question why the State of Bavaria agreed to fund a separate museum to display Brandhorst's holdings as not all private collections warrant their own museum.

The public museum sector may be seen as the most obvious home to secure the future of many private museums and their holdings, I question how financially sustainable this is in the long-term. The viability of the public museum can inevitably be weakened by settlements that are perceived to be one-sided. When viewed in light of ongoing budget cuts and declining government support such decision can put significant public museums and their collections at risk. So, if private museums are constructed as the antithesis of the public museum, to go back to the public museum to ensure private legacies endure for longer periods of time, might appear to contradict the reason why private museums are created in the first place; this would also compromise the *raison d'être* of the private museum and its individuality.

As I have outlined, the Menil Collection's existence was threatened in the years following Dominique de Menil's death (1997). The period between 1999 and 2004 placed the museum's uniqueness and the de Menil legacy most at risk. The Menil Collection managed to avert several attempts by previous board members and directors, who were keen to secure the museum's financial position by institutionalising it and ensuring it conformed to established museum standards and rules. The implementation of distinct bureaucratic and budgetary departments, which are common place at most conventional museums, was seen to be contrary to the Menil Collection's original structure. This clashed with the hands-on approach taken by de Menil and her professional staff, who ran the museum, its curatorial programmes, exhibition schedule and installations. Their informality was not in keeping with conventional museum practice, hence its appeal.

How financially sustainable is the private collector's museum?

Maintaining personal collections intact, and in perpetuity, has and continues to be key to most private collectors' public personae and personal legacies. The sheer number of private museums founded globally in recent times supports such concerns as large endowments are required to financially support them. As we have seen with the Menil Collection, this can be a challenge for many founders. In 1987, upon the opening of the Menil Collection, $20 million was needed to bolster the museum's endowment and offset operating costs. Within two years a further $35 million was needed to avert further financial difficulties. The museum's operating costs rose from $2.9 million in 1987 to $7.9 million in 1992 and according to the Menil Collection's 2017 Annual Report, the museum's annual operating expenses are placed at $18.5 million.[7] The museum's future was finally made more secure through the transfer of $240 million from Dominique de Menil's estate to the Foundation upon her passing, thereby providing the museum with an estimated annual income of around $12 million.[8] Despite this the museum is still left with a shortfall of at least $6.5 million which they have to raise. This scenario is not unique to the Menil Collection as other private institutions struggle to contain escalating costs that are associated with running a museum. What is unique to the Menil Collection was de Menil's ability to muster financial support, from other private individuals and foundations in Houston, to build the museum, save it from the brink of financial difficulty and to ensure it received ongoing support. As de Menil herself exclaimed 'my foundation and my fortune are not bottomless'.[9]

Despite the extremely wealthy status of many collectors, their personal financial position is limited; furthermore, the volatility of the global market can erode the value of stocks, without notice, thereby diminishing the worth of many entrepreneurs and museum endowments that are usually invested in them. This was the case with the slump in oil prices that impacted Schlumberger stocks and ultimately the Menil Foundation's endowment in the 1990s. Similarly, the Museum of Contemporary Art (MOCA) in Los Angeles, and other private and public museums saw the erosion of their endowments during the Global Financial Crisis in 2008. The death of the original founder and creator can also place the future of private museums and collections in jeopardy, as was the case with Karl Ernst Osthaus. Osthaus allowed his heirs to determine the destiny of his holdings and museum upon his death in 1921; by 1922, the collection and museum's naming rights were sold to a group of private collectors in nearby Essen. The Museum Folkwang Essen, was thus founded in 1922.

Seldom do heirs share a similar passion or wish to take on the financial burden of maintaining private museums indefinitely. The future of many private collections and museums risk being sold or dispersed, hence collectors in their later years are looking for a financially secure way to extend the life of what they have created. Their concerns are reflected in a number of recent museum closures: 2015 saw the closing of the Foundation E.G. Bührle Collection in Zürich (1960–2015); in 2014 the Corcoran Gallery of Art (1869–2014) closed its doors as did Villa Flora in Winterthur (1995–2014); after 64 years Museum Oskar Reinhhart 'Am Stadtgarten' (1951) came close to bankruptcy in 2016; the Coninx Museum in Zürich also closed in 2011 after only 25 years. The demise of many private collector museums is inevitably linked to declining endowment funds.

Private collectors and their museums need to look beyond the public sector for a lifeline and consider alternative arrangements: drawing on de

Menil's example of collaboration would be one way to secure the future of private collections. I would argue that David Walsh's Museum of Old and New Art (MONA) is one that may, in due course, pursue a similar path in his desire to ensure the museum endures indefinitely. MONA's annual operating costs far outweigh the income generated by the various retail operations associated with MONA and the Moorilla Estate; thus, running the museum presents Walsh with a significant annual shortfall. As a for-profit institution, MONA may appeal to other wealthy entrepreneurs that admire what Walsh has achieved for his home town and state. Mark Fraser concurs: 'Walsh attracts wealthy fans and supporters. This may be the next stage of development – he may act in this form of community'.[10]

There is no reason why groups of philanthropists cannot band together to support individual private initiatives in the way Houstonians have done. One obstacle is usually differing points of view and interpersonal issues; the other, may be the unwillingness of private individuals to financially sustain an institution that has been created by one individual which may be seen to contradict the corporate nature of community philanthropy. The only other option is to allow private museums to see through their time, however long that may be. As Mark Fraser put it: 'Things should not always be done with perpetuity in mind. We assume museums are forever; museums are not permanent'.[11]

This would ultimately mean the sale and dispersal of personal collections and museums over time – an outcome that would be less appealing to many collectors. Furthermore, this would erode the confidence in the symbolic value of museums.

Art collecting and philanthropy

The boom in private museum building over the last two decades reflects the competitive and dynamic nature of art collecting and philanthropy in the twenty-first century. Grand museum projects like The Broad in Los Angeles, have become global symbols of individual acts of public-spiritedness and entrepreneurship. They attract media attention as founders and their professional staff actively promote their respective museums and holdings. The constant promotional activity leading up to The Broad's opening on 20 September 2015, is an example of this. Not surprisingly, Eli Broad has come to epitomise today's ambitious, engaged and self-assured collector and philanthropist. Broad and his contemporaries look to the private museum model to store and display their holdings and to create a lasting legacy for themselves. It is unclear at this stage how the growing number of private museums will endure over time. Their future remains largely in the hands of their creators and their willingness, or not, to endow them beyond the grave. As we have seen, significant endowments are required to financially provide for the long-term future of any private museum – not all are willing to commit to such a plan. Hence collectors look for alternative arrangements to protect what they have created and to ensure their personal legacies endure. As philanthropy has evolved over time, the private museum's trajectory has evolved with it – to accommodate individual cultural ambitions and the interest in the private museum as a preferred mode of benefaction for wealthy twenty-first-century collectors.

Conclusions: the private collector's museum in the twenty-first century

The Private Collector's Museum has examined several aspects of the private museum including the manner in which many of them have been established. As we have seen, their existence has immediate ramifications on the public museum sector as they are often denied access to works from private collections that may have otherwise been gifted to them or placed on long-term loan. The ongoing financial cost associated with operating private museums, indefinitely, has also been closely examined. We cannot however, underestimate their contribution to and promotion of art and culture to a broader audience. As Mark Fraser asserts: 'Private museums remind us that the art cannot be treated objectively'.[12]

Although *The Private Collector's Museum* has speculated on the private museum's future and long-term financial position, it recognises the degree of public-spiritedness and philanthropy that has prevailed in making notable art collections publicly accessible from the outset and for the greater good.

Notes

1 Mark Fraser, interview and correspondence with the author.
2 Smart, Pamela G, *Sacred Modern: Faith, Activism, and Aesthetics in the Menil Collection*, Austin, University of Texas Press, 2010, p.143.
3 Dr Christoph Becker, interview with the author.
4 Mark Fraser, interview and correspondence with the author.
5 Bruck, Connie, 'The Art of the Billionaire', *The New Yorker*, no. 6 December 2010, p.50.
6 Dr Harald Falkenberg, correspondence with the author.
7 Menil Foundation, '2013 Annual Report: The Menil Collection, Houston', The Menil Collection, 2013, p.31, pp.49–51.
8 Menil Foundation, '2017 Annual Report: The Menil Collection, Houston', *The Menil Collection*, 2017, pp.70–71.
9 Glueck, Grace, 'The de Menil Family: The Medici of Modern Art', *The New York Times*, 18 May 1986.
10 Mark Fraser, interview and correspondence with the author.
11 Mark Fraser, interview and correspondence with the author.
12 Mark Fraser, interview and correspondence with the author.

Select bibliography

Primary sources

Black, C C, *Bethnal Green Branch Museum: Catalogue of the Collection of Paintings, Porcelain, Bronzes, Decorative Furniture, and Other Works of Art in the Bethnal Green Branch of the South Kensington Museum, by Sir Richard Wallace, Bart., M.P.,* 8th ed. London, Printed by George E. Eyre and William Spottiswoode, 1874. The Wallace Collection, London.

Cambridge Review, 'Kettle's Yard: Antimuseum'; 'What Do We Call the Kettle?', 29 May 1970, pp.169–174. Kettle's Yard Archives, Cambridge University.

Daily Express, '£300,000 Art Collection He Can't Give Away', 1966. Kettle's Yard Archives, Cambridge University.

Frick Archives, *The Frick Collection: Documents Relating to The Frick Collection, 'The Frick Collection' Incorporated 27 April 1920.* Frick Archives, The Frick Collection, New York.

——, The Frick Collection/Frick Art Reference Library, 'Document 2: As Revised by Avinoff and Clapp November 1 after Meeting with Mr. Childs Frick 31 October 1931. Report of an Interview with Mr. Joseph Breck, Acting Director Metropolitan Museum on the Subject of Opening the Frick Collection to the Public – 13 December 1931. Frick Archives, The Frick Collection, New York.

——, 'Alternative Suggestions for the Exhibition and Development of the Frick Collection', 1931–1933. Frick Archives, The Frick Collection, New York.

——, 'The Records of the Organizing Director – Frederick Mortimer Clapp Notebooks – Notebooks 1 – Reports – Committee on Organization and Policy, 1931–1935 [1/5], Memo of Some Points Brought up at the Committee Meeting of 20 December 1932. Frick Archives, The Frick Collection, New York.

——, 'The Records of the Organizing Director – Frederick Mortimer Clapp Notebooks – Notebooks 1 – Reports – Committee on Organization and Policy, 1931–1935 [1/5], Minutes of Meeting of Committee on Organization and Policy at Mr. John Russell Pope's Office, 5 April 1934. Frick Archives, The Frick Collection, New York.

——, 'The Records of the Organizing Director – Frederick Mortimer Clapp Notebooks – Notebooks 1 – Reports – Committee on Organization and Policy, 1931–1935 [1/5], Summary Report of the Organizing Director for the Period 14 June 1933 to 28 March 1934, Covering the Activities of Committee on Organization and Policy; Custodian; and Organizing Director. Frick Archives, The Frick Collection, New York.

———, 'The Records of the Organizing Director – Frederick Mortimer Clapp Notebooks – Notebooks 1 – Reports – Committee on Organization and Policy, 1931–1935 [1/5], Doc. Memorandum on Meeting of the Committee on Organization and Policy, 15 October 1935'. Frick Archives, The Frick Collection, New York.

———, *The Frick Collection: Central Files, 1932–1933, Drawings of the Interiors, Collection & Library and Exterior, Library, 1933–1935 [3/10].* Frick Archives, The Frick Collection, New York.

———, 'Conception Adopted', Opening publicity – Complete set Given to Newspapers, 1935, pp. 3–4. Frick Archives, The Frick Collection, New York.

———, '11 December 1935, pp.1–3', In *Opening publicity – Complete set Given to Newspapers, 1935.* Frick Archives, The Frick Collection, New York.

———, '11 December, 1935, pp. 1–3', Opening publicity – Complete set Given to Newspapers, 1935. Frick Archives, The Frick Collection, New York.

———, 'New Construction; Building Procedure; Admission Regulations', Opening publicity – Complete set Given to Newspapers, pp. 1–9. Frick Archives, The Frick Collection, New York.

———, 'Order in Which Rooms Will Be Visited (with Principal Works of Art in Each)', Opening publicity – Complete set Given to Newspapers, 1935, pp.1–5. Frick Archives, The Frick Collection, New York.

———, 'Order in Which Rooms Will Be Visited', The Frick Collection: Central Files, 1935, Opening publicity – Complete set Given to Newspapers, 1935, pp.1–5. Frick Archives, The Frick Collection, New York.

———, The Frick Collection: Historical Note, n.p., 1936. Frick Archives, The Frick Collection, New York.

MacColl, D S, *The Wallace Collection in War-Time and Its Reopening November 1920* [the Report Written by the Keeper of Hertford House – D S Maccoll], Printed by H.M. Stationery Office Press, London, 1920, pp.1–12. The Wallace Collection, London.

Menil Archives, Dominique de Menil, Draft: Notes Dated 1977. The Menil Collection, Houston.

———, Notes by Dominique de Menil, Draft Dated 30 March 1977 with a Second Draft Proposal Compiled 4 December 1980. The Menil Collection, Houston.

———, Curatorial – Museum Storage Records: Exploration Trip for Study Storage 28 June–3 July 1976, Dominique de Menil typed up notes from her itinerary. The Menil Collection, Houston.

———, Curatorial – Museum Storage Records, Articles for Menil Foundation storage space museum. The Menil Collection, Houston.

———, Dominique de Menil Letter of Invitation Draft Dated 26 February 1980 Architectural Competition, Curatorial – Museum storage records, Miscellaneous Research/Travel, 1976–1977. The Menil Collection, Houston.

———, Dominique de Menil Letter of Invitation, Draft Dated 26 June 1980, Architectural Competition, Curatorial – Museum Storage Records, Miscellaneous Research / Travel, 1976–1977. The Menil Collection, Houston.

———, Dominique de Menil's Notes Handwritten by K. Davidson Dated 15 October 1976. The Menil Collection, Houston.

———, Dominique de Menil's Typed Notes Dated 14 November 1979, Curatorial – Museum Storage Records: Museum Overall Purpose. The Menil Collection, Houston.

———, Report on Environmental Conditions and Conservation Requirements for the De Menil Collections in Houston, Texas 23 September 1977 (Copy 2), Curatorial – Museum Storage Records, pp. 1–14. The Menil Collection, Houston.

———, Dominique de Menil Comments on the Menil Collection and Museum, Publicity – Press Releases, pp. 1–3, 1981–1987. The Menil Collection, Houston.

———, Menil Administration: TMC Building Project, Publicity and Opening Publicity – Press Releases, 1981–1987. The Menil Collection, Houston.

———, Bibliographic Sketch of Dominique De Menil Dated 18 June 1984, Menil Archives Administration TMC Building Project and Opening, Publicity – Press Releases, pp. 1–2, 1981–1987. The Menil Collection, Houston.

———, Milestone Dates for Design and Construction, Publicity – Correspondence, 1981–1987. The Menil Collection, Houston.

———, The Menil Collection Dedication Booklet, The Building Project: Opening Brochures, 1987. The Menil Collection, Houston.

———, The Menil Collection, Comments by Walter Hopps, Menil Archive, 1981–1987. The Menil Collection, Houston.

———, Menil Administration – The TMC Building Project, Miscellaneous Files, 1981–2010, The Building Project: Art storage. The Menil Collection, Houston.

———, MacAgy, Jermayne, 'The Trojan Horse: The Art of the Machine (25 September–9 November 1958) Exhibition No. 29, Curated by Jermayne Macagy', Catalogue *essay*, Contemporary Arts Museum Houston, pp.1–49. The Menil Collection, Houston.

Moliner, Émile, *Great English Collections: The Wallace Collection (Objets D'art) at Hertford House*, Vol. II, Two hundred Copies: Edition no: Presentation copy, 1903. The Wallace Collection, London.

The Huntington Archives, *Overview; Institutional Mission Statement; Henry Edwards Huntington Biographical Sketch; General Background Information*, San Marino, Los Angeles, no date. The Huntington Library, Art Collection, and Botanical Gardens, San Marino, Los Angeles.

———, 'Bonds to A.D. Huntington Trust (25 April 1927), Copy Indenture Conveying 1000 Newport News Shipbuilding and Dry Dock Co'. The Huntington Library, Art Collection, and Botanical Gardens, San Marino, Los Angeles.

———, 'Copy Indenture Conveying 1000 Newport News Shipbuilding and Dry Dock Co Bonds to A.D. Huntington Trust [25 April 1927]'. The Huntington Library, Art Collection, and Botanical Gardens, San Marino, Los Angeles.

———, '[8 September 1930] Report on Interview with Myron Hunt Relative to Construction & Residence of H.E. Huntington', pp.1–3, San Marino, Los Angeles, The Huntington Library, Art Collection, and Botanical Gardens, San Marino, Los Angeles.

Secondary literature

Abt, Jeffrey, *The Origin of the Public Museum*, A Companion to Museum Studies, edited by Sharon Macdonald, West Sussex, Blackwell, 2011.

Anderson, John, *Art Held Hostage: The Battle over the Barnes Collection*, New York and London, W.W. Norton, 2003.

Angoletto, Matteo, *The Menil Collection, Houston, Texas, USA, 1982–1987*, Renzo Piano, Milan, Motta, 2006.

Anholt, Simon, 'Some Important Distinctions in Place Branding', *Editorial, Place Branding* 1, no. 2 (2005), pp. 116–121.

Apostolou, Natalie, 'The Art of the Deal', *Charter (Institute of Chartered Accountants in Australia)*, no. June (2010), pp. 40–43.

Araeen, Rasheed, 'Our Bauhaus Others' Mudhouse', in *Making Art Global (Part 2), 'Magiciens De La Terre', 1989*, edited by Lucy Steeds, London, Afterall Books, 2013, pp. 238–247.

Ayres, William S, 'The Domestic Museum in Manhattan: Major Private Art Installations in New York City, 1870–1920', Doctor of Philosophy, University of Delaware, 1993.

Bailey, Colin B, *Building the Frick Collection an Introduction to the House and Its Collection*, New York, Scala Publishers, 2006.

Ballon, Hilary, *Mr. Frick's Palace*, The Council of the Frick Collection Lecture Series, New York, The Frick Collection, 2009.

Barassi, Sebastiano, 'Kettle's Yard: Museum or Way of Life?', in *The Modern Period Room: The Construction of the Exhibited Interior 1870–1950*, edited by Brenda Martin, Penny Sparke and Trevor Keeble, London and New York, Routledge Taylor & Francis Group, 2006, pp. 129–141.

Barkin, Kenneth D, 'The Crisis of Modernity, 1887–1902', in *Imagining Modern German Culture: 1889–1910*, edited by François Forster-Hahn, pp. 19–35, Washington, DC, National Gallery of Art, 1996.

Barrett, Jennifer, *Museums and the Public Sphere*, West Sussex, Wiley-Blackwell, 2011.

Barron, Stephanie, *Degenerate Art: The Fate of the Avant-Garde in Nazi Germany*, Los Angeles County Museum of Art, New York, Harry N. Abrams, 1991.

Beckstette, Sven, 'In Favour of Transparency: A Roundtable Conversation on Collectors and Collections with Candice Breitz, Peggy Buth, Jonathan Monk and Andreas Siekmann, Moderated by Sven Beckstette', *Texte Zur Kunst*, 21, no. 83 (2011), pp. 76–93.

Behnke, Christoph, 'Corporate Art Collecting: A Survey of German Speaking Companies', *Journal of Arts Management, Law and Society*, 37, no. 3 (2007), pp. 225–243.

Belk, Russell W, *Collecting in a Consumer Society*, 2001 edition, London and New York, Routledge, 1995.

Bell, Ford W, *How Are Museums Supported Financially in the U.S.?*, Washington, DC, United States Department of State Bureau of International Information Programs, 2012.

Bennett, Shelley M, *The Art of Wealth: The Huntingtons in the Gilded Age*, San Marino, CA, The Huntington Library, Art Collections and Botanical Gardens, 2013.

Berger, Maurice (ed.), *Museums of Tomorrow: A Virtual Discussion – Issues in Cultural Theory*, Vol. 8 (Center for Art and Visual Culture, University of Maryland Baltimore County), New York, Distributed Art Publishers, 2004.

Blackbourn, D, and Evans, J. Richard (eds.), *The German Bourgeoisie: Essays on the Social History of the German Middle Class from the Late Eighteenth to the Early Twentieth Century*, New York, Routledge, 1991.

Blumenreich, Ulrike, 'Compendium of Cultural Policies and Trends in Europe: Country Profile Germany', Bonn, *Council of Europe/ERICarts*, 17th edition, 2016, pp. 1–70.

Boehm, Mike, 'L. A's MOCA in Deep Financial Trouble', *Los Angeles Times*, 19 November 2008.

Braddock, Jeremy, *Collecting as Modernist Practice*, Baltimore, Johns Hopkins University Press, 2012.

Bradley, Kimberley, 'A Day in the Life: Christian Boros', *Art Review*, November, no. 63 (2012), pp. 138–143.

Bredekamp, Horst, *The Lure of Antiquity and the Cult of the Machine: The Kunstkammer and the Evolution of Nature, Art and Technology*, Princeton, NJ, Markus Wiener, 1995.

Brennan, Marcia, Pacquement, Alfred, and Temkin, Ann, *A Modern Patronage: De Menil Gifts to American and European Museums*, edited by The Menil Collection. Houston, TX, Menil Foundation, 2007.

———— (ed.), 'Seeing the Unseen: James Johnson Sweeney and the De Menils', in *A Modern Patronage: De Menil Gifts to American and European Museums*, pp. 21–37, Houston, TX, Menil Foundation, 2007.

Broad, Eli, *The Art of Being Unreasonable: Lessons in Unconventional Thinking*, edited by Swati Pandey, New Jersey, John Wiley, 2012.

Brown, Jonathan, *Kings & Connoisseurs: Collecting Art in Seventeenth-Century Europe*, New Haven and London, Yale University Press, 1995.

Brown, Julia, *The Museum of Contemporary Art: The Panza Collection*, edited by Los Angeles The Museum of Contemporary Art. Los Angeles, The Museum of Contemporary Art, 1985.

Bruck, Connie, 'The Art of the Billionaire', *The New Yorker*, 6 December 2010, pp. 50–61.

Bryant Jr., Keith L, 'The Art Museum as Personal Statement: The Southwest Experience', Great *Plains Quarterly* 9, no. 2 (1989), pp. 100–117.

Burke, Jill, *Changing Patrons: Social Identity and the Visual Arts in Renaissance Florence*. University Park, The Pennsylvania State University Press, 2004.

Burns, Charles J, *From Medici to Bourbon: The Formulation of Taste and the Evolution of a Vanderbilt Style*, London, The Preservation Society of Newport County, 2007.

Büsing, Nicole, and Helko, Klaas, *BMW Art Guide by Independent Collectors*, edited by Christian Schwarm and Uwe Ellinghaus, Berlin, Hatje Cantz Verlag, 2012.

Cabanne, Pierre, *The Great Collectors*, London, Cassell and Company, 1961.

Cameron, Dan, 'Symposium,' in *Museums of Tomorrow: A Virtual Discussion – Issues in Cultural Theory*, Vol. 8 (Center for Art and Visual Culture University of Maryland Baltimore County), edited by Maurice Berger, p. 25, New York, Distributed Art Publishers, 2004.

Cecil, Robert A, 'French Eighteenth-Century Sculpture Formerly in the Hertford-Wallace Collection', *Apollo Magazine*, no. June (1965), pp. 449–463.

Chong, Alan, Lingner, Richard, and Zahn, Carl (eds.), *Eye of the Beholder: Masterpieces from the Isabella Stewart Gardner Museum*, Boston, Beacon Press, 2003.

Coates, Rebecca, 'The Rise of the Private Art Foundation: John Kaldor Art Projects 1969–2012', Doctor of Philosophy, The University of Melbourne, 2013.

Codman, Jr., Ogden, and Wharton, Edith, *The Decoration of Houses*, New York, Rizzoli and The Mount Press, 2007. (Reprint, 2007.)

Constable, William G, *Art Collecting in the United States of America: An Outline of a History*, London, Edinburgh, Thomas Nelson, 1964.

Coolidge, John, *Patrons and Architects: Designing Art Museums in the Twentieth Century*, Fort Worth, TX, Amon Carter Museum, 1989.

Cooper, Douglas, 'Emil G. Bührle and His Collection', in *Masterpieces of French Painting from the Bührle Collection*, edited by The Arts Council of Great Britain, Exhibition at The National Gallery – London, 29 September to 5 November 1961, London, The Arts Council of Great Britain, 1961.

——— (ed.), *Great Private Collectors*, New York, Macmillan, 1963.

Cuno, James, *Museums Matter: In Praise of the Encyclopaedic Museum*, Chicago and London, University of Chicago Press, 2011.

Dallas Museum of Art, *Fast Forward: Contemporary Collections for the Dallas Museum of Art*, edited by Maria de Corrall and John R. Lane, New Haven and London, Yale University Press, 2007.

Dana, John, *The Gloom of the Museum* Lanham, MD, AltaMira Press, 1917. (Reprinted in Reinventing the Museum: Historical and Contemporary Perspectives on the Paradigm Shift, Edited by G. Anderson, pp. 13–29, 2004.)

Danziger, Danny, *Museum: Behind the Scenes at the Metropolitan Museum of Art*, New York, Penguin Group, 2007.

Duncan, Carol, *Civilizing Rituals: Inside Public Art Museums*, London and New York, Routledge, 1995.

Elliott, Clare, and Lash, Miranda, *The Menil Collection: Art Spaces*, London and Houston, Scala Publishers in association with The Menil Collection, 2007.

Elsner, John, and Cardinal, Roger (eds.), *The Cultures of Collecting*, Melbourne, Melbourne University Press, 1994.

Eskilden, Ute, Fischer, Hartwig, and Olbricht, Thomas (eds.), *Rockers Island Olbricht Collection Museum Folkwang*, translated by Tim Beeby and Sabine Bürger; Brian Currid (preface), Göttingen, Steidl, 2007.

Feinberg, Susan Gail, 'Sir John Soane's "Museum": An Analysis of the Architect's House-Museum in Lincoln's Inn Fields, London', Vols. I and II, Doctor of Philosophy, University of Michigan, 1979.

Feldstein, Martin (ed.), *The Economics of Art Museums*, Chicago and London, University of Chicago, 1991.

Fleishman, Joel L, *The Foundation a Great American Secret: How Private Wealth Is Changing the World*, New York, Public Affairs, 2007.

Folkwang Museum, Folkwang *Museum – Learning by Seeing*, Munich, Berlin, London and New York, Prestel Verlag, 2005.

Foundation Emil G. Bührle Collection, *The Passionate Eye: Impressionist and Other Master Paintings from the E.G. Bührle Collection*, edited by The Foundation Emil G. Bührle Collection. Zurich and Munich, Artemis Verlag, 1990.

Foundation François Pinault, *Palazzo Grassi – The World Belongs to You*, edited by Palazzo Grassi François Pinault Foundation, Paris, Beaux Arts éditions, 2011.

———, *Punta Della Dogana – In Praise of Doubt*, edited by Punta Della Dogana François Pinault Foundation, Paris, Beaux Arts éditions, 2011.

Fowler, Bridget (ed.), *Reading Bourdieu on Society and Culture*, Oxford, Blackwell, 2000.

Franklin, Adrian, *The Making of MONA*, Melbourne, Penguin Group, 2014.

Freeland, Chrystia, *Plutocrats: The Rise of the New Global Super Rich*, London, Allen Lane/Penguin Group, 2012.

Freudenheim, Susan, 'Romancing the Collector: Will There Be a Storybook Ending?' *The New York Times* p. 1, 2004.

Frey, Bruno S, and Meier, Stephan, *Museums between Private and Public: The Case of the Beyeler Museum in Basle*, Zurich, Switzerland, University of Zurich, February 2002, pp. 1–23.

The Frick Collection, *The Frick Collection Guide to the Galleries*, New York, The Frick Collection, 1978.

Frieder Burda Foundation (ed.), *Museum Frieder Burda, Architect Richard Meier*, Ostfildern, Germany, Hatje Cantz Verlag, 2011.

Frumkin, Peter, *Strategic Giving: The Art and Science of Philanthropy*, Chicago and London, University of Chicago Press, 2006.

Fulbrook, Mary, *A History of Germany 1918–2008: The Divided Nation*, 3rd edition, Oxford, Wiley-Blackwell, 2009.

Furjàn, Helene Mary, 'Glorious Visions: The Theatre of Display and Sir John Soane's House-Museum', Vol. 1, Doctor of Philosophy, Princeton University, 2001.

Gaynor, Suzanne, 'Sir Richard Wallace and His Own Collection', *Antique Collector*, no. April (1983), pp. 48–53.

Getty, J Paul, *The Joys of Collecting*, New York, Hawthorn Books, 1965.

Gill, Anton, *Peggy Guggenheim: The Life of an Art Addict*, London, Harper Collins, 2001.

Goldfarb, Hilliard T, *The Isabella Stewart Gardner Museum: A Companion Guide and History*, New Haven and London, Yale University Press and The Isabella Stewart Gardner Museum, 1995.

Graw, Isabelle, *High Price: Art between the Market and Celebrity Culture*, translated by Nicholas Grindell, Köln, Sternberg Press, 2009.

Greer, Judith, and Buck, Louisa, *Owning Art: The Contemporary Art Collector's Handbook*, London, Cultureshock Media, 2006.

Grenfell, Michael (ed.), *Pierre Bourdieu Key Concepts*, Stocksfield, UK, Acumen Publishing, 2008.

Greub, Suzanne, and Greub, Thierry (eds.), *Museums in the 21st Century Concepts Projects Building*, Munich, Berlin, London and Paris, Prestel, 2006.

Gross, Michael, *Rogues Gallery: The Secret Story of the Lust, Lies, Greed and Betrayals That Made the Metropolitan Museum of Art*, New York, Broadway Books, 2009.

Haithman, Diane, 'MOCA Accepts Eli Broad's $30-Million Lifeline, Appoints CEO', *Los Angeles Times*, 22 December 2008.

Harris, John, *Moving Rooms: The Trade in Architectural Salvages*, New Haven and London, Yale Press University Press, 2007.

Harvey, George, *Henry Clay Frick: The Man*, New York and London, Charles Scribner's, 1928.

Hatton, Rita and Walker, John A, *Supercollector – A Critique of Charles Saatchi*, 2000, 4th edition, Surrey, Surrey Institute of Artology, 2010.

Heckmüller, Skadi, *Privat Zu Gang*, Berlin, Distanz, 2011.

Helfenstein, Josef, and Schipsi, Laureen (ed.), *Art and Activism: Projects of John and Dominique De Menil*, Houston, Menil Foundation, 2010.

Helfenstein, Josef, and Piano, Renzo, 'The Menil Museums, Houston, Texas', in *Architecture for Art: American Art Museums 1938–2008*, edited by Scott J. Tilden (Photography by Paul Rocheleau), New York, Harry N. Abrams, 2004.

Hellandsjø, Karin, *The Art of Tomorrow Today. The Collection*, translated by Jennifer Lloyd, Milan, Skira, 2008.

Hickley, Catherine, *The Munich Art Hoard: Hitler's Dealer and His Secret Legacy*, London, Thames and Hudson, 2015.

Higonnet, Anne, *A Museum of One's Own: Private Collecting, Public Gift*, Pittsburgh and New York, Periscope Publishing, 2009.

Hooper-Greenhill, Eileen, 'Museum Education: Past, Present and Future', In *Towards the Museum of the Future: New European Perspectives*, edited by Roger Miles and Lauro Zavala, pp. 133–146, New York, Routledge, 1994.

Horowitz, Noah, *Art of the Deal: Contemporary Art in a Global Financial Market*, New Jersey, Princeton University Press, 2011.

Howard, Peter, *Sir Richard Wallace: The English Millionaire of Paris and the Hertford British Hospital*, Glasgow, Grimsay Press, 2009.

Ingamells, John (ed.), *Wallace Collection the Hertford Mawson Letters the 4th Marquess of Hertford to His Agent Samuel Mawson*, London, The Trustees of the Wallace Collection, Manchester Square, 1981.

Jenkins, Richard, *Pierre Bourdieu*, 2002 edition, London and New York, Routledge, 1992.

Jodidio, Philip, *Piano: Renzo Piano Building Workshop 1966 to Today*, Menil Collection, Köln, Taschen, 2008.

Johnston, William R, *William and Henry Walters: The Reticent Collectors*, Baltimore and London, The Johns Hopkins University Press in association with The Walters Art Gallery, 1999.

Jose, Nicholas (ed.), *Contemporary Art + Philanthropy Private Foundations: Asia-Pacific Focus*, Sydney, Power Publications, 2009.

Jürgen Habermas, *The Structural Transformation of the Public Sphere: An Inquiry into a Category of Bourgeois Society*, translated by Thomas Bürger with the assistance of Frederick Lawrence, Great Britain, Polity Press, 1989.

Klonk, Charlotte, *Spaces of Experience: Art Gallery Interiors from 1800 to 2000*, New Haven and London, Yale University Press, 2009.

Klose-Ullman, Barbara, and Holler, Manfred J, 'Art Goes America', *Journal of Economic Issues* XLIV, no. 1 (March 2010), pp. 89–112.

Kröller-Müller Museum Staff, *Kröller-Müller Museum*, 2nd edition, Haarlem, The Netherlands, Joh. Enschedé en Zonen Grafische Inrichting B.V., 1977.

Lane, Grayson Harris, 'Duncan Phillips and the Phillips Memorial Gallery: A Patron and Museum in Formation, 1918–1940', Doctor of Philosophy, Boston University, 2002.

Lawson-Johnston, Peter, *Growing up Guggenheim: A Personal History of a Family Enterprise*, Wilmington, DE, ISI Books, 2005.

Leat, Diana, and Anheir, Helmut K, *Creative Philanthropy: Towards a New Philanthropy for the Twenty-First Century*, London and New York, Routledge Taylor & Francis Group, 2006.

Lenz, Christian, *The Neue Pinakothek Munich*, London, Scala Publishers, 1989.

Lepik, Andres, *The Architecture of the Museum Brandhorst Museum Brandhorst: The Architecture*, edited by Bayerische Staatsgemäldesammlungen, pp. 37–59, Ostfildern, Germany, Hatje Cantz Verlag, 2009.

Lindemann, Adam, *Collecting Contemporary*, Köln, Taschen, 2006.

Lorente, J Pedro, *Cathedrals of Urban Modernity: The First Museums of Contemporary Art, 1800–1930*, Burlington, VT, Ashgate, 1998.

———, *The Museums of Contemporary Art*, Surrey, Ashgate, 2011.

Los Angeles County Museum of Art, *The Broad Contemporary Art Museum at the Los Angeles County Museum of Art*, edited by Los Angeles County Museum of Art, Los Angeles, Los Angeles County Museum of Art, 2008.

Low, Theodore, 'What Is a Museum? (1942)', in *Reinventing the Museum: The Evolving Conversation on the Paradigm Shift*, edited by Gail Anderson, Plymouth, AltaMira Press, 2012, pp. 34–47.

Maak, Niklas, 'Between Pinault and Pinchuk: The Network and Rituals of a New Transnational System of Collectors', *Texte Zur Kunst*, 21, no. 83 (2011), pp. 38–55.

Macdonald, Sharon (ed.), *A Companion to Museum Studies*, Malden, MA, Blackwell, 2006.

MacGregor, Arthur, and Impey, Oliver (eds.), *The Origins of Museums: The Cabinet of Curiosities in Sixteenth-and Seventeenth Century Europe*, Oxford, Clarendon Press, 1985.

Mack, Gerhard, *Art Museums into the 21st Century*, Basel, Berlin and Boston, Birkhäuser, 1999.

Macleod, Dianne Sachko, *Art and the Victorian Middle Class: Money and the Making of Cultural Identity*, Cambridge, Cambridge University Press, 1996.

Mallett, Donald, *The Greatest Collector. Lord Hertford and the Founding of the Wallace Collection*, London, Macmillan, 1979.

Mandler, Peter, *The Fall and Rise of the Stately Home*, New Haven and London, Yale University Press, 1997.

Marks, Richard, *Burrell a Portrait of a Collector Sir William Burrell 1861–1958*, Glasgow, Richard Drew, 1983.

Marotta, Antonello, *Contemporary Museums*, Milan, Skira, 2010.

Mauriès, Patrick, *Cabinets of Curiosities*, London, Thames and Hudson, 2002.

Mazaroff, Stanley, *Henry Walters and Bernard Berenson Collector and Connoisseur*, Baltimore, Johns Hopkins University Press in association with The Walters Art Museum, 2010.

McClellan, Andrew, *Inventing the Louvre: Art, Politics, and the Origins of the Modern Museum in Eighteenth-Century Paris*, Cambridge, New York, Melbourne, Cambridge University Press, 1994.

———— (ed.), *Art and Its Publics; Museum Studies at the Millennium*, Massachusetts, Oxford, Berlin and Melbourne, Blackwell, 2003.

————, *The Art Museum from Boullée to Bilboa*, Los Angeles and London, University of California Press, 2008.

————, 'Musée Du Louvre, Paris: Palace of the People, Art for All', in *The First Modern Museums of Art: The Birth of an Institution in 18th-and Early-19th-Century Europe*, edited by Carole Paul, Los Angeles, J. Paul Getty Museum, 2012.

Meachen, Vanessa, 'A Guide to Giving for Australians', Philanthropy Australia, 2006, 2010.

Meier-Graefe, Julius, *Modern Art: Being a Contribution to a New System of Aesthetics*, translated by Florence Simmonds and George W. Chrystal, New York, William Heinemann and G. P. Puttnam,1908.

Menil Foundation, *The Menil Collection: A Selection from the Paleolithic to the Modern Era*, Newly updated edition, edited by The Menil Collection, Houston, TX, Harry N. Abrams, 1987.

Merrill, Linda and Lawton, Thomas, *Freer: A Legacy of Art*, Washington, DC, Freer Gallery of Art, Smithsoniam Institution in association with Harry N. Abrams, 1993.

Message, Kylie, *New Museums and the Making of Culture*, Oxford and New York, Berg, 2006.

Miller, Lillian B, *Patrons and Patriotism: The Encouragement of the Fine Arts in the United States 1790–1860*, Chicago and London, University of Chicago Press, 1966.

Mory, Christophe, *Ernst Beyeler – A Passion for Art*, translated by Isabel Feder, 2011 edition, Zurich, Scheidegger and Spiess, 2003.

Moulin, Raymonde, *The French Art Market – A Sociological View*, translated by Arthur Goldhammer, 1987 edition, New Brunswick and London, Rutgers University Press, 1967.

Newhouse, Victoria, *Towards a New Museum*, Expanded edition, 2006 edition, New York, Monacelli Press, 1998.

——, *Art and the Power of Placement*, New York, Monacelli Press, 2005.

——, *Renzo Piano Museums*, New York, Monacelli Press, 2007.

Orlow, Dietrich, *A History of Modern Germany 1871 to Present*, London and New York, Routledge, 2012.

Oxenaar, RWD, Hammacher, AM, Wolk, Johannes, van der, Kooten, Toos, van Bremer, Jaap and Brouwer, Marianne, *Kröller-Müller: The First Hundred Years*, translated by JW Watson, Haarlem, The Netherlands, Joh Enschedé en Zonen, 1989.

Pearce, Susan M, *Museums, Objects and Collections: A Cultural Study*, Washington, DC, Smithsonian Institution Press, 1992.

——, *On Collecting: An Investigation into Collecting in the European Tradition*, London and New York, Routledge, 1995.

Phillips, Duncan, *The Artist Sees Differently – Essays Based Upon the Philosophy of a Collection in the Making*, Baltimore, Press of Norman T.A, Munder, 1931.

Phillips, Marjorie, *Duncan Phillips and His Collection*, Boston, Atlantic Monthly Press, 1970.

Pomian, Krazysztof, *Collectors and Curiosities*, translated by Elizabeth Wiles-Portier, Cambridge, Polity Press, 1990.

Reinhard-Felice, Mariantonia (ed.), *The Villa 'Am Römerholz' – Oskar Reinhart Collection 'Am Römerholz' Winterthur – Complete Catalogue*, Winterthur, Schwabe Basle, 2005.

——, *The Secret Armoire Corot's Figure Paintings and the World of Reading*, edited by Oskar Reinhart Collection 'Am Römerholz' Federal Office of Culture, Munich, Hirmer Publishers, 2011.

Ritchie, Ian, 'An Architect's View of Recent Developments in European Museums', in *Towards the Museum of the Future: New European Perspectives*, edited by Roger Miles and Lauro Zavala, pp. 7–30, New York, Routledge, 1994.

Robbins, Derek, *The Work of Pierre Bourdieu: Recognising Society*, Boulder and San Francisco, Westview Press, 1991.

Rogoff, Irir, and Sherman, Daniel J (eds.), *Museum Culture*, Minneapolis, University of Minnesota Press, 1994.

Roscio, Nicola del, and Sylvester, Julie (eds.), *Cy Twombly Gallery: The Menil Collection*, New York, Houston, New Haven and London, The Cy Twombly Foundation and Menil Foundation in association with Yale University Press, 2013.

Rosengart, Angela, *The Rosengart Collection*, edited by The Rosengart Foundation, Munich, Berlin, London and New York, Prestel, 2002.

Ross, Estelle, *The Wallace Collection and the Tate Gallery*, London, Wells Gardner, Darton, 1908. (Courtesy of The Wallace Collection Research Library.)

Rovers, Eva, 'Monument to an Industrialist's Wife: Helene Kröller-Müller's Motives for Collecting', *Journal of the History of Collections* 21, no. 2 (2009), pp. 241–252.

———, 'Introduction: The Art Collector – Between Philanthropy and Self-Glorification', *Journal of the History of Collections* 21, no. 2 (2009), pp. 157–161.

Rudenstine, Neil L, *The House of Barnes: The Man, the Collection, the Controversy*, Philadelphia, American Philosophical Society, 2012.

Rühl, Anna (ed.), *The Museum Brandhorst*, Munich, C.H.Beck, 2013.

Ryskamp, Charles, Davidson, Bernice, Galassi, Susan, Munhall, Edgar, and Tscherny, Nadia, *Art in the Frick Collection Paintings, Sculpture, Decorative Arts*, New York, Harry N. Abrams in association with The Frick Collection, 1996.

Saarinen, Aline B, *The Proud Possessors*, London, Weidenfeld and Nicolson, 1959.

Sachs, Angeli, and Magnago Lampugnani, Vittorio (eds.), *Museums for a New Millenium: Concepts, Projects, Buildings*, 2001 edition, Munich, London and New York, Prestel, 1999.

Sanger, Martha Frick Symington, Henry *Clay Frick: An Intimate Portrait*, New York, London and Paris, Abbeville Press, 1998.

———, *Helen Clay Frick: Bittersweet Heiress*, Pittsburgh, University of Pittsburgh Press, 2008.

Schaik, Leon van, *Meaning in Space*, Melbourne, Lyon Housemuseum, 2011.

Schaulager, *Schaulager: Preserve, Study, Share*, Basel, Laurenz Foundation, 2012.

Serota, Nicholas, *Experience or Interpretation – The Dilemma of Museums of Modern Art*, London, Thames and Hudson, 1996.

Sheehan, James J, *Museums in the German Art World: From the End of the Old Regime to the Rise of Modernism*, Oxford and London, Oxford University Press, 2000.

Sindelfingen Schauwerk, *Schauwerk Sindelfingen*, edited by The Schaufler Foundation, Schauwerk Sindelfingen, The Schaufler Foundation, 2010.

Sir John Soane's Museum, *A New Description of Sir John Soane's Museum*, 11th revised edition. London, Published by the Trustees, 1955.

———, *Sir John Soane's Museum London: A Short Description*, edited by Sir John Soane's Museum, London, Published by the Trustees, n.d.

Smart, Pamela G, *Sacred Modern: Faith, Activism, and Aesthetics in the Menil Collection*, Austin, University of Texas Press, 2010.

Smith, Rowena Joy, 'H.S. Ede: A Life in Art', Doctor of Philosophy, Cambridge University, 2001.

Smith, Terry, *What Is Contemporary Art?* Chicago and London, University of Chicago Press, 2009.

———, *Contemporary Art: World Currents*, London, Laurence King Publishing, 2011.

———, (ed.), *Contemporary Art + Philanthropy Public Spaces/Private Funding: Foundations for Contemporary Art*, Sherman Contemporary Art Foundation, Sydney, University of New South Wales Press, 2007.

Spielman, Marion H, *The Wallace Collection in Hertford House*, London, Paris, New York and Melbourne, Cassell and Company, 1900.

Staniszewski, Mary Anne, *The Power of Display: A History of Exhibition Installations at the Museum of Modern Art*, Cambridge, MA, MIT Press, 1998.

Storr, Robert, 'To Have and to Hold', in *Museums and Contemporary Art: Collecting the New*, edited by Bruce Altshuler, pp. 29–40, Princeton and Oxford, Princeton University Press, 2005.

Stourton, James, 'Switzerland: Emil Bührle 1890–1956', in Great Collectors of Our Time – Art Collecting since 1945, pp. 187–193, London, Scala Publishers, 2007.

Texte Zur Kunst, 'That's a Given! A Survey of the Relationship between Public Museums and Private Collectors', *Texte Zur Kunst*, September 21, 2011, no. 83 (2011), pp. 128–173.

———, 'The Collectors', *Texte Zur Kunst*, September 2011, no. 83 (2011).

———, 'The Curators', *Texte Zur Kunst*, June 2012, no. 86 (2012).

———, 'Globalism', *Texte Zur Kunst*, September 2013, no. 91 (2013).

———, 'Architecture', Texte *Zur Kunst*, December 2013, no. 92 (2013).

———, 'Speculation', *Texte Zur Kunst*, March 2014, no. 93 (2014).

Thompson, Don, *The $12 Million Stuffed Shark: The Curious Economics of Contemporary Art*, New York, Palgrave Macmillan, 2008.

Thornton, Sarah, *Seven Days in the Art World*, New York and London, W.W. Norton, 2008.

Tilden, Scott J (ed.), *Architecture for Art: American Art Museums 1938–2008*, New York, Harry N. Abrams, 2004.

Timms, Peter, *What's Wrong with Contemporary Art?* Sydney, University of New South Wales Press, 2004.

Velthuis, Olav, *Talking Prices: Symbolic Meanings of Prices on the Market for Contemporary Art*, New Jersey, Princeton University Press, 2005.

———, 'Accounting for Taste', *Artforum International*, April, no. 8 (2008), pp. 305–309.

Walker, Georgina, 'A 21st-Century Wunderkammer: Museum of Old and New Art (MONA), Hobart, Tasmania, Australia', *International Journal of the Inclusive Museum 9*, no. 2 (2016): pp. 1–17.

Walsh, David, *A Bone of Fact*, Sydney, Picador, 2014.

Weddigen, Tristan. 'The Picture Galleries of Dresden, Düsseldorf, and Kassell: Princely Collections in Eighteenth-Century Germany', in *The First Modern Museums of Art–the Birth of an Institution in 18th-and Early 19th-Century Europe*, edited by Carole Paul, pp. 145–165, Los Angeles, J. Paul Getty Museum, 2012.

Wegmann, Peter, *Casper David Friedrich to Ferdinand Hodler: A Romantic Tradition Nineteenth-Century Paintings and Drawings from the Oskar Reinhart Foundation, Winterthur*, Frankfurt am Main and Leipzig, Insel Verlag, 1993.

Weil, Stephen E, *A Cabinet of Curiosities; Inquiries into Museums and Their Prospects*, Washington, DC, and London, Smithsonian Institution Press, 1995.

———, *Making Museums Matter*, Washington, DC, Smithsonian Institution Press, 2002.

Wimmer, Dorothee, 'Bremen-Berlin-Weimar: Cooperation between German Art Collectors and Museum Directors C. 1900', *Journal of the History of Collections*, 21, no. 2 (2009), pp. 203–212.

———, 'Art in Progress: The Woman Collector Ingvild Goetz in Munich', *Women's History Review*, 18, no. 4 (2009), pp. 687–703.

Wood, James N, 'The Authorities of the American Art Museum', in *Whose Muse? Art Museums and the Public Trust*, edited by James Cuno, New Jersey, Princeton University Press and Harvard University Art Museum, 2004, pp. 103–128.

Young, Linda, *Historic House Museums in the United States and the United Kingdom*, London, Rowman and Littlefield, 2017.

Index

Printed in the United States
by Baker & Taylor Publisher Services